The Grateful Soul:
The Art And Practice Of Gratitude

Compiled By Kyra Schaefer

As You Wish Publishing, LLC

Connect@asyouwishpublishing.com

ISBN-13: 978-1-951131-02-9

Library of Congress Control Number: 2020907631

Compiled by Kyra Schaefer

Edited by Karen Oschmann

Printed in the United States of America.

Dedication

To our friends who make every day, a day filled with gratitude.

"Look around, things to be grateful for are everywhere."
Kyra Schaefer

Table of Contents

The Gift Of Life
By Allison Voth

I was born in February in the late seventies in Vancouver, Canada. As if to herald the world with my presence, I arrived nine weeks early. An old photograph I have of my mother holding me looks as though her hands were gargantuan, with my tiny legs dangling over the edges of her fingers' make-shift hammock. The preemie diaper affixed to my fragile body appears super-sized. How delicate to be in an incubator for three months! There's no wonder I developed a complex from the lack of physical touch and connection in those early stages of my life.

Raised in a small suburban town with adoring parents and two older brothers, life was simple. My mother made our clothes, as she was so creative with her hands. I am grateful she taught me to bake and cross-stitch, all great skills that are making a comeback these days. My dad taught me to laugh and made me feel special when he took me to Dairy Queen for ice cream, then told me in the car on the way home, "Don't tell your brothers!" One hot summer afternoon in my young childhood days, Dad turned his next ice cream fix into a lesson. He said I could have as much ice cream as I wanted with one rule: "Pronounce the name on the box first." Out came the brick-style ice cream from the freezer—I recall it had yellow and chocolate in it. The word on the box looked like a foreign language to me—lots of a's paired with lots of n's—it genuinely confused me. Dad smiled with his gentle encouragement, but I kept stumbling with sewing together the letters in my mind, even while audibly spelling

1

it. There was simply no connection to B-A-N-A-N-A. This was like an encrypted word that, if I could understand it, would be the key to opening the vault of the sweet treat within. Many failed attempts later, Dad placed the ice cream back, not allowing me to have any. I felt anxious when I saw the brick going back into the freezer, thinking, "How could he do this to me?" I tried harder, and voila, eventually I understood its meaning. "Banana!" I yelled with excitement as the connection hit my brain and rolled off my tongue. Dad laughed with pure joy, and those unfolding moments were transformed into a priceless memory. I am so grateful for his unwavering dedication to involve me in his firm yet playful teaching stance.

What would I give for that sweet moment in my life now? He passed away suddenly on his birthday in 2015. No warning. No sickness. No goodbye. My heart was torn apart as grief swallowed me up like a T-Rex with one enormous gulp. My parents had been divorced for 20 years, and my relationship with my mother was strained. I didn't feel a heart-centered connection with her. It was like the word *banana,* I struggled with it, so I tried harder to make it work, which only left me feeling more disconnected from the gift. In the past few years, her short-term memory decline wasn't only an easy shrug with, "Oh, that's just Mom," anymore. My brothers and I found out she had been diagnosed with Alzheimer's, unbeknownst to us due to our distant, dysfunctional relationship.

This sudden change in events triggered my deep fears, anxiety, and insecurity around our relationship. It was like the ice-cream box going back in the freezer. I thought, "How could this be happening to me?" I felt the stress building as my thoughts focused on how to deal with having one parent left who has a known medical condition. I wanted it easy, I wanted something other than what was dished out to me, but life is also an unwavering teacher.

During this time, my fiancé and I were on the rocks, and this was the catalyst—the cherry on top—that forever changed our paths as they split like a banana. Single, I embarked on a journey into the unknown by pushing myself outside my comfort zone continuously with new adventures. I learned incredible new life skills with meditation, breathwork, and mindfulness. I began to cultivate gratitude as part of my lifestyle by creating a gratitude jar in conjunction with practicing re-framing my perspective into positives. As I discovered the depths of my heart and brought forth the wisdom from my journey of self-reflection, I have used these gifts to see and feel the world differently as I observe my mother and our relationship in the present.

This *is* the time of our lives now. She gets the gift of being present as each new moment unfolds as though it is new—because it is. Isn't that what we all are striving for—to be engaged with the present? Who am I to judge her life? That is her journey, not mine. I choose mine by letting go of my white-knuckle grip on the past when I watch her enjoy the swings at the park, when she marvels at hummingbirds at her window, and how she treasures a muffin from McDonald's like a pound of gold. Life is simple in these moments. "Isn't this just lovely?" she'll say while reminding me that her grandmother always said that. You see, she is also my teacher, who is showing me patience and tenderness for her generation. She is showing me the way to forgiveness to forgive myself for judging someone else.

This has shaped me to understand a simple truth—she has given me the gift of life. Period. No past and no wanting anything to change. It is up to me to decide which path I take in each ever-present moment. Acceptance, paired with appreciation, is the rich recipe that nourishes our hearts to form genuine connections and heal. The lesson in sharing this personal story with you is that there is one thing I have come to know—I *am* a grateful soul. The journey never ends.

Bio

Allison Voth is an international bestselling author and the owner/creative director of HoneyHeartCo., providing retreat planning and building a platform for speakers to empower others with their gifts through co-creating inspiring events. She is a registered Yoga Alliance teacher and has developed a gentle teaching style to reduce stress and build resilience. She is an independent writer, poet, and love enthusiast. Her passion is serving our global family within the common unity that bonds us together in the expression of unconditional love. She can be reached through her website at www.honeyheart.ca

Be Blessed!
♡ AVoth

The Angel In The Dress Department
By Amy I. King

T he song *Peace Train*, by Cat Stevens, played through the speakers of the CD player as I tried to calm my soul, by swaying to the music while sitting in the pew of the Lutheran church. It wasn't working. No matter how focused on the music, she was gone forever, and my life, as I knew it, was infinitely changed.

My beautiful, tenacious, and loving mother was laid to rest next to my step-father the day before, having lost her life to ALS (Amyotrophic Lateral Sclerosis or Lou Gehrig's Disease). ALS is familiar to the general public due, in large part, to the Ice Bucket Challenge. The Ice Bucket Challenge focused media attention on ALS, which has brought about significant advances in medical research and getting closer to a cure.

We were celebrating her life with a beautiful memorial at the Lutheran church. The officiant was a pastor whom she would have loved. Her best friend, Marci, and I created two poster boards filled with pictures of a well-lived and well-loved life. My mom was a world traveler, having worked in international student exchange, she had many opportunities to feed her desire for new cultures and new experiences. She was fun and adventurous and filled with life. Those pictures were proof. Inside the church, I kept my gaze on the giant image of her on the easel, surrounded by gorgeous, fragrant flowers. She was magnificent both inside and out.

A few days before this celebration of life, I had the task of shopping for a suitable outfit for my mother's burial and another for the memorial. I didn't want to move from the couch. I had returned home, motherless, from the hospital on Wednesday night. I hadn't gotten off the couch much since then. Shopping had been something that my grandma, mom, sister, and I often did together. Some of my greatest memories are of those shopping trips and subsequent lunches out. Now, alone, the task seemed daunting. Feeling devastated and nervous, I gathered my purse and keys. I needed to find two different looks. I took a deep breath before putting on the bravest face a woman who had recently lost her mom could muster. You are never ready to lose your mom—trust me. I got in the car and drove, as if on auto-pilot, to the mall. I was in a fog but had a mission to accomplish. Oh, how I wished I had taken Leslie up on her offer to pick something up for me. It was such a sweet thing for her to offer, but in typical "independent Amy" fashion, I didn't want to inconvenience anyone.

In the dress department, I looked at everything that I could see on the racks that came in black. I rolled slowly through the large rounds of clothes, in my wheelchair, feeling lost the further I got. I could not think straight. After what felt like an eternity and the most futile mission on the planet, I could feel the tears coming. I was trying so hard to compose myself, but I was not in the right place, emotionally, to shop. I found myself outside the personal shopper's office, the door closed. I felt like she must have heard me, although I was silently crying. Before I knew it, Lillian, the petite and lovely personal shopper, was standing in front of me, asking if she could help me. Observing that I was dealing with something substantial, she explained that her appointment had canceled. I told her why I was shopping. She leaned in and gave me the gentlest hug and said, "It's okay, honey. I will take care of you." Her kindness hit me hard, and I began to cry again. I thought to myself when the last time was that I had heard the words, "I will take care of you." Exhausted, I complied. She consoled me, asking me about sizes and style preferences. She handed me a plastic cup of water and told me to make myself comfortable in the enormous dressing room. She said, "I'll be right back." She disappeared in a whisper.

It wasn't long before she returned with several appropriate options. I tried each garment. She was so kind each time I came out of the dressing room and asked what she thought. We started talking more, and she told me about losing her mom. There's a strange comfort in knowing you aren't alone. She helped me choose a beautiful sheath dress with a suit jacket for the burial and a dress for the memorial and reception. We sat and chatted a while longer. She was one of the kindest people I've ever met. She gave me her card and told me to call her whenever I needed assistance in the future.

At the burial, I thought of her, as I returned to my spot, after placing a flower on my mother's casket. The suit fit perfectly and was the right choice for the day. At the memorial and the reception, I wore the black dress, in which I felt beautiful. I had so much gratitude for the woman who made such a difficult task feel a little less overwhelming. I was able to get through those days, in part, because of her kindness.

In the months that followed, I stopped by the personal shopper's office, at the department store, a few times in hopes that I could see her again. I wanted to thank her for her kindness and tell her again how much it meant to me. I never did see her again. Wherever she is, I hope that she is well. She was an angel to me that day and will never be forgotten. I hope that she knows how much her kindness meant to me. I am forever grateful.

Bio

Amy I. King is a certified life coach and owner of Your Phenomenal Life, LLC. Amy's greatest joy is using her experiences and wisdom to help others move past their blocks and outdated beliefs to becoming empowered to live the life of their dreams. She is currently coaching and working on her first solo book, *Messy Wheels: Stories from Where I Sit*, available on Amazon, later this year. She can be reached at (916) 718-0914. She welcomes the opportunity to assist you in discovering and living your phenomenal life.

So Many Blessings!
By Anne Foster Angelou

T he list is long for all of us. Waking up each morning is a gift. Every encounter with humans, animals, and nature is a gift. Do I moan, complain, and sound ungrateful sometimes? Yes, I do, but not for long. When I realize how blessed I am, I am humbled, full of joy, and amazed.

There is so much gratitude, especially for the adversity I have experienced from my early childhood—so many lessons that taught me how to love, forgive, and to acknowledge and nurture my gifts. Over my 76 years, I have been guided through life by so many angels in disguise.

My first angel was my maternal grandmother, who not only raised me from birth, but taught me to sing, dance, embroider, crochet, and nurtured a love of learning and curiosity. She took me to libraries, museums, art galleries, zoos, and parks, and enrolled me in book, music, and science clubs. I first heard Mozart's lullaby on a record I received in the mail. She stepped in when my mother was unable to take care of me. She raised her six children, me, my brother for a time, and then my cousin. She sewed my clothing on a treadle machine and made costumes for my Aunt Helen, a dancer.

My teachers, the nuns at Sacred Heart Academy, and my professors at the University of South Florida and the University of Washington were other angels. They taught me "the basics" and then my beloved choices of music, theatre, linguistics, and foreign languages. I am grateful for two years of mandatory Latin, then French, Italian, and German, that prepared me for singing repertoire in recitals and in the professional resident chorus at Seattle Opera. More angels—choir directors and conductors in University Chorus (USF), Chorale da Camera (Cornish), Seattle Symphony Chorale, and The Medieval Women's Choir. I was also blessed to form an *a cappella* quartet, The Angelou Vocal Ensemble, and sing from 1994 to 2012 for hire with some of the most talented singer colleagues available. Music has been a healer throughout my life.

My friends were and are angels, such human gifts, who reflected me in them and them in me. I say this because a class at the Center for Spiritual Living called *Beyond Limits* had an exercise that separated the class into two groups. Half of the class was in the circle, and the rest of us entered. We were instructed not to touch or speak, but to look into each person's eyes and realize, "You are looking upon the face of God." I sobbed with each person. We were so moved by this simple exercise that helped us realize that we have always been and will remain *one*.

I am grateful for friends of many years—one from high school, one from when we were 17 at USF, some I met in my 20s, and others in the last 50 years. Some came and went even after a long-beloved friendship. The loss still saddens me, but I love them anyway and always will. I am grateful for learning who I am through painful lessons and experiences of joy.

My spouse is another blessed angel. We have shared heart-breaking and joyful events, and have always been committed to each other. My friend and companion shares the love of friends, neighbors, strangers (the Greeks have a word for it, philoxenia), animals, and the earth.

Because of him, I learned a new language, visited his country of birth, and gained a new family. Because of a medical device issue, we did not have children, but we loved all five of our cats, each one with a unique personality, and cried until we ached when they died.

During my last year performing at Seattle Opera, I began to have discomfort in my chest and had breathing issues and pain. My health worsened without being properly diagnosed for over 15 years. By the time I retired early at age 63, I could not walk ten feet without feeling an overwhelming heaviness in my body, breathlessness, and episodes of pre-syncope (fainting). The first cardiologist said one day, "I don't know what to do with you; you keep getting worse." Fortunately, she referred me to the U.W. Heart Center, where I was diagnosed in two visits with hypertrophic cardiomyopathy with a large obstruction on the septum of my heart, a genetic condition. Unusually, I have clear arteries or "zero plaque." I delayed the surgery because I was afraid—until I had a mild heart attack from atrial fibrillation.

After several meditation workshops with Dr. Joe Dispenza, I gained the courage and scheduled a septal myectomy at the renowned Mayo Clinic in Rochester, Minnesota. We bravely flew to Minnesota, and my life was saved by the skilled heart surgeon, Hartzell Schaff, MD. Now I can walk three miles per day if I wish. The recovery was four months with the loving care of Dimitri, and the many years of struggling to stay alive is a distant memory. You cannot imagine how grateful I am. Dr. Owens at U.W. Heart Center is so smart and caring. I am grateful for him and other physicians on my health team

Now we have a pandemic. Dear Lord, what's next! Well, let's make another list—a warm home, food, clothing, water, lots of books and music, a sweet cat, great neighbors, loving friends, intelligence, and a wacky sense of humor—all to be enjoyed with my loving husband. My life's rule is, "Don't hurt any human being, any animal, or the earth." Share, care, forgive, love, and laugh. Experience joy because it's all around you. Be patient, and don't let fear in. We can get through this together, giving each other courage and hope. Maybe I will write that book I've been planning since 1970 (a calendar entry). Have an open heart and mind accepting and celebrating others' differences. Be well, safe, and don't forget to love.

Bio

Anne Foster Angelou, Seattle, Washington, USA, life-long singer and performer, government public servant by day until retirement, a grateful woman for all life's lessons, lover of life, all living beings and the earth, appreciator of humor, music and the arts as great healers. I have lived near "water" all my life—the Atlantic Ocean, the Gulf of Mexico, and now Puget Sound and the Pacific Ocean, and can't imagine being anywhere else. Email: fosterangelou@comcast.net.

Hiking The Trail Called Life
By Anne Joannette-White

While on a hiking trail with my husband in Algonquin Provincial Park, I stopped to pause and reflect on an "a-ha" moment I'd just had.

The hike had started, and I was feeling good. I was feeling ready. And I was feeling positive. Knowing I'm not in the best of shape, I was confident that this type of activity, deep in the heart of the forest, would be beneficial to my body, mind, and soul. I started at a slow, easy pace, taking the time to look up and admire the different shades of green radiating from the trees, the lake's deep blue water, and the pale blue cloudless sky.

I inhaled deeply, grateful for the moment, taking in all the beauty.

The tall trees proudly exuding such strength made me feel grounded and confidant. I saluted some, hugged others, and thanked a few more for "being there" for me when the need arose. Appreciating their wisdom, my mind wandered momentarily. The stories they could tell!

As I took another deep breath, I looked up again!

Water is a paradox for me. I feel the comfort from being near to it, yet fear it at the same time. I don't swim, you see. The water demands respect, and yet, invites us to play. I can see myself on a canoe trip or trusting as I float with a pool noodle. Simply sitting on the edge of a dock and dangling my feet in the fresh water would be just as magical. The lake tells its story: a source of life for so many and a source of joy for me.

I inhaled deeply again. A powerful clean, crisp, and refreshing smell filled my body!

The songs of crows, loons, and blue jays filled nature's auditorium. I stopped to listen. They were letting me know that they were enjoying the environment as much as I was. Mindful of the rustling leaves as the wind traveled through the trees, something caught my attention. I saw little red squirrels chasing each other, chipmunks running toward their favorite hiding spots to unload their delicious treats in their mouths, and snakes gliding and slithering around us trying to get out of our way. In the moment, we let gratitude for the nature around us fill our souls, as a few agile dragonflies and colorful butterflies flew by.

I took another deep breath. My smile widened.

My husband was there, a few steps in front or behind me, reassuring me and making sure I was okay. I was grateful to be sharing space and time with him. I love the moments when we can truly enjoy each other's company, moving together in the same direction, understanding each other's joy of being surrounded by nature. The silent moments are appreciated and healing.

Consciously, I inhaled deeply once again and kissed my husband!

Continuing our hike, I was mindful of every step. Thinking of all the times in my life when I was careful and overcautious, fear has been a shadow in my life—the fear of not being accepted, the fear of not being included, the fear of voicing my opinions, the fear of saying no, the fear of hurting someone's feelings, the fear of making mistakes, the fear of disappointing someone else, the fear of embarrassing myself, the fear of embarrassing someone else. And, the greatest fear of all, the fear of not being enough. Yet, as I walked, there were trips and stumbles, but I moved on, watching for roots, fallen tree branches, small stumps, unsteady rocks, and uneven ground. With each step, I reflected on some of my life's lessons—the stumbles, the mistakes, the challenges, the blessings, the answered and unanswered prayers, and the wishes that came true. It was in this moment that I realized this trail is a mirror of my life. With all its gifts, lessons, and challenges, I now mindfully continue to "watch my step" and enjoy the beauty of life that is.

And as I smelled the pungent pine needles, my body and soul were instantly filled with joy.

Life is like this hiking trail. We start off with good intentions, and along the way, we can get distracted. Sometimes, we get discouraged by obstacles and challenges, and sometimes, we even need a helping hand. We walk on the trail and take the time to feel, smell, listen, touch, and, particularly, see the beauty that surrounds us.

Slow and steady is how I decided to walk on this trail called life. It turns out that these obstacles have been placed on my path with intention. I look straight ahead, I look up, I look down, and rarely do I look back. There will always be other things to do, other places to be and other people to meet. Enjoy these moments. Enjoy life's trails. And for every step, remember to inhale gratitude and exhale fear.

Surrounded by nature, with the deepest of inhales, I yelled: *"Thank you!"*

Bio

Anne Joannette-White is a newly-retired teacher with a passion for continuous learning, both for herself and others. She is an empath who enjoys meeting and learning from like-minded individuals in the pursuit of her interests in energy healing. Anne enjoys discovering her truest self and all that life has to offer her. She volunteers at her local hospice, spends time in nature, and values time with her friends and family. Anne is looking at life as "the best is yet to come" and enjoying every new experience.

Said Yes To It All
By Becki Koon

I thought I was ready.

It was the beginning of a new year, and I wanted to set the stage with gratitude. I had no idea that the first piece of paper pulled from the "gratitude jar" I made a couple of years earlier would bring me to my knees. I read the words, felt my chest get heavy, my heart breaking, my breath shallow and labored, and tears were welling from deep within. Through tear-glazed eyes, I read his words, "I am grateful that the most beautiful woman on the planet is sharing her life with me!" Then, the breath-taking sobs took hold.

It was a strange experience. I felt the enormous swell of eternal gratitude for the love I shared with my soul mate, the love of my life, and at the same time, the heartbreak of his presence leaving the planet. He went way too soon, a mere three months ago.

I was in such a great space that day, feeling motivated, moving forward with a sense of peace in my heart. That is why I felt strong enough, saying yes to reading the notes in the jar. Somehow, it seemed like an essential activity for me to do with the energy of the new year pulsing, pulling me forward. I had no idea the wave of grief would come crashing onto the shores of my internal landscape as hard as it did.

But in those moments of sobbing, I spoke to him, letting him know how much I loved that he thought of me that way, that he loved me so deeply in the twelve years we shared. I am forever grateful for our time together. I thanked him for having a hand in this now moment, this moment of raw emotion that I accepted and welcomed with open arms.

It is so easy for us to sidestep deep emotions, ignoring the body experiences that arise. When we grieve, our heart literally feels like it is breaking. We can love with complete abandon, yet fear vulnerability. We can even be elevated in blissful joy, then hesitate because we somehow fear the moment will pass. It often appears that if we temper our intense feelings, we seemingly function better with an "I got this" kind of non-attachment attitude.

There is nothing wrong with how we approach our intimate internal life. I hope no one judges themselves harshly. We all do the best we can with the life circumstances presenting themselves. But the fact is, the more we choose to ignore or stuff our intense emotions, the more likely we are to suffer stress and anxiety. It can then surface in unexpected ways in moments that seem unrelated to current events or circumstances.

The beauty of this time on our planet is that scientific research is proving what humans have known for thousands of years: our emotions affect our experience of life. Our emotions are a powerful force on the world around us. We can learn to accept our humanness and understand that we are doing a fantastic job as a soul in these dense-feeling bodies. We can learn how to harness and work with those energies in a life-enhancing way.

I have heard it said that intense grief is the flip side of a deep and abiding love. What I did not understand until I experienced it myself, was the reality that these two sides of emotion can be experienced at the same time, in the same moment.

My love was diagnosed with cancer, and 20 days later, he was gone from the physical world. At first, we were in shock but hopeful. After nine days, he told me this was not about his survival but his passing. He lovingly asked me to help him leave this place with as much dignity and conscious awareness as possible. Conscious death was to be our shared journey. At that moment, with my heart completely breaking, I looked into his eyes, and, with all the love and gratitude I am capable of feeling, I told him, of course. I would be there every moment, every precious moment along the way.

We are all so much stronger than we realize, and in the face of adversity, we *find* courage, we *find* resolve, we *find* heart. When we find our hearts and step into the higher-level energies of love and compassion, we often find that gratitude is there—a gentle and silent antidote to our pain. Gratitude has a way of alchemizing and shifting awareness from our individual suffering to seeing life from a bigger perspective, the one connected to source, the divinity within connected to all.

The more I practice seeing and experiencing my world from a state of gratitude, the more peace I find. Does it mean I don't feel the intensity of loss? Absolutely not! What it means for me is that I understand I can feel it all, say yes to it all, and still find comfort in my world. Life throws us curves; the road is wrought with hazards. There is no way to escape from challenges, changes, and being influenced and impacted by the world around us. The critical questions: How resilient can you be? Can you find your grateful soul?

Starting a practice of gratitude is one measure in your control that helps you move and shift your emotional state, your energetic experience. The gratitude jar was a practice we enjoyed, little notes of paper with what we felt grateful for in that moment.

I feel so blessed to have pulled that paper out of the jar, to be able to read the words he so lovingly wrote. I am grateful I have those pieces of him that, when I am ready, will reveal themselves to me. For now, I am happy to know they exist. I feel honored he loved me so deeply, but mostly, I am grateful that I said *yes* to it all!

Bio

Becki Koon is a heart-based intuitive channel, life coach, HeartMath coach, Reiki master, author, and speaker. Through her business, Step Stone, Becki empowers people to activate, energize, and catalyze healing energy, reduce stress, and take charge of their life through remembering and connecting to their divine essence.

Becki has a passion for sharing energy awareness with those seeking a new way to experience their realities. The recent loss of her husband opened her up to an even deeper level of acceptance, love, and gratitude. Contact Becki at: stepstone2you@gmail.com; www.facebook.com/becki.koon.consulting; or www.beckikoon.com.

Mayflies And Feathers
By Becki Koon

I'm missing you as I head home from my trip. I gaze over the wing of the airplane, and I contemplate the beauty that my eyes behold. The sunset is magical; the colors flame in hues of bright orange, red, and peach as the sun says goodbye, kissing the horizon while it slowly sets. I again experience that familiar feeling of sadness that you are no longer here to share these sights with me. And yet, I realize you are there, a part of the beauty I am seeing, a part of the magic I sense and feel. My heart swells with gratitude, even in the sorrow, missing you.

I believe we shared an uncommon love, a combining of souls that is rare in this life and what most people seek to find. How blessed we were to have divine magic a part of our lives in the twelve years we spent together. Your transition from this world was not what we had planned; you left this planet way too soon, my love. And yet—

I have memories!

I will never forget the evening I saw you walking down our deserted country road, lost in the moment. I stepped into the street to watch what was taking place; you were about thirty feet in front of me. The early evening light was setting, and the sun's rays were casting a perfect shadow on the swarm of mayflies that were swirling around you, engulfing you in a dance of movement that was ethereal. You were moving your hands in slow motion in response to the whirling flies enveloping you, and the waves of flow that occurred were like watching water move around your body effortlessly. I observed for several minutes, taken by the sheer beauty of the dance. I then walked into the swarm to join you and, for a few moments, felt the absolute joy of nature caressing us.

You had a way of showing me the connection to all things that I now carry in my soul, a part of the way I view my world, an honoring of the life force that surrounds me always. I thank you for showing me how easy it was to see the beauty in even the smallest or most ordinary of things.

I remember walking by myself downtown one afternoon, finding a beautiful blue feather resting on a window sill of a local shop. I was so drawn to this feather that I excitedly put it in my pocket to bring home to show you. When I started to share that I had found this stunning feather, you stopped me before I could give you any more information. You then described the feather and the location in perfect detail. What I had not known was that earlier in the day, you had found a beautiful blue feather and placed it on the window sill of that same shop. I was in awe of our unexplainable connection and felt gratitude for my awareness of details. Many people passed by the same window sill, and yet the feather remained for me to find, a gift of your making.

Once we were working on a hot summer afternoon, moving some items from one location to another. Due to the heat, a floor fan was running to keep the air flowing. I had music playing loudly in the background and was busy putting games away on a shelf. All of a sudden, I felt the energy shift. I turned around to look at you and see what had changed my awareness. You were gazing intensely at the fan. A feather tied to the outside rim of the fan was blowing in the breeze. Then I saw what had you so mesmerized. I, too, gazed in amazement at the feather dancing in the fan wind, realizing its dance was perfectly synchronized with the music playing in the background. Time seemed to stretch as we both watched the magic taking place before our eyes and ears. I was as much in awe of you as I was the feather in the fan. You regularly saw magic in the smallest of life's details, and because of that, I, too, was blessed to participate in those moments.

We shared that gift of life, the ability to find the higher-level emotions of joy, compassion, gratitude, care, appreciation, and courage in the face of even the most challenging of situations.

The most daunting task we experienced together was your death process. I don't believe many people consciously choose death, but when faced with the irrefutable truth of your cancer-filled body, you accepted your journey with grace and courage, and, to this day, I am in amazement. Gratitude came in waves as the moments carried a sacred energy we both cherished, as your body continued to let go, to shut down to life as we had known. Your soul stayed strong and carried us both, carried me when I found myself in moments of experiencing the loss that was looming, the saying goodbye to your physical form that had become such an extension of me. You never lost focus on your task at hand or your compassion for me.

We both felt blessed you were home for this journey, comforted by your surroundings. The smallest of events took on a depth of meaning beyond words. We embraced while we gazed at the moon, breathing in precious seconds as I buried my face in your neck, smelling your skin still radiating your scent. We held each other close as many times as your body could allow. We performed a ceremony, working with crystals and oils while calling in your soul's strength, the angels, your guides, and your loved ones. Your last words spoken are forever in my heart, "Oh, I have to say goodbye now, I love you!"

Even in the death process, you, my love, taught me to honor life to the fullest, every nuance, every now moment, with grace and gratitude.

Dedication from Becki Koon: The stories shared are in honor of my late husband Jack, who helped me to witness the magic of life, the joy in the simple moments, the healing power of music through his gift as a musician, and the awe-inspiring significance of the natural world. We traveled a sacred journey together, endlessly exploring energy and esoteric thought. Now, we explore communication through the veil, collapsing dimensions to explore new realities, new horizons. Physical death has not finished our journey together; it only shifted how we experience our connection. He is always near me, and I have a grateful soul.

My Lemon Story
By Bilge Gregory

After 13 years together, he looked at me and said, "I don't love you anymore." I was devastated, trying to pick up the pieces, hoping and believing it was a phase. He didn't want a divorce, and he wouldn't leave the house, so we were frozen in time as a couple. What could I do? I could work on myself. So I started to exercise, started seeing a therapist, and quit my self-medicating habits. In my therapy sessions, it was clear that I was dealing with tremendous codependency. I told my therapist one day, "I want to feel elation when I'm alone. I've never felt that way before; it's always been when somebody else was around." It was something I felt I needed to do to release parts of my old self.

Less than a year later, I asked him for a separation. I finally had found some level of independence, and I knew it was time to break away. This man was in my life for a reason, for a season, but not for forever. A month later, in early 2008, I went on my second annual all-girls snowboarding trip. It was the only sport I had learned as an adult at the age of thirty-three. There is something incredibly empowering about learning a new sport as an adult, especially for somebody like me—a physician who relied mostly on her brains growing up.

The problem was, in my second season, I had hit a plateau. I had made it to the blue-square difficulty level on the mountain, but each time I attempted to initiate a turn, I would catch an edge and fall. My coaches were busy helping

25

other students and did not see my frustration building. I was to the point of wanting to give up. It was actually the last day of the course, for that season.

Nancy, one of the more experienced coaches, caught a glimpse of what I was struggling with on the mountain. She approached me and said, "I know why you keep falling. I see that you are too afraid to let go a little bit, and go straight down the hill. I know that sounds extremely intimidating, but it's only for maybe one second, enough for you to have time to prepare for a turn. Just be okay with the speed for that brief period of time. You need to let go, and also, lean your lead shoulder into the mountain. I mean *lean in* to the mountain. That also sounds scary and counterintuitive, but that's what actually gives you control." Little did I realize at the time that she wasn't only giving me a lesson about snowboarding, she was giving me a lesson about life. I was so caught up in fear that it froze my ability to evolve spiritually—or physically, as in this case. Sometimes letting go is all you need to do to achieve a miracle. So I did.

I looked downhill, forced my right shoulder forward, and let go. I made every single turn going down the mountain without error, without falling, without fear. When I made it to the bottom, I threw my snowboard off and started jumping up and down, yelling in joy. In that moment, I realized I was not only elated; I was also alone! This made me scream even louder. I felt like I had conquered the world.

During those years, I had a terrible diet Coke habit. I enjoyed four to six cans per day, and my favorite was to pour it into a glass of ice with a slice of fresh lemon. The fresh lemon was something I insisted on when I drank my soda; however, I had forgotten to purchase any on our grocery shopping trip while preparing for that weekend. We had too much going on, and the grocery store was too far away to make a return trip worth it.

I found my friend Amy, who was also a camp attendee, but in a group of a different skill level. She saw my gleaming smile and asked me what had happened that made me look so incredibly happy. We strapped our snowboards to our backs and started trudging in the snow toward our car in the parking lot. As I was gleefully describing the events of the day, I looked down between my feet, and in the parking lot of the Durango Mountain Resort, was a fresh lemon in the snow! Tears started flooding down my cheeks. I had discovered for myself, and for the first time in my life, synchronicity! It was also the first time in my life that I started appreciating the signs that the universe had been giving me all along, but I was too blind to see. From that day forward, I made a promise to myself to be present to the signs that the universe gave me. Trusting in my heart, I've discovered that my life happens *for* me, not *to* me, and I am blessed with the abundance of synchronicities every single day!

Bio

Dr. Bilge Gregory, MD, is a cosmetic surgeon and energy healer. She helps people transform both inside and out with her skills in high definition liposuction, injectables, and transformational coaching. She is passionate about teaching others the powerful connection between the mind and body. She wants to help people understand how our bodies are miracles and can manifest healing without the use of medication. You can reach Dr. Bilge Gregory at Vital Connection MD, 480-223-9323.

Hidden Treasure
By Brooke Bensinger

Most people have a nightstand by their bed. I never gave its purpose much thought until recently. If you have a nightstand, take a close look at the items on it. I imagine there's a lamp. Perhaps a box of tissues. I'm sure those who enjoy reading have a pile of books on theirs. A co-worker says she keeps lip balm on her nightstand during the cold, dry winter months. Mine has a pen and a small pad of paper to record fleeting thoughts I need to remember. They're treasures of sorts. Each item is valued and serves a purpose. In my case, they make life easier and comfortable in some way.

The drawer of my nightstand became a junk drawer over time—a place to store odds and ends that don't seem to belong anywhere else. They lost their value or purpose, yet I wanted to keep them for some reason. I hadn't looked through the contents for a while and took the time to purge some items last month. Pushed toward the bottom of the drawer was a wall calendar from 2015. That was the year I was intentional about practicing gratitude on a daily basis. Before I went to sleep each night, I reflected on the day and wrote at least one thing for which I was grateful. After a quick glance through the first month or so, I decided to take a closer look.

The first thing catching my eye was the names of people mentioned. Reminiscing about them and the reasons for which I was grateful made me smile. I remembered a William Arthur Ward quote, "Feeling gratitude and not expressing it is like wrapping a present and not giving it." I decided to contact those individuals to inform them they made my gratitude calendar. What a fun and rewarding experience that was! Doing so brought joy to our lives. My email to one friend encouraged her to share her gratitude with others. Another friend stated she was brought to tears reading my text because she received it on a day when nothing seemed to be going right. Expressing gratitude is contagious and good for your well-being.

There were a few names I chose not to contact. One was a man I had dated. He recently got married, and I thought it best not to inform him. Another was a former co-worker with whom I had a contentious relationship. Including that individual in my gratitude calendar was a way to cope and combat the negativity. Reading those entries stirred some uneasiness. Expressing my gratitude to my former colleague would probably be beneficial, but I cannot find it within me to do so right now (Note to self: unpack that baggage). Then there was Weston. Sadly, I do not recall anything about Weston, but "Meeting Weston" was listed on September 4th. The encounter must have made an impression if it was recorded. How important is it to remember the specifics for which I was grateful? I decided the reason didn't matter because Weston made my gratitude calendar. At the moment his (or maybe her) name was written, I was appreciative of the fact I met Weston.

I then turned my attention to other details. There were fifty-five entries of gratitude in January. My first entry was "Surprise phone calls." I had gotten an unexpected call from a long-distance friend who wished me a happy new year. Some entries were specific, while others, for example, "laughter," were generic. The months of February through October had anywhere from seventy-four to eighty-two entries. Wow! There were days I wrote three or four reasons to be grateful. One day in September had five entries.

Although there were seventy-seven reasons listed in October, there was an entire week with blank spaces. I was puzzled. I'd been on a roll, and then nothing for seven days. This caused an emptiness in my gut. Based on my reason listed for October 31st, "Eucalyptus essential oil helped with congestion," I assume I wasn't feeling well. That's not an excuse to stray from my habit. In fact, that's when I should have found reasons to get my mind off my illness. The emptiness, however, didn't compare to turning the page to November. There were twenty-two reasons listed on only sixteen days. Those fourteen empty spaces were glaringly obvious. In the last ten days of the month, I wrote nothing. My last entry for November noted I picked up Armstrong, my dog, who is now four years old. Granted, having a puppy is time-consuming and exhausting, but is not a compelling reason to stop recording my gratitude. Turning to December was like getting punched in the gut. Only six reasons were listed in a span of four days at the beginning of the month. My emptiness from viewing the previous two months was replaced with feelings of grief, loss, and sorrow. No wonder the calendar was hidden at the bottom of my junk drawer. It lost its purpose. Perhaps I relegated the calendar there due to shame or embarrassment of falling short.

I couldn't take my eyes off those empty white spaces. Why did I disappoint myself? I tossed the calendar on my nightstand. After a few days, I realized I never read the reasons for which I was grateful in December. My next to last entry was, "Never too late to start the day over." Tears came to my eyes. A reality check, a powerful reminder.

My 2015 calendar was a hidden treasure. Uncovering it reminded me of my gratitude practice. No longer hidden, the calendar has once again taken a rightful place on my nightstand. I have added a new treasure: a 2020 calendar. The first entry for January 1st is "Finding my 2015 gratitude calendar." The second for that day is, "Never too late to start the day over."

Bio

Brooke Bensinger believes it is never too late to pursue your dreams. As a school counselor, entrepreneur, and agent of change, Brooke believes in the power of faith and action. In her 50s, Brooke started a tie-dye business and became a published author, both of which she had envisioned for many years. Her passion is to use creative arts as a catalyst for self-discovery and transformation, so individuals of all ages gain self-confidence, resilience, and a sense of empowerment as they transition through life's milestones. You can reach Brooke at bsquaredtieydye@gmail.com for tie-dye classes, creative wellness workshops, and conversation.

Roses Have Thorns
By Carmen Jelly

"Gratitude unlocks the fullness of life. It turns what we have into enough, and more. It turns denial into acceptance, chaos to order, confusion to clarity. It can turn a meal into a feast, a house into a home, a stranger into a friend." ~ Melody Beattie

Why is it difficult to feel grateful? It takes great courage to embrace gratitude. As a psycho-therapist, I witness human pain, suffering, trauma, grief, despair, and all shades of darkness. As a human, I also experience both light and darkness. We have all felt physical, emotional, and mental discomfort.

In his book, *A New Earth*, Eckhart Tolle talks about our inherited dysfunction and the collective manifestation of insanity. He also suggests that if we look at human history as if it was the history of a person, we would be looking at psychopaths, complete selfishness, greed, and violence. This is our reality of human history, ever since the beginning of time. When we look at the world, we can see oppression, injustice, greed, and corruption. However, this is only one side of the truth. There is an old Buddha saying: "Pain is inevitable, suffering is optional."

The other side of the truth is that we have people who teach and practice peace, awareness, love, connection, and gratitude. We have beauty all around us. The reality is that the world is exactly the way it is. Just because a rose has thorns doesn't mean it is broken or harmful. The barbs also communicate and teach us how to handle what we love with care and attention. Our thorns in life are a constant invitation to read how we are holding ourselves. Are you holding yourself in pain and judgment or with self-compassion?

At our true core is a desire to appreciate life and beauty, like the rose, thorns and all. Such a state of being is possible, but it doesn't come from experiencing the perfect life. The way to discover joy isn't through pushing away the unwelcome afflictions. Being grateful is not about trying to feel good all the time, or feel anything in particular. The prickles to our fingers can be the painful holes or portals to gratitude. I invite you to examine your portals purposefully and intentionally. Our holes are an invitation to our hidden, grateful souls. These wounds are the gateways that take us from chaos to calm, holes to wholeness.

People cannot be in defensive mode and growth mode at the same time. Growth mode takes courage and a shift in perception from fear to faith. Are you willing to consider a shift? In each person's life, there is a time when they choose to pursue growth. I invite you to step into this healing and transformative exercise.

Beneath the Thorns:

Get into a comfortable position and take a few deep breaths. Feel your attention dropping down into your heart and into your lower belly. Feel what it is like to be seated more deeply in your inner authority and your inner knowing. Trust your deeper knowing as you ground into the earth. As you breathe, feel your legs and feet, and sense into the ground beneath you. Imagine that you are held and deeply rooted by the ground, like a rose. Feel a sense of both opening, like the petals, and grounding, like the roots. Sense the rose putting its roots deep, deep down.

Take a few deep breaths. As you feel increasingly grounded, stable, and open, sense your heart. Feel it supported by this ground and recognize that it is safe for your heart to open like the petals of the rose. It is safe for your heart to radiate out its true nature. The natural radiance of your heart shines. Take as long as you like sensing your heart.

Focus your attention on your chest and heart area. If you have experienced neglect, abuse, grief, sadness, or anger, your heart might be a deeply sensitive area. Pause and take as many deep breaths as you need. Imagine that your heart is a blossoming rose. As you take in a few deep breaths, imagine warm sunshine beaming over your heart with warm healing touches. The rays brush up against a few thorns. The barbs are wounds and pain you may feel. Allow yourself to feel the prickles inside your heart. These tiny holes are a portal to look deeper into our hearts. Imagine that the hot sun is gently caressing and soothing your tiny holes. Sense the wounds allowing you to look deeper inside. Shiny jewels lay beneath the thorns and wounds. Inside the portals are your forgotten qualities, like seeds waiting to be nourished.

The buried seeds are our essential qualities, parts of our true self, which have been hiding. Beneath one wound, you may discover your quality of creativity, and behind another your quality of self-worth. If you lean into fear, shame, or guilt with willingness, the seeds will emerge. With your inner eye, look at the hidden and buried seeds and let the warm sunlight in. Discovering these seeds can be deeply gratifying. Welcome these parts of yourself. See your beautiful soul qualities. This is the space to recognize gratitude for life.

Excavate the seeds from the wounds. Bring them to the surface of your heart and out through the holes. They are expressions of your true self. In our ordinary lives, we can engage with our true selves with an inner radiance and sense of being grateful. The heart is infinite in its capacity to hold gratitude.

Roses have thorns. Like the rose, your heart will always have thorns, these scars. On a deep level, we can appreciate how the thorns came into our lives. This gratitude brings a sense of meaning to what we do. Relax into your breath, join your hands together at your heart, and with a deep sense of gratitude, move into your day. Heaven is right here in the midst of you.

Bio

Carmen Jelly Weiss is a daughter, sister, wife, mother, and grandmother. As an author, registered psychotherapist, and clinical supervisor, she empowers people to move from wounds to wellness. She specializes in attachment, trauma, depression, anxiety, grief, addictions, and many other life transitions. She is passionate about mindfulness and empowering clients to rediscover their true selves and to speak their truth. She brings over 25 years of experience to her private psychotherapy practice. Connect with Carmen at carmen.jelly@newperceptions.ca and www.newperceptions.ca.

The Grateful Divorced Soul
By Carolyn Mackey

The deepest gratitude came after I survived my greatest fear. Divorce. One and a half years ago, the love of my life dropped a huge bomb on me. He was leaving. He wasn't happy anymore, and his mind was made up.

I was glad the truth was finally out. I didn't like it or want it that way, but I'd be lying if I said I didn't see it coming. But I was in shock. How could he leave me? I was the one protecting the relationship illusion. All I could think about was how unfair it was that I was the one "walking on eggshells" that *he* carelessly scattered about the floor of our "happy" home. And then he leaves me! At the time, I believed I was tolerating *his* bad behavior. The reality was I had abandoned myself. *I* was behaving badly because I allowed his behavior to repeatedly disrespect me, our promise, and our binding legal contract of marriage. I was aware he wasn't happy. I was also in a voluntary denial that we were living in an uncomfortable, energy-clenched, holding pattern. He no longer resembled the man he was when we were married. However, I truly never thought he'd leave. I especially never imagined he would blame me for the deep disconnect he was feeling with his inner happiness. I ignored all the red flags. All because I selfishly and naively didn't want to lose *my* life partner. I was terrified by divorce. It thought it meant failure. It was against everything I was taught, and against the traditional moral values I was taught to believe early in life. I was determined long before I ever got married to not be a divorcee. As a good Capricorn should be, I'm a loyal and committed partner. As it turns out, I was loyal to a fault. So loyal to him, I abandoned myself and sacrificed my peace of mind and emotional safety.

After he moved his stuff out of the house, I spent many weeks in complete and utter disbelief. I was sad, confused, and upset that my entire future was a big, involuntary, blank slate. The thing I feared the most had happened. I was living the experience of abandonment by way of the dreaded divorce. Time felt painfully slow and endless.

Yet, in my solitude, I had no other choice but to process what happened the best I could. I realized that I was responsible for one hundred percent of the misfortune I perceived I was enduring. I would think to myself, "If only I would have been more assertive in that argument." I regretted not saying, "No, that doesn't work for me," or, "I will not accept that kind of treatment." If I had tried to say anything like that, maybe we could have duked-out a fair battle. But I didn't. All of the excuses I had made for my crumbling marriage stemmed from a deep fear of loss.

My ex and I spent three months minimum with almost no communication. The only things ever spoken about were the brief details of finalizing the requirements for the divorce filing. My heart hurt so deeply, but I signed the petition without hesitation. I would never chase him or beg him to stay. I won't be, and never will be, with someone who does not wholly want to be with me. So, I humbly reclaimed my maiden name, like a long, lost relative. I embraced my next chapter with deep, unwavering gratitude because it was mine. I stepped fully into my spiritual practice and committed to healing my pain. I knew my heart's desire and my intrinsic motivation. I was a willing partner and had so much to offer, even though I realize now that I never learned how to be in a healthy partnership.

After a year of practicing continuous, committed self-care, and radical acceptance, I've determined that the divorce I feared so much was the absolute best thing that has ever happened to me. It was the best thing that ever happened because I found my perfectly imperfect self on the other side. I found clarity about my true responsibilities. I found an authentic, vulnerable, strong, honest woman inside of me. I had no other choice but to commit to my happiness and show up for me! I had to show up humbly, and unapologetically, in a way that felt admittedly messy, uncertain, and forced into total surrender. I had to put one foot in front of the other, and bravely march in the direction of the unknown. It required so much courage and humility. But I was determined to accept my fate as it was. I knew that I wouldn't be alone forever. I knew God would send me the loving partnership I deserved, admitting that the person I chose to be my one and only, was mistakenly not "the one" for me.

The divorce was like a rebirth. I have deep gratitude in my heart that I was able to experience my worst fear, to overcome it and remember my true essence and strength, and remember who I am. After the divorce, I became committed to myself in a whole new way. I committed to my career, my inner peace, and my new life chapter with vigor. I had surrendered so much of myself to try to preserve my marriage, and that was the dark truth behind the divorce. The gift I received from my now ex-husband was the greatest gift of self-love. And for that, my soul will be forever grateful.

Bio

Carolyn Mackey is a Reiki Master and full-time teacher of *A Course in Miracles*. She helps individuals find their unique spiritual path and purpose. She is passionate about sharing the ideas from *A Course in Miracles* and helping others learn to read it in a way that makes the lessons and ideas more fun to learn. You can connect with her at carolynshares@gmail.com or carolynshares.com.

Gratitude: A Key To Manifesting
By Catherine Cates

My childhood was tainted by emotional and verbal abuse from my father. When I was in my twenties, I made a decision that he didn't agree with. He took it upon himself to write me a long letter detailing his points of contention. The one line that stood out in the letter pretty much summed up how he felt about me: "You will never amount to anything."

Yes, you read that correctly.

Being a parent now, I can't imagine ever saying that to my son, but that is what my dad said to me. At that point, I had two options. I could wind up on the floor in a puddle of tears, or I could do what I did, which was to get mad. I ripped up the letter and refused to take on his belief about me.

Just because he believed I would never amount to anything, didn't mean I had to believe it. That's part of the unconscious programming our parents give us when we are kids. We take on their beliefs because our parents are the authority, so it must be true.

Beliefs aren't called "make-believe" for no reason. They are not real. As such, we can choose to take them on or not. The good news is we can get rid of them at any time. First, you have to know what yours are.

After my dad wrote that to me, you can imagine he wasn't high on my list. If I had taken on his belief about me, I probably wouldn't be writing this chapter. Nor, probably, would I have created my thriving sixteen-year-old business or had an award-winning sales career. Instead of internalizing his beliefs about me, I refused to take them on. By not taking on that toxic belief and clearing out others I held about myself, I was able to have a successful career. Incidentally, many years later, after I had created my business, he told me that he was proud of me for doing so.

When I became a parent, I realized it was time to forgive my dad and be thankful for all he had done for me. If I had not, I doubt we would've gotten to that point in our relationship where he would admit he was proud of me. Once I let forgiveness and gratitude into my heart, we were able to have a loving relationship. In all of the years he had acted abusively, I was never grateful for all the handy-man projects he did for me. In my world, his abusive behavior canceled out any help he provided me, even though my mom had always insisted that is how he showed his love for me.

Since he recently passed away, I am even more grateful that I forgave him all those years ago, as it paved the way for our relationship to turn into one of love and respect rather than only animosity and hurt. It also allowed us to have a heartfelt, tearful final conversation as I told him how much I loved and appreciated him. Now more than ever, I am grateful for all the things he did for me, even if I didn't appreciate it at the time.

With his passing, I am particularly grateful for every loving and respectful interaction we had these past several years. My heart fills with love and gratitude every time I think of our final interaction the last time I saw him alive. As I was leaving, I bent over to hug and kiss him goodbye. He reached out, squeezed my hand, and said, "I love you very much." Those were words I rarely heard my dad say, but what a joy to hear them then! They are even more precious to me as they were the last words he said to me in person.

In forgiving my dad and being grateful for our relationship in recent times, I was able to let go of the old negative messages or beliefs he had given me about myself. When we let go of the negative beliefs, we free up space to manifest. Part of manifesting is feeling good about ourselves. Limiting beliefs about ourselves or things we want to manifest, such as love or money, hold us back from getting what we desire.

Become aware of what old beliefs you may be hanging onto. Instead of holding onto those old tapes your parents planted in your head, clear them out. Know they are not real. In doing so, you'll be amazed at what you can manifest.

Gratitude can be used to unlock manifesting, particularly when we are grateful for whatever it is we want to manifest, whether it's relationships or things. In the case of my dad, being grateful opened the door to manifest a loving relationship.

When practiced daily, gratitude raises our vibration. The higher our vibration, whether it's joy, gratitude, or love, the easier it is to manifest. When we are in worry, doubt, or fear, our mood or vibration is lower, thus making manifesting more difficult.

How do we raise our vibration into gratitude?

Gratitude journals have been all the rage. It's great to be grateful. However, writing words down on a page doesn't often do much to shift our mood. Neither does talking about what we're grateful for. Talking and writing about it can be a precursor. The best way to shift our mood into gratitude is to evoke the feeling of it. Think about what you're grateful for, feel it, and then let that feeling fill you up. Now you have raised your vibration into gratitude.

I am grateful for the loving relationship I cultivated with my dad in the last decade or so of his life. As I write this, I can feel the gratitude filling me up.

What are you grateful for?

Feel it, own it, celebrate it. Now you have raised your vibration, and the sky is the limit for manifesting or merely having a great day.

Bio

Fear kills more dreams than failure ever will. Catherine Cates has helped thousands go from doubt to making their dreams come true. Primarily business-minded women find direction, focus, and success with her unique blend of intuition and twenty-five-plus years in the business world. As an intuitive visionary with her feet on the ground, Catherine gives you easy strategies on which low-hanging fruit to pick first, getting results faster, building confidence, and inspiring you to achieve even bigger successes. Transform your mindset. Turn your life and business from ordinary to extraordinary! Reach Catherine at www.catherinecates.com, me@catherinecates.com or 469-850-2204.

A Grateful Heart
By Chantalle Ullett

"My world has changed, and so have I. I have learned to choose, and I have learned to say goodbye." ~ Pocahontas

During the last 10 years of my career as a licensed massage therapist, I have experienced many changes, shedding layer upon layer of old versions of myself that no longer suit me.

I learned a concept many years ago suggesting that when we are born, our souls map out the life we wish to lead, and make agreements and contracts with other souls, such as our parents, siblings, coworkers, and random people, to help us learn the lessons we choose to experience in our waking lives. Then—poof—we are born, forgetting all we have mapped out. We then spend the rest of our lives trying to figure out which lessons we asked to learn. To this, I add the concept of reincarnation, which maintains that after we pass away, our soul returns to earth in another body. But I also postulate that we should live without regret, so when our soul returns to earth time and time again until it fully comprehends the lessons it chose to learn in previous lives, we may pass through without regret.

There was a time when I felt lost—no hope, no love, and no future. Then in one moment, there were opportunities allowing me to learn and grow, and all the negativity, hate, vengefulness, and difficulty changed. Each of my experiences had arisen at the right moment in time, creating many "a-ha" moments and takeaways. Interestingly, these junctures often happened after I attended a class, seminar, or conference from which I learned that conscious awareness is crucial, and as mine changes, it permits me to shed old belief systems that no longer serve me. This allowed me to heal, and realize there is no right or wrong, good or bad, or me versus them, but rather, a oneness.

I grew exponentially in my conscious awareness when I learned to forgive myself for my feelings. Talk about a strange concept. How does one go about forgiving oneself? First and foremost, you need to know it is okay to feel resentment, anger, bitterness, disheartenment, and negativity toward varying situations or events, and understand that these are all lessons we asked for. Some lessons are more difficult than others; however, viewing them as obstacles along life's journey (thank you, Prince, for this reference) helped me tremendously. You see, our life is a path with numerous twists, curves, hills, straightaways, and forks on which we can choose to turn left or right, or even go straight. We must know that we will encounter obstacles along the way, but it is how we tackle these obstacles that will determine our course. You see, we can choose to go around, over, or under without ever truly seeing the challenge for what it is. Growth and awareness happen when we choose to tackle the obstacles head-on, layer after layer until we reach the core.

To tackle negativity and overcome obstacles, I have found that breathwork is one of the most effective techniques to release stuck energies. It begins with a deep breath inhaling all the way down to the abdomen, where your solar plexus chakra is located, with the understanding of breathing in peace, love, and light. Next, you want to hold the breath for a moment and focus on the event, person, feeling, or thought. Finally, you exhale swiftly in one breath, forcing out the thoughts and emotions we have chosen to hold onto that are no longer serving us. While having used this technique countless times on myself and others, the heaviness the body holds onto due to these emotions seems to dissipate with each deep exhale, resulting in a lightness felt throughout the body. It still astounds me every time.

For the many people who have asked how I have come to these perspectives, here's my answer: I am forever grateful for everyone who has come into my life. First and foremost, to the Creator for His support and guidance. He is integral to who I am and who I am yet to become through all the events, lessons, experiences, and growth I have chosen to receive in this lifetime, as well as from the people I have encountered along the way. I am also grateful to powerful teachers, mentors, and guides, among them: Loesje Jacob, for teaching me to listen and learn from the vast knowledge of the African and Asian elephants, dolphins, orangutans, and countless other animals we encountered on our trips together throughout the world. Carolyn Myss, Greg Braden, Dr. Bruce Lipton, Dr. Darren Weissman, Dr. Joe Dispenza, and numerous other authors, for their incredible seminars and wise words. Last but not least, I am blessed beyond words for the endless support of my husband, Jim, as he grows and gains experience through his own personal journey. My daughters, Kayla and Hailey, for not only being two of my guides, but for also allowing me to be theirs. To my mom, Marie, I am so proud of you. You have inspired me with your strength, tenacity, and boldness for pushing thru one of the most difficult decisions you made this past year.

To everyone else throughout my life thus far. This quote from Anonymous sums it up best: "People come into your life for a reason, a season, or a lifetime. When you figure out which it is, you know exactly what to do."

Bio

Chantalle Ullett is a licensed massage therapist, having earned her degree in 2010 from Cortiva Institute for Massage Therapy. French-Canadian born, she relocated in 1997 to McHenry County, Illinois, where she now lives with her husband and their two daughters. Here, she practices her therapy, continuing her lifelong healing journey, which includes traveling the world, working with sentient beings, and experiencing deep, transformational healings with animals of all kinds. She specializes in treating the body, mind, and spirit through a variety of modalities, including Linking Awareness creating heart-to-heart connections with sentient beings. You can contact Chantalle at chantalleullett@gmail.com.

Thanks+Giving: A Recipe For Living
By Dr. Cheralyn Leeby

It was Monday, January 16. My boyfriend, Doug, knocked on my dorm door. I remember looking over the banister, smiling at how cute he looked with his wind-blown hair, ripped jeans, and motorcycle helmet in hand.

As I peered closer, I noticed Doug's expression was somber. Something was wrong. Trying to shake that feeling, I cheerily asked, "Why are you here so early?"

At that moment, the phone rang. I can still hear the familiar "brrrrrring" and feel the heavy handle of the corded phone. Doug already knew what the call was about.

Doug held my hand while my dad told me that my younger brother, Matthew, had ended his life. I remember screaming, "No!" while tears flooded my face. I felt a nauseating emptiness. Matthew was 18, a freshman at the University of Alaska, and I was 21, a senior at Vanderbilt University.

Losing sweet Matthew 32 years ago was the most raw and real time in my life. There was no hiding from the all-consuming shock, sadness, anger, intense guilt, and questioning that comes with suicide. Without knowing that I would experience grief in this way, I had registered for a "Death and Dying" class that semester. Miraculously, I had the opportunity to simultaneously live through loss while studying it.

In processing my grief, I realized that my favorite holiday, Thanksgiving, contained the essential ingredients for turning my debilitating darkness into light (and it had nothing to do with pumpkin pie).

When I greet life with Thanks and Giving, I gracefully manifest peace, love, and purpose.

Adopting Thanks+Giving as a prescription in perception nurtures inner freedom and ease with the outer world. For me, grieving was the result of attaching to expectations and living in the land of "shoulda, coulda, woulda." I mourned Mathew's past and the future I thought he deserved. I wanted the present to be under my control. Thanks+Giving, in contrast, is a process of relentless allowing, while stepping into acts of service that ignite passion and purpose.

Thanks

When I give thanks for all things, I surrender my battle sword wielded in my egoic experiences, and the dualities of expectations and reality, blame and responsibility, judgment and acceptance. When I consciously choose gratitude, I commit to seeing *all* things, situations, and people with ruthless compassion as part of a masterfully woven tapestry. Even the hardest human experiences are held in appreciation for the lessons and blessings. Short or long, knotted or golden, every strand of human life is essential to the divine whole that can only be seen from an all-encompassing view. Full with grace, I remind myself to find awe in *all* (awe-all) as opposed to describing a few things as "awe-*some*."

For many years, I searched to understand why Matthew's life thread was tattered, jagged, and cut short. I spent sleepless, weepy nights questioning why any child battled depression, abuse, starvation, or war. Today, I accept

Matthew's death without having answers, and I thank him for being the catalyst for my professional path as a marriage and family therapist. I now surrender the notion that I can or should prevent anyone from their experiences.

There is a story about butterflies that I love. Caterpillars safely reside in cocoons for a time until eventually, the butterfly is ready to emerge. An observer may notice that there is pulling and stretching as the butterfly contorts and labors through a small hole into its new en-*lightened* life. An outsider may feel prompted to assist. However, scientists confirm that if the cocoon is cut to "free" the butterfly, it does not develop the wing strength to fly. Saving the butterfly from its necessarily difficult moments keeps it weak. The lesson here is that *all* of life—the pain, and the glory—are worthy of praise as essential steps on the journey.

The Japanese art of Kintsugi, meaning "golden joinery," is the process of transforming something broken into a more valuable gilded heirloom. Like the butterfly, this up-cycling renders the brokenness worthy. The butterfly and the Kintsugi artist do not have to *think* their way through transformation. Instead, they co-create their "master-peace" by aligning with divine design and the natural laws.

Giving

When I consciously savor and serve with intention, I transcend sorrow and disappointment. When I choose to give of myself, I experience unexpected abundance and deep connection in return. Giving is the test and testament for true grace and gratitude. Beyond simply wishing someone well, salvation and freedom follow the "Golden Rule" embraced by many religions and cultures. We are advised, "*Do* unto your neighbor," not simply co-exist and say, "Thanks."

There are times I notice a gap for myself between the thanks and the giving. When I choose to translate gratitude into loving action, I feel elevated and energized. Serving others turns my struggles into gifts, just as foundations, charities, and humanitarian organizations are born from trials and adversities.

A key directive in life, therefore, might be to uncover how our suffering can illuminate a path to purpose. Although the ways and means are unique for each of us, it has been my experience that joie de vivre or *life joy*, is where our sense of gratefulness, presence, and purpose meet.

With this recipe, I remind myself to see every moment as one of Thanks+Giving. The buffet is plenti-*full* when I can say "yes" to the following questions:

1. Am I living with grace, allowing all to simply "be" without judgment, expectation, or desire for change?
2. Am I inviting gratitude in every moment, appreciating the lessons and blessings as part of the universal weave of life? Can I affirm my difficulties and complete the following statement: "I am grateful that (adverse experience) happened because—"
3. Am I moving from awareness into actions that serve others?

Beyond the tender turkey and savory mashed potatoes of our American November holiday feast, my daily meal for healing is one of conscious Thanks+Giving. I invite you to join me at this table of awakened living.

Bio

Dr. Cheralyn Leeby, Licensed Marriage and Family Therapist, has over 30 years' experience working with individuals, couples, and families, guiding them to actualize their heart-healing with Thanks+Giving. She earned undergraduate and graduate degrees from Vanderbilt University and her Doctorate from UF. She has specialized training in Art Therapy and Holographic Memory Resolution. Dr. Leeby created Soul Life, an innovative wellness education and prevention platform with workshops and retreats in the USA/Mexico. Dr. Leeby is deeply grateful to her brother Matthew, her family, and her beloved husband, Doug, for their love and inspiration.
www.soullife.us

When The Mourning Dove Whispers
By Cheryl Peterson

We were enjoying one of those simple and uncompli-cated Sunday dinners together. As usual, Dad had insisted on joining us at the table even though he couldn't swallow. He had a medical condition that prevented him from doing so. We quietly nibbled at our food, pretending to be unaffected as he pushed liquid dinner through his feeding tube. On this particular night, he looked up at me and said, "Isn't that the most beautiful bird you've ever heard?" I glanced at the clock he'd been given that hung on the dining room wall, which made different bird songs every hour. Dad seldom spoke, and the tenderness of his words was perfectly unpredictable. Right then, I felt an overwhelming sense of gratitude. My intuition nudged me to make a mental note of the sound of the mourning dove. At the time, its relevance was unclear.

Fast-forward several months. According to his doctors, Dad was a medical miracle. Some of the family had gathered for the weekend. It was a perfect day—sunny, relaxed—and I was grateful that we were together. We went to a restaurant that overlooked the reservoir. It was one of Dad's favorite places. Then, I received the phone call. I excused myself from the table to take it. Sensing the apprehension in the doctor's voice, I knew what his words would reveal. "Cheryl, your father has six months or less to live. Frankly, we're not sure why he's still alive, since we believe that he's had esophageal cancer for the past several years." His words pierced my soul. I glanced over at Dad sitting on the deck, enjoying the view, and he looked so peaceful and content. The doctor asked, "Cheryl, do you want me to tell him now?" I paused briefly, trying to absorb the information, but asserted, "No. I'll share the news with him."

As we ended the call, I looked again at the deck, where my family was laughing and enjoying time together. In the distance, I heard the whisper of the mourning dove. I knew that spirit was with me, encouraging me and reminding me of my strength to move forward through this life-altering moment. I felt an overwhelming sense of gratitude. "Okay, spirit. What should I do next?" I asked. My intuition urged me to simply enjoy the day. The still, small voice inside me said, "Everything will be okay. Everything is okay."

After discussing his diagnosis with my siblings, we all agreed it made sense for me to be the one to tell him. While watching television with Dad the next day, I decided that now was as good as it would get. I thought, "Spirit, you have quite the sense of humor. I'm the youngest of six kids and, according to Dad, the least responsible of the bunch." I laughed out loud at the irony of it all and forged ahead, powered by spirit. "Dad, I have some news from your doctor." Once again, I heard the whisper of the mourning dove in the distance. Dad kept his gaze on the television, and without emotion, said, "I'm going to die soon, right?" Silence filled the moment. The light was shining through his window, and I noticed his amazing blue eyes, which were always gleaming. Dad glanced at me and, with a smirk on his face, said, "I'm going to hell." I asked him why he thought that. He grinned at me. "Because that's where all of my friends will be." Grateful for the moment of levity, we both let out an exuberant laugh.

We were hospice bound. As soon as I entered the facility, I was overcome with the feeling that I'd entered sacred ground. As Dad began his week-long journey, I thought about the many hours I'd spent quietly at his bedside at home. As usual, Dad wasn't interested in talking. He much preferred watching television and gazing out his window. My mind was occupied with thoughts of the past 40-plus years I'd spent with him. I reflected on the times I'd withheld saying, "I love you," because I knew he wouldn't say it back to me. He never used words to express love. I thought about how many times I'd wanted to offer him forgiveness for what he considered were mistakes he'd made when I was a child and a young adult. But I didn't. I never told him how grateful I was that he'd sacrificed so much of his life to ensure that our family had a roof over our heads and food on the table. He'd worked extremely hard at his job, and the stress of it all resulted in many late nights and binge drinking to release what he couldn't verbalize to any of us.

Knowing that he'd be uncomfortable having a discussion with me, I decided to write him a love letter of gratitude and forgiveness. I left it on his bedside table and felt grateful that spirit had prompted me to do this. When I returned the next day, he was sitting up in bed, blue eyes shining brightly, looking peaceful and relaxed. I sat down quietly, took a deep breath, and asked him if he'd read the letter. He said, "Yes. Thank you." Without a word, we both gazed out the window. In the distance, we heard the mourning dove whisper. My heart was filled with gratitude.

Dad made his transition peacefully. I'll be forever grateful for the time I was able to spend with him as he completed his journey. It's been 20 years since he passed. And, to this day, the mourning dove still comes to whisper. I know that his spirit is with me, and my soul overflows with gratitude.

Gratitude is one of the greatest gifts you have to give. Give it without reservation.

Bio

Cheryl Peterson has worked for a non-profit organization and has defended women's rights for the past 36 years. She enjoys her work as a fiber artist and creates wearable art for sale at art shows and online. Cheryl is a Reiki practitioner and practices guided meditations with individuals and groups. Powered by spirit and inspired by *A Course in Miracles*, she enjoys sharing her love and light with the world. The amazing journey continues. Contact Cheryl Peterson, Morning Dove Designs at cherylswearableart.com or cherylmdd@gmail.com.

Another Day In Paradise
By Cindy Mallory

Live life as if everything is rigged in your favor. ~ Rumi

L ife is a miracle. Once we feel this truth, gratitude for every part of our existence will be a given. The feeling our deepest gratitude provides is beyond words. It is a way of being, a path of love. It is faith. It is about trusting there is something bigger out there, even in the midst of our greatest darkness.

We are told that cultivating gratitude makes us happier. So, how do we get there as we go about our daily lives, with its myriad of challenges? We need to go beyond the trappings of life to a place of being, where we notice the magic all around us. Then we will see all that life bestows upon us with a clear mind.

Our thought patterns affect our emotional health and how we experience our lives. There are always two paths in front of us, no matter how difficult our lives may be. The first is when we perceive only obstacles and let old fearful thought patterns dominate our lives. This is where our minds will go when we are without attention and focus, like well-worn grooves in the brain. We get lost wishing for our lives to be better or different and miss the inherent beauty of what exists right in front of us. This unconscious flow of negativity blocks our ability to experience our lives and makes gratitude impossible. The second path is when we choose to believe in our soul that everything is a gift, no matter what we are dealing with, and that life will never give us more than we can handle. This is the road less traveled, the hero's journey. This is the route to gratitude.

With practice, we can learn to catch negative thoughts as they are occurring. At first, it feels like you are working a muscle that would prefer to be left alone. Then, one day, you notice you feel happier and lighter each time you replace a negative thought with a loving one. It gets easier, and eventually, gratitude permeates every facet of your life, transforming your world.

Yet, for those who have experienced significant trauma, especially during their early years, finding a way to feel grateful for life's struggles can be especially challenging. Those negative grooves in the brain may be deeply embedded. Finding the courage to acknowledge and wade through our deepest pain is the only way to get there. Otherwise, we drag our hurts behind us while they continuously recreate our pain. Facing these traumas is an act of self-love, a message to ourselves that we are worth saving. It's this message of love that is a prerequisite for true gratitude.

As we walk along this path of healing, we begin to notice how we are being transformed, and we recognize that this journey is taking us to places inside ourselves that open our hearts in ways we could not have imagined. We find beauty at the bottom of our deepest suffering. This is the gift that exists beyond words, and from which love and gratitude extends outward to everything and everyone.

I learned this from the inside out, beginning my path of healing 32 years ago. If I had instead chosen to circumvent this learning experience, limping through life, gratitude would not have been possible. I would still be living in the dark.

I was separated from my mother at an early age. Her leaving was followed by many years of sexual, physical, and emotional abuse. When there is no one to tell us differently as children, we believe the worst, and it becomes our reality. The only answer I had to any question was that I was completely unworthy of love or even living.

By the time I was 13, I was an empty shell. I lived outside of my body in a world that was colorless and hollow. Being looked at or touched caused physical pain, and I believed I was hideous inside and out. Yet I had learned to be a chameleon, to blend in, so people only noticed how quiet I was. Everything had been taken from me before I even knew what it was.

It took many more years, and the love and support of my amazing husband, before I was able to embark on the uphill journey of healing. Healing was demanding and boundless, like climbing a mountain. Each time I stopped to take a look, the view became less terrifying and more breathtaking. Over the years, the walls around me slowly melted away, and the world began to shine again. Healing from this early loss of self has become my life's work. Trauma has been my teacher, and its lesson is gratitude. My life is truly miraculous.

Suffering can be the golden path to your healing. It can be one of the most powerful energy forces in the universe. You have the choice to keep trying to avoid it by pushing it away and refusing to acknowledge it, or you can choose to transcend your greatest traumas. Let go and surrender. Go to the bottom of your deepest pain, and feel your despair, your hopelessness, your brokenness; only then can you walk forward in life without your traumas crippling your happiness. As a result, you will be able to climb out of the darkness and find joy, peace, and gratitude for all of the experiences that created your unique self. Then your light will shine bright, and gratitude will flow like your breath. You will truly live the miracle of your life.

There is a truth about life that we often fail to notice. As we change our thoughts, our outer circumstances change to reflect our beliefs.

You have the power to be the change in your life, and dance through each day as if it were merely another day in paradise.

Bio

Cindy Mallory is a yoga teacher, Reiki Master, and writer. She is on a lifelong healing journey, transforming her past into her life's work. She aspires to help others find their individual path to healing. You can reach her at cindy.mallory@utoronto.ca.

How Gratitude Changed Me
By Darby Purcell

The simple act of gratitude not only changed my perspective on my life today but also my future. While I was growing up, being thankful was something that was required by my parents. I had to say thank you when someone held the door for me, and thank you to my father for working almost 70 hours a week. By focusing on the things that I was thankful for, it brought me to an optimistic state of mind. I have learned that offering a simple "thank you" can not only show my appreciation but also make me feel good about myself.

The journey of finding my grateful mindset may seem complicated, but considering I am a 16-year-old writing part of this book, I think anything is possible.

Entering my freshman year of high school, I had the mindset that these next few years were going to be the best ones of my life. Little was I aware of the many roadblocks I was about to encounter. The school work was hard, but what challenged me most was my environment. There were many different types of people in my school, which meant there were just as many people who made smart decisions as people who made dumb ones. I was being picked on by people who were three years older, and by people I thought were supposed to be standing up for me. The majority of my freshman year consisted of me losing my self-identity, any self-confidence I was beginning to build, and most of my friends. Isolating myself alone in my room seemed to be one of the only things that brought me any sense of peace.

The following summer break was extremely chaotic. I had no idea who I was, who I wanted to be friends with, what love was, how to express it, and so many other soul-searching questions. Although, summer did make me feel a little better because I could choose who I did and didn't want to be around. Still, it felt like it only lasted a few days. Before I knew it, I was in my sophomore year class orientation. The beginning of my sophomore year of high school was full of unexpected issues that I had no idea how to deal with. My animosity for school had grown significantly, and being there felt like I was trapped in a prison. Anxiety and depression became a problem and started to take over. It came to the point where I simply refused to get out of bed because I felt so empty inside. I didn't want to do anything outside of my (small) comfort zone. I lost friends, and I lost any sense of the self-identity I had once gained. During my whole entire first semester, I felt like a puppet incapable of taking hold of the strings. Overall, it was a bad start to my experience of high school, and I was desperate to find ways to make myself feel better.

The relationship between my journey of mental health and gratitude begins with my journal. I am not one to journal every single day, but when I have something to say and cannot say it out loud, I do not hesitate to open up my journal and begin writing thoughts. I had a counselor at school who introduced me to the idea of having a gratitude journal, and I decided to try it, considering I was feeling extremely desperate and eager for something to change. Writing in it brought my attention to the positive aspects of my day. For example, even if I thought that the day was the worst day I had ever experienced, I recorded the time a nice lady waved hello to me. It was an opportunity to direct my focus on the things that brought me joy, and it brought me closer to an optimistic view of the world around me. My mother always told me that if 20 people tell me my appearance is ugly and one person tells me I look pretty, to focus on the compliment. Naturally, my tendency is to focus on the 20 people, even though their negative opinions should not matter. My point is that, as humans, we naturally tend to focus on things that are negative because they trigger our worst fears about who we are. We do not practice kindness toward ourselves enough. Convincing myself to be extra thankful and focus on positive outcomes has taken time, but if I can do it, anyone can. When we radiate positivity through our own energy, we invite more of the same in return, leading to an all-around happier environment.

Moving forward, my final point to express is the gift of gratitude to those around me. An example of this could range from a simple compliment to bringing my loved one a bouquet of flowers. Simple acts of gratitude towards yourself matter as well. If I achieve something that I am proud of, and I want to reward myself, I might dedicate my night to myself and do something that I don't normally get to do, but that brings me joy. Doing this has helped to increase my self-esteem and self-confidence by appreciating my accomplishments.

To conclude, the gift of gratitude is confusing but powerful. Making ourselves feel complete while giving other people the same feeling is something that truly goes a long way. Personally, one of the only ways I have successfully dealt with my struggles with depression and anxiety is by using gratitude. Making other people feel better about themselves while also appreciating my good attributes, leads to a feeling that fills the hole of negativity drilled by feeling down and stressed. A social entrepreneur named Mary Davis once said, "The more grateful I am, the more beauty I see." Those few words speak a powerful truth. I hope with my words, I can help others and influence a positive, happy, and healthy outlook on this world. The gift of thankfulness is one that lasts forever.

Bio

My name is Darby Purcell, and I'm proud to say that I am officially an author. I'm also a daughter to my amazing parents, Kim and Ken, a sister to two brothers, Bryce and Parker. I am also a granddaughter, and am particularly grateful for my grandfather, Dr. Edward F. Droge, Jr., Ed.D. for all of his help with writing this chapter. I love my family very much. I am an athlete on the Ponte Vedra High School girls' lacrosse team, and have been dancing for 13 years. I am also active in my church and volunteer with younger children.

Soulful Message Of Gratitude
By Debbie Helsel

To have a grateful soul, one must be a grateful soul. We live the things we learn throughout life. Our living conditions and situations, how we are raised by our families, or even how treat each other or are treated throughout our lives—in both good and bad situations—can have a major impact on how we see the world and how the world sees us. This can play a huge role in our level of gratefulness, whether we choose to admit it or not.

Embracing what life has to offer and has given us while working towards creating the life we desire can seem like an impossible task. Life is what we choose to make of it through our decisions, actions, and experiences. I believe that we can create our experiences based on choices and being open to opportunities and our attitude towards them. It can be hard to find the positive in situations that are out of our control or are delegated by default. Many times, we don't see the reasoning because we only have a vision toward what we see or desire. Faith plays a big role, as well as letting go of things outside our control, and sometimes another person's vision enhances what ours was.

Having a grateful soul starts inside us all. We should express gratitude for everything and everyone in our lives because it is all intertwined and has a purpose. There are messages in each and every area of our lives. Although they may be subtle, they are there. If we pause for a moment, step back, take a deep breath, clear our minds while opening our hearts, and listen, maybe we will even receive a message.

When our wildlife refuge was growing, and we were so close to seeing it come to life in a new way, with relocation and a new chapter, things kind of stalled. It seemed that everything that could get in the way of it happening did. Many issues arose, and it began taking a toll on me and all the people working so hard to make it happen. I took it personally, though. I felt as if it was my fault for not working hard enough or doing more than was humanly possible to do. It simply wasn't enough, no matter what I did. It affected me on many levels, physically, mentally, and emotionally. I was completely drained, and I finally dropped to my hands and knees and submitted. I prayed to whoever was listening out there in the universe, and I released the burdens I was carrying in feeling like it was my fault. I came to terms with the fact it might all end for the refuge and never reach the potential it had, but I had to let it go. I was devastated and emotionally drained, heartbroken and exhausted, but I had to believe that if it didn't work out somehow, I had done my part to ensure its success and that there was something else waiting for me—another adventure I was supposed to be a part of or someone else I was supposed to help. When you know that you were put on this earth to be of service, you always know you will be needed. But at that time, I had nothing left to give, I was getting sick by that point, and I had to come to terms with it all. I realize through it all that I had forgotten to actually stop and ask for help from God and the angels. I guess I thought I had asked, but not truly asked with the core of my being.

After I let the burden and control go, the blocks and barricades began to fall, and things rolled along in motion. Our organization is in its 31st year, we are growing and thriving, and are about to achieve yet another milestone this year. It has been quite the ride and so much better than we could have imagined. Being grateful for what we had achieved, and accepting that it would be changing again was hard. But being open to new ideas and concepts even if we had our heart set on one thing was tough since we needed to realize there was a lesson in it and always growth from it. We need to remember to set our ego aside (we all have one that creeps out occasionally) and listen for guidance, definitely listening to each other also, so everyone may contribute something.

Isn't life supposed to be for us to help nurture each other and help each other grow and see one another achieve our greatest aspirations, even if they seem small or insignificant to others? For some, they are grateful to have another day, and maybe watch the sun rise or set. For some, it is surpassing the daily goals they had set for themselves or landing their dream job. For some, it is merely making it through one day without being affected by an addiction, or maybe even walking a single step when you were told it would never happen, or beating the odds on a dis-ease all the doctors said wouldn't be possible.

We are the ones who create possibilities! Our thoughts and actions and being grateful for each moment that life has given us, good or bad, are blessings that help mold us into the most amazing person we can become if we are open to it. Change is hard, but having a grateful soul is easy.

You know what I am grateful for? I am grateful for me, and I am grateful for you. I am grateful for my family and friends. I am grateful for opportunities and living my passions in life. I am grateful to be chosen to be of service to Mother Earth. I choose to have a grateful soul, and you can, too.

Bio

Rev. Dr. Debbie Helsel is a Heart 2 Heart Healing and Heart 2 Heart Connections Practitioner. She is additionally trained in reconnective healing, Reiki, spiritual response therapy, and is studying rose alchemy, flower essences, and essential oils. While working with her guides and angels, she seeks divine guidance on healing with crystals mostly through self-study and discovery. She has a Doctorate of Metaphysical studies through The Alliance of Divine Love Ministry, studying with the Center for Healing in Orlando. She enjoys digging crystals and attending drum circles.

Debbie is the Executive Director at Back to Nature Wildlife Refuge in Orlando, Florida. Since 1990, Debbie has dedicated her life to caring for injured and orphaned wildlife. Learn more at www.BTNwildlife.org, or contact Debbie at BTNdebbie@gmail.com.

A Grateful Heart
By Debra Kahnen

How do you cultivate a grateful heart?
A grateful heart is cultivated over time. You could call it a spiritual practice—because it takes practice.

It is easy to be grateful for the good things in life—kindness, a helping hand, a financial windfall—but it is harder to be grateful for the difficult things in life. When you suffer a loss, the degree of pain is equal to the degree of love. My gratitude practice was invaluable when I was blindsided with the news that my husband did not like being married and was moving out the next weekend. I was happy in my marriage and grateful to have him in my life. While there were aspects that were not working optimally, I chose to focus on the things I was grateful for. I was cultivating a grateful heart. There was not much I could do during the period of shock and the responsibility of packing and sorting belongings. Luckily, we had never combined our finances since we were married later in life.

A dear friend of mine recommended that I use the process in *The Grief Recovery Handbook* to heal. It was an amazing book, and I diligently worked the process to not only heal the loss of my husband, but other losses in my life. It was like recovering parts of myself that I had lost, while restoring my wholeness. I was able to later set up a meeting with my soon-to-be ex, and we wrote down all the things we had been grateful for during the time of our marriage and relationship and shared them with each other. I remember back to my wedding. It was so magical. We married 11/11/11, and at 11:11 p.m., we stopped the celebration for a moment of silence, and I literally felt like I could float off the ground. We went to Italy, swimming with the dolphins, on my first cruise. I learned what it felt like to have someone that was caring and kind in my life. I discovered my love language was acts of service, which he so easily did daily. There were so many joyous experiences. I decided to be grateful for those and realized that without that marriage, I would not have had those amazing experiences. We were able to acknowledge, appreciate, and celebrate all the good that was made possible because of our union. Amazingly, in the courtroom, it was him falling apart and me holding his hand. I think looking at the good and being grateful for that, as well as looking at the lessons I learned, allowed me to move forward as a bigger, capable human being. My grateful heart kept me from getting stuck in the loss, or emotions such as blame, anger, or resentment.

The degree of frustration is also equal to the degree of desire. When my son turned 18 and was in high school, the support money provided by his dad was paid directly to him. Rather than being grateful for the money, I was so resentful that my son was blowing through the money that he should be saving for college. I wanted to successfully launch him on his own, and he was completely unwilling to listen or be told what to do. What he valued, I found a waste of money because he had no idea what the real world was going to be like—how much things cost and what could be easier by saving now. That money could be used for college tuition, a down payment for an apartment or a car. How many generations of parents and kids have not seen eye to eye? It is not easy to move something with that much resistance to gratitude. How could I look at this from a different point of view?

As my resistance built, the relationship between my son and I became increasingly troubled. The more I tried to get him to save—the more he would spend. I knew I had to let go and find a place of non-resistance and a way back to gratitude. Abraham Hicks says to find the next thought that feels better. Saying the opposite doesn't work if the thought does not make you feel better. Saying I don't care when I do care will not make me feel better. However, I could say, "I am glad he is getting to enjoy this time before he has to work the rest of his life." That didn't feel quite right. "I am glad his father was able to provide this support for his son." That felt somewhat better, but I kept pulling back to the resistance, "Every dollar he wastes now is going to make the future harder." I struggled to find the point of gratitude. I decided to try focusing on other areas. "I have a nice home with everything I need, a job with a good salary, my son and I have our health. I have wonderful parents that are still alive. I have many talents and have had many accomplishments over my lifetime." As I started to feel better, a new thought found its way into my mind. "If you take the support and subtract the bills he pays between now and graduation, it's only several thousand dollars." I then asked myself, "Is that money worth damaging my relationship with my son and my well-being?" Recognizing that I had wasted more than that buying things I barely used, my resistance subsided. I felt much more present and able to live in a state of gratitude. Once again, my home became a peaceful place to live.

My son and I are a lot closer. Other things will come along and try to throw me out of my grateful heart state. But I have the tools to put myself back on track.

Bio

Debra Kahnen is a registered nurse and naturopath. In recent years, she has completed research to help chronic pain patients and nurses deal with stress using mindfulness. She has presented her research nationally and internationally. As a column editor for a professional nursing journal, she wrote about healthy practice environments and resilience. She is the author of *Power of Clarity: What to Do Today to Create Tomorrows You Love*, available on Kindle. As a Theta Healing practitioner, she assists individuals in healing. She can be reached at debrakahnen.com.

Grace. Gratitude. Freedom.
By Donna Kiel

As I drove my mother to the doctor, we chatted. Our roles were familiar. Since the age of six, I took on the role of caretaker and counselor to my mom. In a diagnostic manner, I asked questions about her physical symptoms. I offered a calm and detached reassurance that she would be fine. Mother and daughter relationships are always complicated. Our relationship was no different. From my mother's perspective, I was her college-educated, professional daughter who was smart, had a strong work ethic, and who was the one she could rely on. To me, my mother was an anxious, often needy, beautiful, funny, unorthodox woman.

I discovered early on in life that if I became knowledge-able, articulate, well-read, and confident, then I could shield myself from being vulnerable and wounded. If I was the one my mother or others came to for guidance and solutions, I wouldn't need to face the deep longing or hurt that frequently filled my heart. The result was a distance between my mother and me, and from most others.

I didn't start life that way. My earliest memory of my mother was her gentle touch and soothing voice singing me to sleep with a song I think she made up. The words, "Good night, sweet Jesus, keep us at rest," were like a warm blanket of safety. I adored my mother. My love for her was steadfast and clingy. I never wanted to be without her. All that changed when I was six. In one afternoon, when I was left in the care of my uncle, my trust, security, and open-heartedness came crashing down. I look at my daughter, and now my granddaughter, and my soul rages with anger at the thought of anyone violating them the way my uncle violated me.

It wasn't so much the abuse that changed my world as it was my mother choosing not to believe me. The deep wounding of my mom's inability to believe me launched a lifetime of trying to prove I was worthy and believable. I longed to be worthy of my mother's comfort and admiration. In the process, I built a wall around my heart. Yet, like most walls, freedom was on the other side. Friends would tell me, "Donna, your mom loves you and is so proud of you." I never believed them. I wanted her love to be true, but my heart said no—don't let her love you—it will hurt.

As the doctor examined her, my mother asked the doctor about her life, her children, her ethnicity, and her age. My mother never met a boundary she didn't cross with a type of loving engagement that would have even a cardiologist tell my mother of her struggles with her children. As the doctor shared her life story, her face grew concerned as the stethoscope moved around my mother's chest. She interrupted my mother's questioning, long enough to say, "Fran, we're going to need to admit you to the hospital, you're in the midst of a heart attack." The doctor was calm, assuring, and took my mother's hand gently, saying, "Your daughter and I will be with you, and this will be fine."

The nurse brought a wheelchair to take my mother to the emergency room that was in the building next to the doctor's office. The three of us got in the elevator. As we all faced the elevator door void of eye contact, staring ahead, I put my hand on my mother's shoulder. I told her things would be fine. I jumped right into caretaker mode, saying I would get her belongings, take care of my dad, and make sure she had her nightgown. The nurse leaned into my mom and said, "You're one lucky woman to have such a loving daughter." Without even a pause, my mother said, "I guess so, considering I never even wanted her."

What did she just say? She never wanted me. Really? Is this how one finds out? She never wanted me. All I ever wanted was to have her want me.

It took enormous control to wait two days before I asked my mother to explain her comment. Years of fearfully avoiding feeling connected to my mother were now replaced with rage. I worked so hard to take care of her, and she didn't want me. I had to know why she didn't want me. I was not her first child—rather, I was her middle child, and for all intents and purposes, I was the good one of the three. I was the one who went to school, worked hard, did well, and who took care of her.

My mother easily shared the explanation of her statement. She described her life with my alcoholic father and her unstable family. In that moment, as I took in the information, I searched for understanding.

Mother and daughter relationships have unspoken expectations. I expected my mother to cast aside her fears of her family, of my father's addictions, and of life and give me unconditional love. My mother expected me to be the daughter she needed. In that moment of truth, when my mother spoke, her words gave me freedom. It is gratitude for that moment of graceful truth, which transformed my life.

My mother, like all mothers, was a woman whose imperfect life was complex and confusing. She gave me the love she was capable of giving. It is grace that gives me gratitude. Grace for my mother's humanness. My mother's weakness became my strength. Her need to be cared for gave me the opportunity to become strong, resilient, and caring. Grace, with gratitude, is the key to freedom. It is when we can find the moment of grace, the moment of thankfulness, even for that which we believed we did not want, that we are set free to fully love ourselves and love those who tried their best to love us.

Bio

Donna Kiel is a life coach, speaker, and university professor. Donna has inspired thousands in finding purpose and living a life of meaning and impact. Her vast experiences as an educator, counselor, and leader have resulted in her expertise in designing the life you want. She holds three degrees, including a BA in psychology, an MA in counseling, and a doctorate in leadership. Donna's specialties include achieving personal and professional success, achieving peace and personal fulfillment, anxiety reduction, and aging with vitality. Donna offers free assessment and consultation. She can be reached at drdonnakiel@gmail.com or through her website at www.donnakiel.com.

One Journey To An Attitude Of Gratitude
By Dorothy Welty

I grew up in the middle-class suburb of Park Ridge, Illinois, an idyllic community outside Chicago. Growing up in Park Ridge in the 1960s was quite the *Leave It to Beaver* existence where fathers worked hard, and mothers stayed home to run the household. Saturdays were about household chores and manicured yards. Sundays were about attending church and welcoming extended family for Sunday dinner. Everyone had an intact family, nice homes, and nice cars. Everyone's father had a decent job. Everyone's mother was devoted to her husband and children. All the children went to good schools and were raised with a common set of morals and values that the whole community held dear.

I was aware I had landed quite a bit of good fortune being born into this all-American suburban life. I knew many people across the country and around the world were not so fortunate. Though I was aware that I had much to be grateful for, I grew up lacking a heartfelt sense of gratitude. For inside this idyllic-appearing home was a pervasive fear that squelched any seeds of gratitude from sprouting forth.

Raised by parents who had grown up during the Depression, their parental approach was a "pull yourself up by the bootstraps and work to prove your worth" mentality. No matter how hard we all worked, the fear that all could be lost by circumstances beyond any individual's control pervaded everyday life, preventing any sense of gratitude. This culture of fear bred judgment as well. I was told I wasn't attractive enough to marry well. I wasn't smart enough to go to a university. I wasn't gifted enough to devote financial resources to develop my creativity. I was told I was average. I was discouraged from seeing myself as something unique and special. I was encouraged to learn typing and shorthand so that I would always have a job and be able to support myself. When I was bullied at school, my mother told me it only affected me because I let it. When I cried at the dinner table because my brother picked on me, I was banished to my room until I could stop crying.

Growing up was like a slow death by 1,000 cuts to my soul. My mother's message was clear: to protect myself from the never-ending emotional torture, I needed to toughen up. I took her message to heart. I buried my sensitivity. I distanced myself from others and used my strong will and intelligence to advance myself in a culture where accomplishment was valued. I mastered the "pull yourself up by the bootstraps and work to prove your worth" mentality. I grew a strong armor. At the slightest hint of feeling vulnerable, I took a "get them before they get me" offense.

As a result of how I was raised, I became what I had lived, fearful. By age 50, I despised who I had become. I knew I could not spend whatever time that remained in this life living in betrayal of my true spirit. Little did I know the power of my intention to live authentically would, over the next seven years, strip away everything I had known my life to be up to that point. I would lose my financial investments, my marriage, my home, my friends, and my career. Some of the losses were by choice, while others came by way of the Universe, teaching me to let go of fear and have faith. Living inauthentically for decades had brought me to a state of despair so deep that I braved shedding my armor and found the courage to embrace the unknown.

Up to that point, the armor I had worn to protect me from emotional vulnerability had left me unable to shed a tear for 25 years. As the life I knew was stripped away by loss after loss, I had to face many of my worst fears. Day after day for several years, I could hardly stop the tears from flowing. I found myself crying not just for all my current losses, but all the emotional wounds I had experienced as a child. When I allowed myself to fully experience all the hurt and pain, while it took several years, all the despair eventually did pass through me. I emerged on the other side of all the chaos and pain finally able to reconnect with my true spirit.

I committed to giving myself all the love and compassion that was not given to me growing up. I consciously chose to begin responding to the events in life in a loving way rather than reacting to life from a place of fear. Since living more authentically, I experience a calm I have never known. In the serenity of living as one with my true spirit, I am more kind and loving, and I receive more kindness and love in return. In giving myself the love that I had not received as a child, the middle-aged woman I am now recognizes that I do not have to be affected by any unkindness or judgment that comes my way. The sweetness of life has slowly returned.

I live at a much slower pace now, experiencing heartfelt gratitude daily. From my home and my work, I gaze upon the mountains that seem a visual metaphor for the obstacles

I have overcome, and I experience peace. Releasing the fear, living in the moment, and consciously choosing to respond from a place of love and compassion is the commitment I make in living each day. I am so grateful for my long, uncomfortable journey to developing an attitude of gratitude.

Bio

Dorothy Welty is a community college administrator and teacher. She holds an MS in psychology from Illinois State University. She is passionate about the power of education to change individual lives and the world in which we live. In her free time, Dorothy enjoys meditation, hiking, kayaking, writing, baking, and a variety of other creative pursuits. You can reach Dorothy at dwelty50@gmail.com.

Peace, Freedom, And Forgiveness
By Douglas Roland Smith

In March of 2003, a powerful snowstorm swept through the Front Range of Colorado. Days later, and through a series of events, I'd wind up meeting Adriana at a public recreation center. Like that storm, she was both powerful and deep. From the moment I met her, there was an instantaneous connection, as if we'd traveled this world together once before. In the days, months, and years that followed, my gratitude for our connection and relationship would grow, transform, and mature into a relationship beyond my wildest imagination.

Adriana was from Venezuela. She'd immigrated to the USA about ten years prior to my meeting her. She was full of spice, love, and the Latin way of being. I had no idea how she would impact me at the time, but I knew from the moment I met her that she was amazing. Coming out of a failed relationship, I was wounded to the core, shy, insecure, and—from my perspective—lost in many ways. I wasn't ready for another relationship, but there was something mystical and spiritual about Adriana. I'd soon discover that she, like me, had multiple relationship failures in her past. She also, like me, had decided relationships weren't her strength.

Hours into our first conversation, we started exploring the topic of spirituality. We found out quickly that we had a love for the Christ consciousness and a deep desire to grow our relationship with source. Weeks later, and as if on cue, I discovered a book called *A Course in Miracles*. At the time, a class, based on the book, was being held in a small Unity Church just east of downtown Denver. After going alone a couple of times, and with a little nervousness, I invited Adriana. She loved it. I loved it. So, we kept going again and again. For 17 years and counting. Little did we know in those early days that *A Course in Miracles* (the Course) would have a profound impact on our relationship.

After a couple months of attending the classes and reading together regularly, we began to realize that the Course is actually all about relationships—and all kinds of them—with our romantic partners, our kids, our parents, our bosses and everyone in our lives. It's also about our relationships with everything around us. For Adriana and me, the Course was especially important for our relationship with each other. Since our past relationships had turned into love/hate relationships—as most do—we were wary of recreating the same dynamic. The Course would teach us that what we'd experienced in the past didn't need to reoccur.

One of the new perspectives that the Course offered us was the importance of setting a relationship goal at the beginning. In our past relationships, we'd both tended to jump into the physical dimension without first knowing why. Like all new relationships, Adriana and I initially dealt with all the normal challenges resulting from a "me first" perspective. We'd evaluated our previous relationships based on how much security and sex we would get from our partners. In fact, our previous relationships were based on the scripts we imposed on them. If our partner didn't meet the script, it was over.

This time, we decided we wanted a relationship that had peace—or total fulfillment—as its central focus. We learned that total fulfillment meant peace. Peace meant total fulfillment. Once we committed to each other's total fulfillment, it was much easier for each of us to show up and manage our expectations. We each celebrated both each other's individual desires and those we had for our relationship.

In addition to gaining a new understanding of peace and setting it as our goal, we chose freedom and forgiveness to round out our core relationship principles. Freedom in a relationship is typically interpreted as freedom of the body. We learned to see freedom from a completely new perspective. It was much more about the freedom of the mind. We learned that this meant being present in each "now moment" and engaging in conversations with as little story from the past as possible. It also involved releasing the future. This allowed us to be less fearful and, consequently, freer. Freedom requires releasing the past and future. This became our mantra.

From a Course perspective, our third key principle, forgiveness, is about seeing a grievance—or perceived harm—as if it had never happened. Once we fully understood this concept, it became much easier to release each other from all the typical trappings of our egos: "I'll forgive you, but I'll never forget what you did. And I can bring it up over the course of our relationship as often as I want." This is the ego's use of guilt to cause harm to a relationship. With our new way of looking at forgiveness, our grievances were able to dissolve almost immediately.

Relationships aren't easy. And ours hasn't been perfect by any means. Our previous relationships had led to incredible loss and pain. Together, with the help of *A Course in Miracles*, we've helped each other relearn the purpose (at least from one particular perspective) of relationships. By combining peace, freedom, and forgiveness, Adriana and I have thrived. Our relationship wouldn't have lasted without them. Our path may seem hard to believe, but I can truly say that I've never been happier to share a life experience with someone. Over the last 17 years, the Course has had an incredible impact on not only our relationship with each other but our relationships with everyone. For this, I'm deeply grateful.

Bio

Doug is a lover of humans and an explorer of life. He spends his time working in the technology connectivity space, building virtual reality worlds, and providing consulting and coaching for individuals, couples, and organizations. If you'd like to reach out to Doug, please send inquiries to virtualdoug2017@gmail.com.

An Artist's Vision And An Author's Heart
By Elicia Raprager

Life is beautiful when you witness the magic in ordinary scenes. Life is more empathetic when you carefully choose your words. This is why I am an artist and author. I'm grateful for these special gifts.

I remember the first time I looked outside in our second rental house and saw fireflies. I squealed.

"Oh, my God! Honey, look!"

You would have thought I saw a mythical creature. My excitement was spontaneous and boisterous. The fireflies' luminance glinted like glitter and sunlight. As these mystifying insects hovered and blinked across the lawn, I felt a wave of nostalgia and gratitude.

When I was a little girl, my mom used to lift me to gaze out the kitchen window. We would watch the sunset or sunrise. She would point out salmon, lavender, creamsicle, and other fun colors from the painted sky. My mom is an artist. She taught me the proper names of hues. My dad had me looking up a lot too. He set up the telescope on clear nights. We looked at the moon's craters, Cassiopeia, the Big Dipper, and sometimes Mars. We went on scenic motorcycle rides near mirrored lakes and thick woods. This engaged my poetic mind. When I needed to free the verses, my dad parked the bike and handed me scrap paper. I'm thankful to have strong relationships with my parents. As they grow older, I appreciate them more.

I like to think my artistic brain has helped keep these memories vivid. I can recreate the images in my mind and make it even more beautiful on paper. As my mom said, "You paint what you see, not necessarily what's there." Most of the males on my mom's side of the family are colorblind. I'm thankful I can appreciate the last hint of amber in the blackening embers. I notice how the snow looks white and shimmery in the sunlight and appears periwinkle as the sun retires. It's amazing how color portrays time and tone.

I share my paternal aunt's love of writing. She wrote poetry and is starting to write again in retirement. This hobby connects us. I used to be quiet and timid. I shared my ideas and concerns in writing and art. I have found I better understand how I feel about a situation after I write about it. As a teenager, I painted tornadoes, playing cards burning, and butterflies on flowers. I wrote poetry about my parents' divorce, bullying, and nature. Both these outlets have been there for me, and I've taken both for granted as well.

Writing and artwork allow me to understand and express myself. I'm glad to have both forms of creativity. Both have revealed my purpose and self-identity. Writing and painting are as close as I can come to realizing my dreams. My compositions have benefited friends and strangers, and I'm grateful for it.

"You're a good artist, but a better writer. Practice both." Thanks for the advice, Dad.

I was warned I wouldn't make a living on art and writing. I've seen my mom have successful months of sales. Those are inevitably followed by months of empty inquiries. It's difficult to budget and save on an artist's income. I was encouraged to get a stable job that allowed me to enjoy both art forms. I'm thankful I have that job and these opportunities.

I start each journal entry with three good things that happened or three things I'm thankful for. This was the beginning of an improvement in the quality of my life and the softening of my tone.

Gratitude has changed me in many ways. The biggest one was giving me peace of mind and a resilient heart. Life is whimsical when you don't restrict your imagination. That's how greatness happens.

I have additional time in the day for activities I enjoy and mindful practices that benefit me. I think the elementary school version of me would be happy to know art and writing are still an important part of my life.

I want to make the world happier and brighter. When practicing gratitude, I think about my family, friends, and employer. Recently, I added my creative and artistic abilities to that list.

These give me the confidence to make connections with similar minds and talents. That community gives me a sense of belonging. I've taken risks and felt the ecstasy and queasiness from starting something new and learning as I go. I used to write in private. Now, I'm a blogger and author. I used to doodle on my homework and try to draw as well as my mom. Now, I'm trusted with commissioned designs.

When I focus on what I have and what I can do, my perspective changes. This rewires my current circumstances for positive experiences and a sunnier outlook. I remain realistic but open my eyes and heart to hope and kindness.

I've gifted gratitude journals and affirmation calendars, hoping to guide their recipients. Writing monthly reflections in my planner helped me see progress and notable highlights.

In times of uncertainty and fear, you can rely on gratitude to maintain balance. You can start as I did with journal entries, search for methods, or create your own. Gratitude is effortless.

I can write to process the most bothersome issues. I can write to organize my thoughts into something logical when I'm excited and thinking faster than I can comprehend. You may have been so absorbed by a book that you missed lunch and phone calls. That's what it's like when I'm at my art table. Time passes, and the only indicators are the development of my work-in-progress and change in lighting. The result reflects my efforts.

I'm grateful for the life I'm living. I'm especially grateful for the people living it with me. Thank the people in your life. Nurture your abilities and make opportunities. I'm glad to have an artist's vision and an author's heart. Gratitude is my nature. Reflection is my soul.

Share a smile. Stay inspired.

Bio

Elicia contributed to the bestselling book, *Inspirations: 101 Uplifting Stories for Daily Happiness*. Her story, "The Huron Suite," was published in the July/August issue of the *RAC Magazine*. Elicia's blog focuses on mental health support, personal development, gratitude, and more. Elicia's favorite thing to hear is, "You inspired me." Elicia received encouragement and gratitude when she opened up about her mental health on social media. She prioritizes self-care for her mental and physical well-being. Elicia will share more of her story in her future book, *Share a Smile: Thriving in Life and Treatment*. Please visit www.eliciaraprager.com.

C'est la Vie!
By Evyh Cerhus

I created a TV series with X, based on my original idea. We did some research, and I was doing much more work than X, but X "bought books" and gave me some money to keep going. When we began to write the pilot, X insisted, as X's mother language is English, to type instead of me. I ignored all the red flags because I wanted so badly to break through, but the real reason was the fear of not being "good enough" by myself.

With gratitude, we pitched the show around, starting with Krysanne Katsoolis. Their comment: "Why is your commitment, your energy stronger than X?" Then, I discovered that X had claimed the copyright. X stole it! I'm so grateful I solved the issue. (Hush! X doesn't know.) A producer wanted to develop it. Would X be okay to do a rewrite? I'll type too! I confronted X about everything, except the copyright—X would get back to me later, and said, "You betrayed me! Can you look at yourself in the mirror?"

Later, a beautiful coyote popped out in my yard and stuck around for a while. A Native American friend of mine said, "X is 'the Trickster.'" Well, guess what? X never called me!

At first, I was floating in emptiness, like being suspended in time, then I was hit by a wave of sadness, followed by a swell of anger at X, but I was also mad at myself, for giving my power away! I got sucked into the deadly gravity of a mega black hole, and I was at the mercy of a terrifying energetic vampire!

I was a total failure and I wanted to die. All my family and closest friends were in Europe. I took refuge, deeper in this lethal Dracula, hoping that once dead, I'd be rocked by a relieving gratitude into oblivion.

But lightning struck my never-ending abyss. The phone rang. Argh! The liberating end was so close. "Evyh, it's Krysanne, I was in Australia, are you okay?" I told her my story. She wasn't surprised at all and said that she never felt X, that it was obvious I was the creator of the show—and that I should be grateful to X! My life was shattered by this so-called friend and "co-writer." Legally, I had no show, I couldn't develop it by myself, and I had to be grateful?

The sweet call of the seducing Nosferatu again! I could feel its poisonous fangs in my brain, so I hung up, sinking in an ocean of tears, submerged by violent surges of pure rage. Krysanne called back and said that I would be able to create my show, and that this time it will be better without X. I got rid of a toxic person. Period.

Then a vibrating sound: "I believe in you, Evyh!"

My heart was filled with incredible gratitude for such selfless kindness and love. She was my Van Helsing fighting the formidable bloodsucker. With four words, she brought me back to life. But you have to do the work; no one can change you, except you.

Instead of lots of Valium, I went on a ten-day meditation retreat. As I was drifting in a senseless void, my ego started to melt away, my black hole gave birth to a mighty, glitzy

Quasar. Illuminating my mind with thousands of sparks, it woke me up to my true higher self, the one connected to the whole, and I took my power back!

I went back to work, I asked my late native spiritual mentor, Star Mother, for help. Her first message was, "Trust, white girl," and with profound gratitude, I began to be channeled with tons of ideas. I created a new TV show, which Krysanne optioned. We're developing together my first feature script, *The Rez*, and a short film, *Jane and the Rose*, that I'll direct. To be continued.

She even encouraged me to write a book, which is the reason why I contributed to this one—my first step in this direction.

From this awful challenge, I made a new, genuine friend and ally. Instead of collapsing, I became more productive than ever, and because of this tsunami of emotions, I have more compassion and understanding of human nature. I'm more able to convey all that in my writings to help others.

This is what it is to be human, and let's face it, humans are complicated.

"C'est la vie." Life is difficult. Who said it would be easy? The reason why we are here is probably to learn our lesson and ascend spiritually—that's "the hero's journey" (J. Campbell).

As a woman, an artist, and an activist, everything I do is to contribute to raising consciousness. That's my mission on this beautiful planet.

I'm now so grateful to X, as the experience forced me to face my darkness, accept it—instead of reacting to it—and use it as leverage to blossom.

I'm grateful for all the pains and the joys, the conflicts and the harmony. I follow the Buddha's teachings, and as he says, "It's easy to take a path, difficult to stay on it."

I'm grateful for Antoine Trebouta and Colette Le Lay, Brigitte D, all the good and bad people, past, present and future. I am grateful for my friends, family, they're *all* in my life for a reason!

Antagonists are my Buddhist friends, because in the end, "I transform the poison into medicine."

Gratitude is about receiving and surrendering to the law of the universe, the quantum field.

Gratitude doesn't need a reason to be expressed. Every day, I offer pure gratitude, it connects me to the higher good, the universe. I guarantee you that magic happens. Gratitude sends vibrations out there into the invisible, links you to similar souls, and miracles will happen.

I highly recommend that you try it every day. Open your heart to gratitude, no matter what, and wait and watch!

With much love and light to y'all.

Namaste.

Bio

Evyh Cerhus is a multi-lingual, French-American producer, actress, writer, singer, and lyricist. Her producing and writing credits include two worldwide-distributed documentaries and several short films. She also has a few projects in development, including a feature film and a scripted TV series that she created, among others. As an activist, she supports all minorities, like Native Americans, and encourages women to protect and fight for their rights. Her lifetime goal is to contribute to art and humanity, to make our planet a better place, promoting peace, education, and tolerance through dialogue.

To Jaeger, With Love
By Felicia Shaviri

To have a dog is to know what it is like to be unconditionally loved. ~ Unknown

It was on a Friday, June 13, 2014, when out of the blue, my daughter, Micah, suggested we take a trip to the Tacoma Humane Society located in Tacoma, Washington. Dogs and cats have always been a part of my life growing up and, well, it seemed only natural to have either one or both living in our home to make our family complete. Little did I know this trip to the Humane Society would begin and end in a way that would leave a forever paw print on my life.

We first stopped by to see the cats, then we proceeded to enter the dog kennels. After looping around twice, we decided to head out. As we went to exit, I heard a sound that called me to stop in my tracks. My attention was immediately drawn to the kennel directly behind me. I walked over to the gate and asked, "Are you talking to me?" and again, he spoke. I looked at my children and said, "I think he is trying to talk to me." I asked the dog again, "Are you talking to me?" and again, he responded.

I looked at my children and shouted, "Find me an attendant!" I simultaneously stood in front of his kennel, looking like a human X. I then said to my children, "I think he is talking to me. This dog wants to chat with me, and I want to talk to him too." It was love at first sight. I asked if he would like to go home with us, and he began to jump up and down on all fours as if he was a kangaroo, so I took that as a yes.

From the moment I brought him home, all chaos broke loose. There was an incredible amount of resistance, resentment, and even anger projected. Each time he made someone's favorite shoes, the leather sofa and ottoman, charging cords, or designer handbags his new chew toy, I would hear about what he had done. I would scold him and ask him, "Why?" Then I would kiss his forehead and tell him to not do it again.

The pressure was beginning to wear on me, so I decided to talk it over with one of my dear friends whom I respected greatly, Ms. Jeanne. I told her that I was thinking of returning him, and she simply responded by asking, "So, is that what you are going to do with your kids and husband too? Would you try to return your children if they did something that you did not like? He is just a baby, you have to take your time with him, like you would your children." I didn't need to hear another word. I didn't care about the grumbling or complaining—he was a member of this family, like it or not, and he was going to stay.

From that point on, Jaeger and I were on a path that would lead our hearts to bond like I had never known. He did have some challenges with separation anxiety, but that was part of the reason he would chew up whatever was left out. We began to run together in the mornings and sometimes in the late afternoons, and he loved it. He was quite playful, and when it was time to go out for a walk, I would have to insist that he calm down because he would jump so high in the air and twist his body that I was afraid he would eventually throw out his back. It was clear to the other members of my family that he was becoming more and more attached to me. Each time I returned home from having been out, regardless of the amount of time I had been away, he would greet me as if he hadn't seen me for weeks.

It was through the eyes of my dog that I began to see the meaning of true love. ~Shaviri

Flash forward to the fall of 2015. After completing my shift at the sheriff's department one day, I knew for certain that I would not be returning. I didn't know what was in store, and it may sound strange, but it didn't matter because I knew it would be okay. Yes, my life was about to take another huge shift that would lead me on a journey that was full of twists and turns that I never saw coming.

As I began to follow a series of "coincidences," and what I believe to be nudges from the Universe, there was a feeling of freedom, liberation, and a sense of awakening to a level of life that I had yet to experience. I would also find myself coming through many dark, cold, and lonely tunnels with a pain that was almost unbearable. Through it all this amazing soul, my ride or die was in the form of a dog. He rode the wave with me and assured me time and time again that all was well, and that was my Jaeger. He was so much more than a dog—he was my running buddy, coach, therapist, healer, and, most importantly, my soulmate and best friend.

My soul will forever be grateful to this angel for loving me and showing me the true meaning of unconditional love. I have never felt such pain and heartache until this moment. I will always remember the nights we would sit and chat into the wee hours of the morning, taking naps during the day on the sofa, and giving you the last bite. My heart feels like it has cracked in a million pieces, and I struggle to catch my breath when I think of him. I am grateful for the forever paw print he has placed on my heart.

Jaeger Shaviri ~ June 13, 2014 - March 30, 2020

Bio

A former correctional deputy turned best-selling author and transformation coach, Felicia believes every person can turn their life around regardless of the circumstances. "I stand fast with an unbending belief that there is always an opportunity to learn and grow with every experience. Each experience offers us endless possibilities to live the life we desire." A native of Chicago's South Side, Felicia lives between Seattle, Washington, and Henderson, Nevada with her husband and three children. Felicia is a professional fitness/wellness coach, certified life coach, voice-over talent, research assistant at DePaul University's Department of Innovation, and founder of SheRox Fitness and Wellness, based out of Henderson, Nevada.

Gratitude Every Day
By GG Rush

When I open my eyes every morning, and I become aware that I am awake, I close my eyes again, take a deep breath in, and exhale it out. I then say a thank you to the Universe that I am alive and well. I gently rub my cat, who is always curled up on my legs. I feel and hear her purring. I then say out loud, "I am grateful for this opportunity to live another day to the best of my ability." I get my coffee, feed my kitty cat, and sit with soft music to begin my morning meditation. I prepare myself for my day ahead. I read for 20 minutes, and I write in my journal for 20 minutes. I do some yoga stretches and wake my body up. This is my daily morning ritual.

On my drive to work, I call my 92-year-old mom, and we chat about the day ahead, how we slept, and how we are feeling. I tell her I love her and that I am grateful for having her in my life. Every day.

When I arrive at my place of work, I tell the Universe, "Thank you for this job that provides me with money to support myself, to travel, to give back to the world community, and to pursue my writing." This job is my livelihood, and I am grateful for it.

Throughout the day, I take an opportunity to look at the pictures on my desk of my daughters, who are grown women now. I thank the Universe for my beautiful, healthy, and successful girls. I am blessed and grateful, and I know that to be true.

When I return home from my workday, I am greeted by my cat, who is happy to see me. Or she wants treats. Either is fine, for she is my companion. And I tell her I missed her and I love her, and I am grateful for her company.

My mother always calls me from the senior living facility, and tells me what she had for dinner and shares funny stories about her dinner mates. I am grateful she can afford a nice place and that it is nearby so I can see her often. I am grateful for my daughters having Sunday brunch with her and spending time with her.

At the end of my day when I snuggle into bed, I look back at my day with gratitude. I pull out my gratitude journal and I write five things that I am grateful for. Often they are the same things I have written before, but I write five things every evening.

This is how I experience gratitude every day. It isn't hard to do—you just need to make it a daily practice. You can easily find things to be grateful for several times a day. Try it for one day, and I guarantee you will feel happier with your life no matter what is happening, for there is always something to be grateful for.

Bio

GG Rush is a perpetual student and seeker of knowledge, experience, and enlightenment. She is a Wayfinder life coach-in-training. She attended Martha Beck's African Star Program at Londolozi Game Reserve in South Africa. She is certified Reiki II, as well as studying aromatherapy and learning the ancient art of pulse reading. She has traveled the world solo and is currently working on a book about her journeys and self-discovery. GG, aka Gail Rush Gould, resides in Cary, North Carolina, with her cat, Bella.

Gratitude In Times Of Fear And Uncertainty
By Grace Redman

I had my mind set on writing a particular story about gratitude. But as I sat down to write on Sunday, March 21, 2020, my thoughts shifted. Instead of that story, I'd like to share my experiences over the past seven days being homebound due to the "shelter in place" order, enacted to halt the spread of coronavirus. I've learned that even amongst a terrifying time—one the whole world is navigating through—there is still much gratitude to be found; you need to be committed to look for it.

When I first heard about the order, it felt surreal (and still does). What do you mean we all have to stay indoors? What do you mean we have to close our businesses unless they're deemed essential? It was almost unfathomable, and a story I'm sure future generations will study in the history books.

The fear and panic were ever-present. The news didn't help alleviate it either, heightening it with conflicting reports from multiple sources. People flocked to Costco and grocery stores, greedily hoarding items like toilet paper. My TV screen and social media feeds were filled with images of completely empty shelves. I couldn't believe what I was seeing, and my heart immediately went out to all those infected with the virus, the small businesses, as well as those who lost their "secure" jobs overnight. I felt overcome with sadness, and with empathy and compassion too.

On a professional level, the shelter in place order hit hard. I own a staffing agency, and after being attached to it for almost seven days a week over the past 21 years, in only 24 hours, I also had to close until further notice. I had always imagined the days when I wouldn't be attached to my work 24/7, but I certainly didn't envision it this way! The loss of income also loomed large in my mind.

On the home front, we are an active family. My husband, teenage boys, and I are used to being out and about. The boys and I spend a lot of time at the gym, and they also enjoy being outdoors in the evening with their dad, practicing golf. On the weekends, we always have a birthday party, a family dinner out, or gathering with friends. Connecting with others is part of our being. Suddenly, this all ground to a halt. Now, our only outing is a quick walk down the block to get some fresh air. If absolutely necessary, I take a careful visit to the grocery store. I can tell you I've never been so excited to go shopping for a few groceries!

I'm also a success and transformation coach, so I understand the law of attraction well, in that, what you focus on grows. But this event was on a scale I'd never imagined, and I found myself perpetually caught in waves of fear and anxiety, like so many others. I felt it sweep through my heart and spirit, but I knew it was best to ride it out.

Yet over the past seven scary days, I have noticed something beautiful happen. I have seen families out in my neighborhood that I've never seen before, all of them walking, talking, and laughing. I have seen people step up to support those around them via Zoom, Facetime, and other video apps. I have seen an abundance of funny and uplifting videos shared. The outpouring of kindness and compassion is truly heartwarming. And it's not merely a human effect; it's an environmental one too. There are many reports that the waters in Italy have never been so clear, and that for the first time in many years, you can see the blue sky in China.

I know for certain our lives will never be the same. But I don't think it's necessarily a bad thing. Even though I have no idea what the future looks like, I do know that this pandemic is happening *for* us, not *to* us. We are all having the exact experience we need to help us expand, grow, and evolve. Perhaps it will teach us to be kinder to Mother Earth, each other, and ourselves.

Maybe this will give us the chance to finally turn inward and recognize all we truly need is within us, not outside us. Maybe it will teach us we are worthy, even if we're simply relaxing at home instead of hustling and grinding. Maybe it will teach us rest isn't lazy, but necessary to keep our tanks full. Maybe it will teach us how to connect and look people in the eyes, being present with them instead of our phones. Maybe it will teach us to be grateful for all of the little things we unknowingly take for granted.

Through all of this isolation and uncertainty, I have found so much to be grateful for, turning from fear to faith. I am grateful for the clean water that we have access to in our homes. I am grateful for the opportunity to be able to go outside and be connected to nature. I am grateful that my husband, boys and I are healthy. I am grateful for the healthcare workers who are putting themselves on the line and working extremely long hours. I am grateful for the grocery clerks working hard and risking their health to keep us stocked with food and supplies. I could write about so much more that I'm grateful for, but I think you get my gist.

It's true I can't wait to get back to seeing my friends and loved ones and hug them. For a hugger like me, the struggle is real right now! While we are still in the storm, and we don't know for how much longer, I still have faith and confidence that from this intense uncertain situation, beautiful possibilities and outcomes will be created. And so it is.

Bio

Grace Redman owns and manages one of the most successful employment agencies in the San Francisco Bay Area for the past 20 years. She is also a success and transformational coach who helps guide others to diminish their negative mental chatter and create the lives they have been dreaming of. If you are interested in learning more about Grace, and scheduling a discover call to see how she can guide you to diminish your negative mental chatter and create a life you love, submit a request to connect with her at www.daretoachieve.com You can also reach her at grace@daretoachieve.com.

Gratefulness As A Way Of Being
By Iulia Mihai

L et me ask you—when was the last time you were grateful for no reason? Or better yet, when was the last time you were grateful even when you didn't get what you wanted? Because, let's be honest, it is easy to be grateful when your wish comes true, but what about the rest of the time?

In our culture, gratitude seems to exist primarily in the presence of desire. You want X and, when you get it, you feel grateful. It's an exchange, a quid pro quo of sorts. A formula that teaches you early on in life that getting what you want is the required ingredient to feel grateful.

The truth is, your life doesn't have to be perfect for gratefulness to be present. In fact, there is a strong possibility that your life will never be a hundred percent perfect. And that's okay. Gratefulness is not circumstance-dependent. It can exist by itself, without any props.

The question is, how do you embrace gratefulness, not in exchange for more or something different, but rather as a way of being? How do you switch from gratefulness as a transaction to gratefulness as a way of living?

Simple. It starts with the decision to be grateful. You don't need to learn how to be grateful, what you need to do is allow gratefulness to come through. It is already inside you; it has been there all along.

You see, what gratefulness does for you is quite remarkable. It allows you to transform and evolve because it requires you to focus on what you have, not what you lack. The human mind has a natural tendency to focus on the negative, on everything that you don't have, doesn't work, makes you unhappy, or does not fit your expectations. And the more you focus on all these things, the more you silence gratefulness.

When you switch to a grateful way of being where you allow gratefulness to come through regularly, your mind becomes familiar with the feeling of being grateful. And the mind loves what is familiar. The more familiar this grateful feeling is, the more your mind will recognize and embrace it.

Apart from your mind's predilection for the familiar, your mind also has a penchant for pictures, real and imagined. In fact, reason can be easily overruled by imagination, and your brain is able to process images much faster than words. They don't say "a picture is worth a thousand words" for no reason.

Imagine then, how powerful a daily gratitude practice would be, where you take a few minutes every night to reflect on the things, small or big, you are grateful for, things that perhaps you often take for granted. Imagine falling asleep as you recall everything that went well that day, all the blessings, the people in your life, the pets who bring you joy, the wonderful book you read, the workout you enjoyed, the great dinner you shared with a loved one.

We've been taught to expect the outcome first before we feel grateful, when, in fact, gratefulness should precede the desired outcome. When you start and end your day feeling grateful, you start from a place of power, abundance, and inspiration. And what you focus on grows.

Your mind will loudly remind you of all your fears, all the reasons why it won't work. That's what your mind does, that's its job. Your heart, on the other hand, will gently nudge you to remember all the ways it could work. Listen to your heart, even if it's barely a whisper, because that is where gratefulness resides—in your heart, not in your head.

If you already have a daily gratitude practice, give yourself a pat on the back. You are way ahead of most people around you. If you don't or if you want to try something a little different, here's an idea you can experiment with.

You may have heard of the *Wheel of Life* exercise, which is a tool often used by coaches to help their clients evaluate various areas of their life, and assess how happy they are in those areas, what is missing, and how to bring balance to the life areas that are out of sync.

The areas covered in the Wheel of Life exercise can vary slightly, but generally speaking, they tend to be around these categories (in no particular order):

- Career/Business
- Friends/Social Life
- Family Relationships
- Romance/Love
- Wealth/Money
- Recreation/Fun
- Health/Fitness

- Personal Growth

- Spirituality

- Community/Contribution

I like to use the Wheel of Life concept to reflect on something I am grateful for in different areas of my life, and I do this every night before going to bed. Instead of looking at what is missing, what needs to be "fixed," I choose to focus on what is going well in each area—what brings me joy.

Sometimes, what I am grateful for may seem like a small thing to the outside world, but it doesn't matter, because I am not looking for external validation. This is for my soul only, and my soul doesn't use the same measuring stick the rest of the world does. Between you and me, if I worry about something being too small to be grateful for, I know it's my ego talking.

It is easy to make this a regular practice, because no matter how challenging things may seem, there is always something you can be grateful for. All you have to do is decide to be grateful, and choose to focus on what you have, not what you lack.

I encourage you to look for the silver lining and embrace gratefulness as a way of being every single day. When you transform your thoughts, they transform your feelings, and together they transform your life.

Bio

Iulia Mihai is an internationally respected mindset coach and clinical hypnotherapist. She is the founder of Success Path

Coaching and Hypnotherapy, located in Vancouver, Canada. Iulia has over 25 years of experience in the area of human psychology and behavior. She offers coaching, hypno-therapy, and meditation programs for personal growth, and for those wanting to clear their blocks and limiting beliefs, experience personal transformation, and achieve career breakthroughs. Her passion is helping women get out of their own way and stop sabotaging themselves to create a life and career they love. You can contact Iulia Mihai through her website, www.successpath.ca.

Pathway To Gratitude
By Jae Hart

Someone once said, "You've survived all your worst days, keep it up!" This quote helped me realize that I've already made it through the toughest times in my life, and I will get through the next challenging time as well. I've had several of the same experiences as many of you—failed relationships, infertility, sick children, money trouble, job issues, family or friend let downs. I'll admit when these situations arose in the past, I felt they were happening *to* me. I'd say things like: What did I do to deserve this? Why is life so hard? Was it my fault, or do I get to blame someone else? Some events took months or years to get over, only to reinforce my victim mentality of how challenging and unfair life can be. Now, as I reflect on the hardest times in my life, I can see the reason for going through these struggles. I'm full of gratitude for the ability to see the benefits of those hard times, and even when I can't, I still have faith. It is powerful to know I can rise above any situation and look at it from a different perspective. I can be grateful for the blessings that I know will come from all experiences.

I've decided that I want to live a life with as little regret as possible. I've found the best way to achieve this is to have gratitude for all experiences and release the need to label them as good or bad. In the end, they shape who we are and give us the ability to love and accept ourselves.

Another tool and path to gratitude is through forgiveness. I've made many mistakes and will continue to—how else can I grow and get to the field of gratitude? However, when mistakes are made by me or others, I try to forgive myself and them as quickly as possible. In doing this, I'm releasing judgments that do not add value to any situation. It's a far better life when we see through the eyes of gratitude and forgiveness. "When we know better, we do better!" I believe this quote. Accepting our situations and using the power of gratitude and forgiveness, propels us to greater heights than we could imagine.

I've discovered a daily routine that has delivered the gracious gift of gratitude in my life. These are several simple steps I've devised that have made a great difference. I've changed from being someone who would become emotionally stuck because of bad situations, to a grateful, forgiving person who does not ruminate or allow tough times to get the better of me. Every morning I say a prayer of gratitude, and over time it has become a kind of mantra. I'll add to it if there is something special happening that day. Each night I either go onto my grateful app or journal what I'm grateful for from that day. It's short and sweet and allows me to end the day on a positive note.

I also cultivated this life skill of daily gratitude with my sons. When my boys said their prayers at night, I'd also have them tell me something they were grateful for, but I created a rule that they could never repeat. This forced them to think beyond the typical gratitudes, like family, pets, health, and home. I believe this practice helped my boys to see life differently and continues to help them cope with the ups and downs that come in their lives. Here is a sample of their lists:

Jake: mattress, umbrellas, winter break, good breath, that my cousin Madalyn is healthy, humor, laughter, patience, kisses, air-conditioning, pressure points, happiness, dog's tails because they show emotion, and smoothies.

Jaren: fabric, clothes, fans, bugs, basketballs, sleep, blankets, medicine, fingers, windmills, pillows, Camp Geronimo, colors, summer, hooks, wood, bees, ribbons, and windows.

Another strategy I practice to maintain gratitude is to look for the positive layers around a challenging situation. I'll use the example of a flat tire. My first thought when a tire goes flat used to be something like, "Of all days for this to happen!" Now that I've learned to foster gratitude, I start with being thankful that it is not a day when something more challenging is happening. Next, I'd ponder how grateful I am that I'm safe and not injured and that my car isn't damaged. From there, I move to the thought that I'm grateful that rubber exists, and therefore, that someone had the foresight to invent rubber so that we can even have tires. I'm grateful that we have towing services, tools, and cell phones, that my car has three good tires, and that I have the money to replace the bad tire. I'm thankful that I have my job, patience, and so on.

Remember, at any point, in any situation, you can impact the outcome by shifting to a mindset of gratitude. I'm not going to tell you this is always easy, but if you can approach a life of gratitude, it will allow you to take control of a situation instead of the situation controlling you. This gives us the ability to step into our power and use our skills to move more quickly and easily through the hard times. Gratitude makes life more enjoyable. It can decrease our stress levels, which has a direct impact on our health, it can diminish the duration of the challenging event, and it allows us to rest easy at the end of the day. If you fall back into the old way of thinking, please don't blame yourself, always show grace, and have patience for yourself. A life of gratitude is a work in progress, but believe you will get there. Your gratitude and forgiveness skills will grow stronger and become second nature, the more you practice. Before you know it, you'll hear yourself often saying, "I am so grateful!"

Bio

Jae Hart earned her certification in hypnotherapy from the Southwest Institute of Healing Arts in 2001. Since then, she continues taking classes and attending seminars to further her education. Jae currently uses hypnosis, EFT, and Reiki to help her clients achieve their personal goals. Her main focus is to encourage people to embrace compassion and forgiveness for themselves and others so they may ultimately love themselves fully. You can contact Jae by either emailing her at om567@live.com or visiting her website, www.RisingHart.com.

Bouquet Of Blessings
By Jaime Lee Garcia

"Thank you for another day to wake up and shine my light on those around me," I whispered, with my eyes closed and a smile on my face, after snuggling down in bed for my much-needed night of sleep.

I learned that the first thoughts in the morning set the tone for the entire day, and your last thoughts at night set the intention for the next one. Having a grateful heart truly transforms your life. Considering this, I made it routine to start practicing the art of daily affirmations. This is incredibly important, especially when going through times of grief, fear, or stress. Warmth fills my heart as I think about how gratitude has gotten me through the darkest of days, and the recent loss of my brother, due to an unexpected tragedy.

During tough days, when gray clouds seem to surround your life like a huge turbulent storm, and you think there's no way you will ever see the light shining down upon you, remember, there is always something to be grateful for. Start by closing your eyes and expressing thanks for one thing, or even one person, who made your day better. Next, think of a second thing, a third, and so on, until you have a bouquet of blessings in your hands. Hold on tight to that bouquet. Nurture and lovingly handle it with care. Put that bouquet of blessings in the most beautiful and colorful vase you can imagine, and let it blossom close to the light of your heart. Think of how much you love these blessings, and more will follow. Pretty soon, you will need a bigger vase to hold your growing bouquet.

My daily affirmations continue to grow. Some of these I wish to share in hopes that they will help you build your bouquet. So, here it goes:

I am grateful for each day that I wake up, and my feet touch the ground because it means another day to share life with my tribe and to shine my light upon this earth.

I am grateful for my Mom, who gave me life and showed me what it means to be a giver and not a taker. She showed me the importance of taking pride in my space and anything I call my own, as it's a direct reflection of myself. She taught me the love of holidays and family traditions, and how to build memories to cherish. She showed me how to be a fighter, even while dealing with Metastatic Breast Cancer. She taught me how to persevere and how to love big. I am thankful she is my Hallmark movie partner-in-crime. I adore those movie nights with her.

I am grateful for the gift of motherhood and for my two daughters, Kortni and Haylee, who fill my heart with pride and joy. They have taught me what it means to love unconditionally. I am grateful for my darling granddaughter, Aria, that Kortni brought into the world. She carries on my ancestry. Looking at her precious face brings me back to the years of raising her Mommy, which went by way too fast. I am filled with pride and gratitude that my girls will continue my legacy when I can no longer walk this earth.

I am grateful for my sister, Michelle, and for my brother John, who is now my angel above. They were my first friends in life, and I will always cherish the many memories of growing up together. I am grateful that even when we would fight as siblings do, we still always had each other's backs.

I am grateful for my supportive husband, who taught me that love has no expiration date, for the many laughs that he gives to me each day, and for loving my daughters like his own. I am grateful for the home we have made together, as it's my sanctuary at the end of a tiring day. Having a roof over my head means I have shelter, which I am thankful for.

I am grateful for my stepdaughters, Christy and Jessi, for welcoming me into the family and for giving me the cutest grandkids to love and dote on.

I am grateful for my extended family, who has made my heart so full, and for always surrounding me with a tremendous amount of love and laughter. I will always cherish the many holidays spent together building memories.

I am grateful for Momma G, the best mother-in-law that I could ever ask for, for loving me like her own and treating me like family.

I am grateful for each of my amazing friends. You have held me together during times when I thought I would crumble. You love me unconditionally and set me back on course when I falter. I love you all more than words and will always cherish the memories we continue to make together.

I am grateful for my fuzzy blanket and steaming cup of hot chocolate, which makes cuddling on the couch that much more fun while watching my Hallmark movies.

I am grateful for many road-trip adventures because it means I get to see new parts of the world and broaden my horizons.

I am grateful for the amazing smell of "Serenity" essential oil filling my room because it means a peaceful, tranquil ending to my challenging day.

I am grateful for my many scars, as they remind me that I have persevered through many storms, that I am alive, and have a purpose.

I am grateful for the sun, the moon, and blue skies because they remind me of the beauty that God created.

More than anything, I am grateful to you for reading this chapter, as it means that I'm fulfilling one of my many dreams.

And now, my friends, it's time for you to start building your own bouquet of blessings. Let your bouquet be filled with much abundance, gratitude, beauty, and love.

Shine on, my friends!

Bio

Jaime Lee Garcia has been a certified law of attraction practitioner through the Global Sciences Foundation since 2015. She loves to inspire others through inspirational blogs and writing, has a passion for seeing people truly happy, and aspires to teach others the law of attraction principles that helped manifest great things into her life. You can reach Jaime by email at secretwayoflife@yahoo.com or on Facebook @secretwayoflife.

#17
By Jaime Lee Garcia

"**W**hy is Mom calling so early on a Saturday?" I muttered while lying in bed and discussing breakfast plans. It was 8:30 a.m. in my time zone and two hours ahead of my mom's. I had a feeling that something wasn't right as I answered, "Good morning, Mom!" Silence followed, as my heart started beating out of my chest. I heard sobs, as she choked on words she was trying to say. She finally whispered, "John was in a motorcycle accident last night, and he didn't survive." Those words would change my life forever. I quickly sat up, praying that this was a bad nightmare. "What? No!" I sobbed while trying to grasp the reality that my big brother was gone forever. I had told myself just two nights prior, that I would call him over the weekend and check-in. The reality was sinking in that there would be no more phone calls, no more cooking up delicious meals together during the holidays, and no more of his amazing hugs. Memories would be the only thing to hold on to.

In a haze, I began to cram clothes into a suitcase, while flight arrangements were made to get me home to my mom, daughters, and niece. Sitting on the plane, grief-stricken, memories of 47 years shared with John flooded my head. We were two years and one school grade apart. We shared friends and even married each other's best friends during our first marriages. All my life, he protected me like five dads, much to my chagrin, but I knew I would miss that. The flight home was long, and memories continued. The image of John walking me down the aisle during my second wedding came to mind. When the time came for the ceremony to start, I came out of the dressing room to find my brother waiting for me. Tears welled up in my eyes as he looked at me and mentioned how beautiful I looked. "Don't cry, Sis!" he muttered as he reached for my arm. I looked over at him, only to find his eyes welled with tears, which made us both chuckle. We were both empaths who wore our hearts on our sleeves. I would carry this moment in my heart forever.

Life with John was interesting and sometimes turbulent. His piercing blue eyes and charming smile always made him a popular guy. He was short, with a big attitude. His presence was always known, good or bad. John had a large personality and often had an audience of people surrounding him as he told one of his stories. He could imitate anyone and often brought many laughs to those around him. Growing up, our weekends were spent attending many soccer and baseball games. He was a stellar athlete, an all-star most of his life. Number 17 was proudly embroidered on all athletic uniforms. He was born on the 17th, and it was his favorite number. How ironic that he passed away in 2017.

I have always believed that gratitude is the antidote to depression, anger, and grief. I live my life with gratitude, but wondered if I could find it through grief. The answer revealed itself when we planned John's celebration of life. Over 200 people showed up to honor him. Each face that walked through the door represented different phases of John's journey. We were overwhelmed by the love that surrounded us, as people told their favorite memory of him. We realized how many lives John had touched. So many people loved number 17. The gratitude we felt was profound.

Friends soon attested how John had visited them in spirit. One mentioned they were woken at midnight to the sounds of water splashing in their pool, only to see no one present. They knew it was John, showing his love. Another friend saw one of the ball-chains on her ceiling fan moving rhythmically for several minutes after saying his name. Her fan had been turned off. The most astonishing happened when I attended a seminar held by a psychic medium, whom I had never met. She approached me in a crowd of one hundred people with messages that were undeniably from John. We were all filled with gratitude from his signs.

Two years later, we still look for signs from John. I recently flew across the country to be with my daughter, who needed emergency surgery, and I was worried. At her age, I also had the same surgery and experienced complications. I said prayers and asked my brother to look over her. Several hours after surgery, the staff had not returned Haylee to her original space, and the nurses had no update. I hadn't slept in 24 hours and was panicking. The hospital was crowded and chaotic. I began roaming to see if I could locate her myself. A nurse decided to help me find her. I mentioned that my daughter should have already been taken back to space #35. She discovered where Haylee was recovering and led me down several hallways to find her. The nurse was confused about why Haylee wasn't returned to her space and mentioned a miscommunication with the surgeon.

I looked down at my daughter, still asleep from the anesthesia, and was filled with gratitude that surgery was successful. Then, I happened to glance above her head, and my eyes widened in shock. The space number on the wall displayed 17, my brother's number. This was no miscommunication after all. I instantly began sobbing while explaining to the nurse why this number was so significant to us. Her eyes welled up in tears as she came over to hug me. I knew then that John was leaving us a sign that he had been looking over his niece. I will forever be grateful that we have such a beautiful guardian angel on the other side. Gratitude through grief will shine through by remembering that our loved ones are always with us.

Bio

Jaime Lee Garcia has been a certified law of attraction practitioner through the Global Sciences Foundation since 2015. She loves to inspire others through inspirational blogs and writing, has a passion for seeing people truly happy, and aspires to teach others the law of attraction principles that helped manifest great things into her life. You can reach Jaime by email at, secretwayoflife@yahoo.com or on Facebook @secretwayoflife.

Learning To Swim
By James Masters

This story started 15 years ago when I was moving from Michigan to Missouri to go to Bible School. I had two dreams right before the move. In the first dream, I went to live on a boat. I learned all about the boat, and in the rest of the dream, I taught others about the boat. The second dream started off in the same way. I went to live on the boat, but as I was learning about the boat, I jumped off and swam across the ocean. I swam back to Michigan, and I taught people about the ocean.

I believe that the Universe was giving me a choice in this dream. In retrospect, the boat clearly represented my religious education. However, at this point, I am not sure this was ever actually a choice. Looking back, I never was truly cut out for boat living.

I chose Missouri because of a school that had "the best" conversion therapy program in the nation. This was my third conversion therapy program. If you are unfamiliar with this term, conversion therapies are pseudoscientific forms of psychotherapy that promise to change the orientation and gender identity of LGBT individuals.

At the time of the move, I was already questioning the efficacy of this form of "treatment." I saw too many lives and families being destroyed from the practice. This program just offered more of the same, so I ended up *jumping off the boat*, with a little help from the religious leaders who were determined to push me off. The God of my understanding was becoming bigger and quite different from the God of my youthful religion, which led to many questions that bucked up against the religious establishment.

I swam as best as I could in this new ocean of life. At times I thought I was going to drown. At one point, I even became physically ill. Losing my religion meant losing everything I knew, including support and community. In my 20s, this trauma eventually began playing out in my body.

I went from doctor to doctor, and the conclusion was I needed surgery. My body was attacking itself, and the consensus was to remove my spleen and part of my liver. Even with surgical intervention, the long-term prognosis was not great, but this was a short-term solution.

Then I came across a teacher named Louise Hay. Her entire message was that a change in mental patterns could facilitate healing. She also talked about how to love myself, something I had never considered. I took her message seriously, and I did the recommended affirmations regularly. Every day I would look in the mirror and say, "James, I love and approve of you exactly as you are."

My entire world began to change. I found a non-surgical alternative to facilitate healing in my body, and I was able to create a *fantastic* life for myself in Missouri. I went from saying affirmations to believing them, which changed everything. I was *learning to swim.*

I thought this newfound liberation would last forever. Then my father died. My husband and I moved back to Michigan to help my mother.

Along with the experience of grief, I was also reexperiencing the trauma of my past. These familiar surroundings brought up all kinds of unresolved emotions, particularly the isolation and fear I felt when I came out as a gay teenager.

I had a lot of support in Missouri, but in small-town Michigan, I began to relive the challenges I faced as a young person, once again, experiencing the isolation as a gay teenager, as well as the trauma and self-loathing that developed through conversion therapy programs.

I became isolated and agoraphobic. I couldn't even work. By this time, coaching was my full-time job, but in this frame of mind, it felt disingenuous.

A few months into this darkness, I watched a video that reminded me that I could change my life if I was willing to change my thinking patterns. I didn't know what to do next, but I knew that if I focused on love, a solution would appear. So, I started with the affirmation, "I am willing to change."

I also decided that I was not going to isolate myself any longer. I picked up a deck of affirmation cards and took them everywhere I went. Anytime I felt anxious, I would hand out a card and had people read them back to me. In this way, every person became my teacher. Many started crying or expressed shock because they would pick a card that was relevant to their situation. Eventually, when I went to the grocery store, I would hear people yelling across the aisles, "Hey card guy!" They would then proceed to tell me a story about how the card impacted their life.

As I put one step in front of the other and began to see the light, communities began forming around me, and I was able to actively contribute to them. I realized that I *swam home to teach my inner child about the ocean* and others along the way.

Psalm 139 says, "If I go up to the heavens, you are there. If I make my bed in hell, you are there. Your hand always guides me." I often think that the difference between religion and spirituality is that religion tries to escape hell, and spirituality transforms it back into a heavenly state.

When we face challenges, there is a temptation to think we have failed in some way, but sometimes we go into those dark places as ambassadors of the light. Even if it is only for the inner child that is still frightened. I know this was true for me.

Louise said, "Whatever you are experiencing in life, it is only a thought, and a thought can be changed." If you are not sure what to do next, focus on love, and please, *love yourself.* You are worthy of your love.

Bio

James is a spiritual/soul coach and a Master Emotional Freedom Technique (EFT) practitioner. Since 2012, he has helped individuals gain a better understanding of their soul's purpose by clearing out old patterns that may be blocking them from achieving their goals. He is dedicated to helping others find meaning and value in their lives. You can reach James at www.jamesmasters.net or on Facebook by going to www.facebook.com/spiritcoachjames.

Abundant Gratefulness
By JamieLynn

To know there is abundance in life and believe in it, we can then be grateful. We live in a world that has taught us there is a lack of love, money, and opportunity. With this view of lack, we live small. What if we could live and be big? What if we could experience an abundance of life and have more of that every day?

In my experience, I tend to get what I think about it. When I think with gratitude, wonderfulness comes into my life. When my thoughts are focused on what I can't do or can't have, I see what I am lacking, and it seems I lose out, miss things, and feel stuck.

As a child, I wished I could have my dad for just a bit longer. He worked nights so we could be cared for during the day when there were school holidays and over the summer. I was about ten when I watched him leave for work and felt tears on my cheeks because I missed him so much.

I put worry before joy, I worried he would die on the way to work, and I worried how alone he must feel during the school year when he didn't see us as much. Worrying about him hurt my heart.

The more I worried, the less it seemed that I was able to see him. My mom would fight to keep me in the house to clean on the weekends, when all I wanted was to be outside with him, working on cars, or doing yard work.

Instead of crying, I started to say *I love you* frequently. I would call him at work, if only to hear his voice. On occasion, I would put a letter in his lunch box or save him leftovers from dinner for his lunch. I didn't know it at the time, yet I was practicing gratitude for having him in my life.

When I was twelve, something amazing happened. A new connection was formed over a holiday that he didn't appear to care about, Halloween. In the past, he would take plenty of pictures and help us with costumes, but I didn't know he loved the holiday so much. It started with a karaoke machine I had gotten for my birthday.

He sat in our friend's house with the microphone, and I sat on the steps with a bowl of candy next to a large pumpkin. Between the two of us, we freaked out a few kids, even teenagers, by convincing them the pumpkin was actually talking to them.

Over the past 22 years, the tradition has grown. He built a coffin and an electric chair. We created a tent and lighting with a creepy science lab, and even hung a large bat and "Michael Myers" from a tree. Dad played Michael Myers, of course, twitching and grunting to freak people out who thought he was a mannequin.

We spooked parents and were gentle to little kids, and now it is a tradition shared with so many people it's tough to give each a job. His grandkids have fallen asleep in the coffin and were thought to be dolls.

The gratitude I started with when I was ten years old grew into a loving event that connects more than my dad and I—it's an expected part of the community for trick or treating. People come from an hour away because they know we will be there.

Showing love and appreciation for the time spent with my dad, even moments spent with him, turned into abundant years and wonderful planning and conversation.

There are other ways to keep gratefulness in your life, and it starts with your thoughts. How you think leads to how you act and how you act leads to how your life looks and feels.

To get started, it is great to create a habit. First, pick a time of day that works best for you. Ten minutes to start is a great amount of time. Take out a sheet of paper and a writing utensil you enjoy using.

Make a list of ten items you are currently grateful for. Then a list of five items you wish you could have in your life right now. Go ahead and write that right now, I will wait.

Okay, are you ready for the next step? Choose ten of the fifteen items that stand out to you the most. Write them out like this: I am grateful for the abundance of *fill in the blank*.

When you have completed that, read on to the next step.

Here we go, now that it is all written out, read each one out loud like this:

I am grateful for the abundance of love, thank you, thank you, thank you abundantly!

Feel the words in your heart as you say them and take time to see what each one might look like. Feeling it in your being does make a difference, and missing this step takes away an opportunity for you.

In all honestly, fifteen minutes should be the time you allow—at least five minutes to recall and truly feel what you are grateful for. I add in the word *abundance* every time to help my subconscious learn and understand that I am seeing the abundance in the world and want that for my life.

Thank you abundantly for taking the time to read each of these articles. As an empowerment coach for the sexually abused and traumatized, I lovingly support anyone who wishes to create a life they love.

I am abundantly grateful for you, and all that you do, have done, and will do for yourself and others in your life. You are amazing and deserving! You are worthy!

Bio

JamieLynn is an empowerment coach after ten years of transformational and leadership training. JamieLynn founded Arise Empowered LLC, which supports those who have experienced sexual abuse through empowerment coaching. She is a public speaker and host of the *Breakthrough & Thrive Summit*. JamieLynn is attuned to Reiki, an artist, illustrator, graphic artist, wife to an amazing man, and mother of two wonderful children. You can visit JamieLynn at Arise EmpoweredLLC.com or search Arise Empowered LLC on Facebook.

Gratitude in Death
By Jan Wilson

You would think being grateful is something we embrace every day that we wake and draw new breath. Yet this simple act of being happy for what we have in our lives gets pushed aside daily, hourly, and many times by the minute by fear, sadness, or whatever emotion might overtake us. Our "feelings" take over, and once again, we ride the rollercoaster that we allow to become our routine. But oftentimes, the most unexpected moment can help us find gratitude and realize the gift we have with each breath and beat of our hearts.

I woke to a beautiful morning on April 23, 1993, ready to go about my normal day. Like always, I got ready for work and walked to the bus stop for the 90 minute ride on two different buses to the office. I settled into my seat and did exactly what I did every day: I began to read. I had no idea that halfway into this ride, my life would dramatically change. Arriving at my bus transfer point, I started to walk from one bus to the next and suddenly felt something pound into my back. As I turned to see what had hit me, I felt a driving force into my right arm.

"I'm dying."

I feared these were going to be my last thoughts. I stared at the paramedic at my feet as he pulled out the defibrillator. I looked up into the eyes of the paramedic near my head as he shook his head. "She's there. We don't need that," he said. "Let's get her loaded." I felt them lift me up on the gurney.

129

I closed my eyes, and everything went black until I woke to a room full of people rushing about.

I gazed at all the people in white coats around me, realizing that two were at my side working vigorously to close the wound on my right upper arm. One of the doctors saw that I was awake.

"We have to get you into surgery," he said as he worked. "Just relax—everything's going to be okay…"

Once again, I closed my eyes, and everything went black. I woke to friends and family in my room, and just like that, everything changed. From that moment onward, I walked with gratitude forever in my heart.

I am grateful to those doctors and paramedics who worked hard to save me from this traumatic incident. I am grateful to God for allowing me to pull through the surgery to repair the damage to my body. I am grateful to my family, who supported me on my long road to recovery. I am happy for all those who assisted in my survival and recovery, yet there is one person to whom I am forever and eternally grateful—that person who gave me the ability and the desire to truly change my life.

I am grateful to the man who tried to kill me. I'll never know if the man who attacked me by stabbing me five times was intent on taking my life or if he was simply out to do harm. I'm sure he would be surprised to learn that while it was painful and certainly something I'll never forget, I have forgiven him and am everlastingly grateful.

No, I didn't see a white light. I didn't visit the afterlife as some people describe after a near-death experience—yet until this happened, I moved through life as someone else. I lived life the way others wanted me to, listening to people who supposedly knew better—people who told me what to do, what to say, how to live. None of them knew the true me. After all, how could they know when I had never allowed myself to be who I truly was?

I'm not the first person to experience a life-altering event, nor will I be the last, but it is something that I've been looking for my entire life. I was looking for the guidance of the spirit to speak to me and tell me who I was, only to learn that it was inside me all along—it needed to be jolted awake. Even the worst of times can open your eyes to the gratitude that is not whispered about but lived.

Finding gratitude in tragedy is not new, but it was certainly new to me. I was thrown into a moment of absolute fear, thinking I'd never recover, only to discover that it empowered me to come into my own. After that, I jumped into life with both feet, considering every possibility I had only previously dreamed of.

This is not to say that I've become one of those people who is always smiling and seeing the silver lining. After all, even when you have a heart full of gratitude, you can only control yourself. Many people don't realize that we allow external pressures to drive us instead of listening to ourselves.

Walking through life in gratitude takes work, like everything else worth accomplishing. You must work at setting your intent every day, and it only takes five seconds. It's as easy and simple as smelling your morning coffee, tea, or whatever you use to start your day. Take a deep breath, inhale the aroma, and set your intentions for the day. Think or verbalize a simple statement—a mantra if you will, such as, "Gratitude turns what we have into enough." There are several simple ways to keep gratitude in your heart. Did you know that if you lift your head and look forward when you walk, it can magically lift your heart? Another simple way is to smile—this small positive act will eventually move from your lips to your heart.

I pray that you find gratitude in a much kinder way than I did, but however you find it, may it stay with you for eternity, and brighten the lives of all you encounter.

Bio

Jan Wilson embraces a life of natural and holistic health. Jan is trained in a variety of Yoga formats, Acupressure, Reiki, birthing services, herbal, and aromatherapies. Jan uses her life experiences and desires to inspire, with the hope that they help others to understand that it is easier to overcome adversity when we embrace our strengths and abilities. She empowers others to create a safe and comfortable space in which to receive healing and support. Contact Jan at every.body.matter@gmail.com or via Facebook at www.facebook.com/EBMPE.

Gratitude In Flow
By Jane Berryhill

It was one of those days. No, actually, it had been one of those weeks. Everything I thought about seemed to come into being, as if by magic. People, places, opportunities were popping up everywhere, all presenting a sense of joy and love of being. I had been struggling with staying where I was versus moving back "home" to Montana. I realized we are almost always given choices to grow and expand wherever we choose to be. We create them with intentions and awareness.

Today, heading for the market to refresh my refrigerator, I stepped up on the free bus and immediately got a big smile and wave from the bus driver, who was new to this iconic little town of Steamboat Springs, Colorado. Having been one of his first passengers in the last week, he quickly recognized me. I smiled back and waved, feeling such appreciation for living in a small town despite it being a world-class resort as well. Everyone here was family, the type that is happy and willingly communicates with excitement and a sense of wonder and gratefulness for the experience. The people here come from all over the world in anticipation of an amazing adventure and are rarely, if ever, disappointed.

Despite my love for Colorado, Montana is truly my home. There is an amazing sense of wonder there as well, for the sky, the land, the waters, the trees, the people. Never have I ever developed such a group of women friends who felt like my tribe, my family, as in the Bitterroot Valley of

133

Montana. I raised my kids there, and they chose to remain, while I chose to run off and have a few adventures. Now it was time to come home, and I started the process of looking for work.

During my time in Colorado, though a fun adventure almost every day, the workpiece was a struggle. There were jobs everywhere along with some great people to work with, but rents were high, and pay was low. I loved it anyway. However, when it came time to return home to Montana, first resume out, I received an immediate call and offer to come and join a therapist team in the town of Missoula. This was nothing short of amazing to me because I had struggled to make this happen in Colorado for nearly five years, and it was akin to pulling teeth.

As a counselor who has written a workbook on flowing with life, I recognize when I am experiencing blocks and resistant energies within and around me. There had been a lot of blocks in my life in Colorado, but there were also lessons for me to dig deeper, become more intuitive and to listen more thoughtfully to my life energy patterns in this place. Steamboat was a place for me to contemplate who I was at the core, and move through my resistances, and back into my power center. It was downtime from a life filled with busy activities and responsibilities. There had been a close friend I adventured with, off and on, over the five years I was here; he chose to back away, allowing me to release my expectations and bring back the flow to my life.

More time in meditation helped tremendously. I also was aware that I could create what I wanted wherever I found myself to be. Before I could leave Colorado, a number of doors opened up as if the universe was offering me a choice. The lesson I took from this was we are given what we need wherever we find ourselves to be. Montana was certainly one of my options if I was sure I wanted to be there. We do have choices, even when we feel ourselves standing behind what feels like a big wall, mostly made up of our preconceived ideas and resistances.

My greatest lesson during my time in this amazing place of Colorado was to learn and experience love as a state of being. So many experience love as an emotion, but that is not what it is at all. Love as a state of being is when you feel this expansiveness for all things, and nothing external can waver that energy, that sense of peace within your core. At your core, there is this sense of wonder and bliss that does not shift and change with experiences. The bus driver this morning was living in that sense of bliss, and he again made me laugh before stepping off the bus to walk home. He was a storyteller, and every story he told expressed a form of joy. You couldn't help but feel his deep sense of appreciation for the new adventure he was on. I think it would have been hard to rattle him—he seemed to carry this sense of being with him that surrounded and enfolded every person who stepped onto his bus.

Life is truly amazing when we open our eyes and allow ourselves to take in not only the beauty of the planet, but the people, the animals, the plants, the interconnections of all things. Connecting to soul friends (wherever we go) happens when we are tuned in and paying attention. I am so appreciative of my time here in Colorado, the lessons, the experiences, and the daily adventures. Was it all fun and games? No. But now it is time for me to re-ground myself in a place where I can once again spread my toes and expand my roots into a place of beauty that I have called home for many years. To be able to throw a kayak out on the waters and simply float in stillness, as life flows below the water's surface in silence.

I whisper to myself, thank you universe, for bringing me back home, to a sense of peace within my core, wherever I am. It's been real.

Bio

Jane received her master's in clinical counseling with a specialty in biofeedback in 1990. She received a second master's in behavioral physiology in 2001. She specializes in teaching others how to get in touch with their physiology, increasing consciousness of how their thoughts and physiology interact to create health as well as what they draw in as life experiences.

She currently has three publications out: in 2017, *Forging the Flow*, a second in 2018 entitled *Emptying the Soul*, and her third book, published in February 2019, is entitled *Your Bumper Car Life*, a humorous book on personality and biofeedback. You can contact Jane at coloradojaneb@gmail.com or 970-761-5963.

The Deer Man
By Jeannine Welton

Sixteen years ago, we packed up our lives in Southern Ontario and moved to a small Northern Ontario town. There are many things that we love about living in the north and our new way of life. One is the untouched wilderness and the abundance of wildlife. You feel a closer connection to mother earth here, and it's the fresh air and the trees and the rocks and the water everywhere you look. At first, the transition was difficult, but I believe that the journey is always made easier by the people you meet that enrich your lives. This is a short story about one particular individual who made a lasting impact on our lives in the north.

The area we moved to is part of a community known as ARGYLE, which is represented by the communities of Arnstein, Restoule, Golden Valley, Loring, and Port Loring. Within these communities, there is an area known as the Loring Deer Yard. This is where hundreds of whitetail deer migrate for the winter. Thanks to one dedicated and longtime resident, Elmer, the deer continue to thrive. He is affectionately known as "The Deer Man." Elmer is one of the people who have deeply touched our lives. As a young man, a fire tragically touched Elmer's life and took away his mom and other family members. The tragedy inspired him along with some others to start the first volunteer fire department for the area. The members of the community bought the first fire truck for $700 in 1954. They had to drive the open cockpit truck up from Toronto, with no paved highway back then, and it was a ten-hour trip! In his 42 years of volunteer service, he also accepted the position of Fire Chief. In 1997, he was recognized with an award from the community for his years of service and dedication.

I'm sure if the deer in the area could do it, they would also give Elmer an award for his caring and compassion. For over 40 years, Elmer fed the deer to help them survive in the harsh winters. We had the privilege of helping Elmer, as it had become a lot of work for him, and we were more than happy to help. It was an awesome feeling to be surrounded by the deer. One little deer lady, in particular, had a unique personality. She would wait close by as we placed a special pile of feed specifically for her. Sometimes we would put out 100 pounds of feed a day! Then there was the happy hour crowd that always came about a half-hour after we would begin to feed. You could almost set your watch by them. A group of up to fifteen deer would come prancing across the field toward the feeding crowd, emerging from the forest at the same time and same spot every day. At times we would be surrounded by hundreds of deer.

There is a real gentleness about the deer. Surrounded by them, I almost feel insignificant in their presence. An honor to gain their trust, they would get to know you, and wait for you to arrive. It puts a real perspective on your life and brings you back to being present in the moment. Meeting Elmer has also left a lasting impression on me. At the time we met Elmer, he was a gentle man of 77 years. The harshest words you would ever hear him say were "holy whistling," which always made us laugh. You would never know that he had many tragedies that affected his life. You never once heard him complain about his life, always happy and smiling.

When we would visit, he always had a pot of tea on and a sweet treat for us. You could also see how the deer loved him. One day while I was helping him feed the deer, I saw him sneak a picture or two. You would think he would have had enough pictures by then. When I asked him why he still takes them, he replied, "Well, it's time to get some new ones!" It was one of the things that brought joy to his life. I once asked Elmer why he fed the deer, and he told me it warmed his heart to watch the deer getting healthy and watching the little ones grow. He loved to sit and watch them run, jump, and play. They are exercising, he explained, as they are preparing for their long journey home. Once they feel it is time, they move back to their home territory up to 60 kilometers away.

It has been an honor getting to know Elmer and his deer. Sadly, Elmer passed recently in his 90th year. He was a proud and independent man, and when he could no longer be in his home or feed his deer, I felt he thought it was simply time to go. Like the deer, he was ready to make his journey back home. Elmer was like the grandfather I never had. He was always there to listen and to offer friendly advice. He was the only person I knew who could give advice by asking you a question. He enriched my life in more ways than he will ever know, and I miss him and his deer terribly.

One thing for sure that I have learned along the way is that the north is now our home, and there is no looking back. Maybe it's the fresh air, maybe it's the wide-open spaces and lack of concrete, maybe it's the laid-back, unhurried atmosphere, or maybe it is the deer and the connections I have made along the way. Whatever it is, we are glad to be here. Thank you, Elmer, for adding to our lives, and I am sure there are many more who could echo our sentiments and add pages of *you* to this short little tale of The Deer Man.

Bio

Jeannine Welton, CYA-RYT 200, is a yoga instructor living in Northern Ontario. She is passionate about helping people heal their bodies and minds through mindful movement and sound. You can find her classes and workshops in Callander and Mattawa under her business name, Mind Body Heart Yoga. She also uses a variety of healing modalities, which she infuses into her classes, such as therapeutic touch, Reiki, and sound healing. Jeannine has always enjoyed writing stories as a way of creative expression. To contact her or to find out more about healing events offered visit: www.mindbodyheartyoga.ca or email Jeannine.mbhy@gmail.com.

The Happiness Jar
By Karen Gabler

In 2018, I read an article by author Elizabeth Gilbert about her "Happiness Jar." She described her daily practice of jotting down moments of joy on paper scraps, which she then placed in a jar. In moments of difficulty, she would pull out a scrap of paper and read a snippet of happiness, quickly reminded of the "momentary gems of life" that would otherwise have been forgotten.

Eager to launch our own "Happiness Jar" experience, we found a large glass canister reminiscent of a cookie jar (because what could possibly bring greater happiness than a giant jar of cookies?). My daughter created a label decorated with intertwined flowers and hearts. I explained to my family that we would each create daily happiness notes, which we would then fold up and put in the jar. At the end of the year, as we waited for the proverbial ball drop in Times Square on New Year's Eve, we would open the jar and review the moments of joy we experienced over the prior year. My family dutifully created daily notes, and the jar filled to the brim with documented evidence of our happy lives.

At the end of the year, we rushed to open the jar, eager to review the greatest moments of the past twelve months. We began to read each note one by one. Some of the notes brought laughter and delight, reminding us of heartwarming moments we shared over the year. My husband taught our daughter to catch a baseball. We found a new waterfall on a hike we'd never tried before. We closed escrow on a retirement property we had coveted for several years.

Other notes brought...bewilderment. "Had fun walking the dog." "Great time at the mall today." "Found a pretty rock today." While we had to assume that each recorded moment held a special place in our hearts when the note was added to our Happiness Jar, we no longer had any idea why that was the case. Our desire to preserve our most notable moments of joy turned into a fairly innocuous list of random activities we could no longer identify and emotions we could no longer evoke.

Research tells us that cultivating gratitude allows us to experience more satisfaction, love and joy. It protects us from negative emotions, reduces anxiety and depression, and allows us to trust that our lives are filled with goodness. It enhances our physical health by reducing anxiety, improving sleep quality, increasing immune function and dissipating depression. Gratitude also helps us to connect with others as we recognize our interconnectedness and shared human bonds.

Engaging in a daily gratitude practice reminds us to pay close attention to the myriad of events and thoughts in our day-to-day lives that bring us joy and uplift our spirit. There are numerous methods of tracking gratitude, including the Happiness Jar, journaling, photos and videos. Regardless of the chosen method, many attempts at a gratitude practice are ultimately unfulfilling, not because of a limited supply of inspiring moments, but simply because we miss a few key elements required to turn our gratitude practice from a rote exercise into a soul-enriching endeavor.

The first key to creating a meaningful gratitude practice is to develop a sense of being present and mindful about our daily life experiences. This requires that we pay attention to what we experience, and then allow ourselves to really feel the emotions rising within us as we have that experience. To do so, we must drop out of our human brains and into our souls, to recognize those emotions within us. We typically rush from conversations to errands to tasks without noticing what we are doing, seeing or feeling. If we can become present in our bodies and truly experience our lives from moment to moment, we recognize the tiny details that make up the fabric of our lives.

It is often easier for children to access this awareness; they are inherently more mindful about their surroundings and eager to focus on whatever might capture their attention in the moment. On a busy Monday, I rushed to make breakfast before my family scattered to school and work activities. My daughter stood at the back door, staring into the yard. She said, "Mommy, look at this!" As I approached her, I realized that she was awestruck by the sky, awash in shades of pink, purple, blue and gold as the morning sun appeared over the hills. I was stunned into my own astonished silence as I put my arms around her, and my heart swelled with love as we watched the sunrise together.

The second key to a meaningful gratitude practice is to document not only the event itself, but the feelings that arose within us as we experienced that event. Our mistake in dropping notes into our Happiness Jar was that we neglected to write *why* the recorded moment was meaningful to us. When we walked the dogs, did we notice that our golden retriever rushed ahead of us but then checked to make sure we were still with him, or that our toy poodle looked up at us adoringly and liked to smell each new flower on our path?

143

When we found a new waterfall on our hike, did we notice the sunlight sparkling off the water pooling in the lake below? Did we hear the birds calling to each other over the thundering falls?

When we remember to note the experience for which we are grateful as well as the reason it struck us in that moment, we recall not only the facts of the situation, but also the tug it created on our soul when it occurred. The event itself is not what inspires the gratitude. Instead, it is the feelings stirring within us that remind us of what brings delight to our hearts and beauty to our lives. By reliving those feelings, we are lifted by our gratitude, and we continue to carry the joy within us.

Bio

Karen Gabler is an attorney, intuitive coach, and psychic medium. She is also a published author and inspirational speaker. Karen is passionate about encouraging others to live their best lives. She provides clients with intuitive guidance regarding personal and business questions, facilitates connections with their loved ones in spirit, and conducts workshops on a variety of spiritual and personal development topics. Karen earned her Bachelor of Science in psychology and her Juris Doctorate from the University of Hawaii. She enjoys reading, horseback riding, and spending time with her husband and two children. You can find Karen at www.karengabler.com.

What Is Your Lack of Gratitude Trying to Tell You?
By Karen Gabler

My role as an employment attorney might be described as "busy." Mornings begin at sunrise with the dings of email notifications and emergency text messages. Lunch, if eaten at all, is a snack grabbed during a short break—a "power meal" of cookies, crackers, or chips on the fly. Evenings find me exhausted from a long day of client service, promising my young daughter once again that I will play with her "tomorrow," after I've "had a chance to rest." Weekends become a much-needed opportunity to catch up on what I haven't yet completed on my task list, as I promise myself that if I can "get through this week," everything will surely calm down again.

As I complain to my co-worker about our endless workload, she casually responds with, "I know, but at least we have jobs, right?" Guilt washes over me as I realize that I'm feeling sorry for myself instead of appreciating my good fortune. Shouldn't I be exceedingly grateful for what I have? I have a continuing source of income in a reasonably secure position, and I can take care of my family. How can I possibly justify wanting more than I already have when so many people have so little?

Gratitude is important, to be sure. Our ability to remain present, stay grounded, and appreciate this beautiful life depends upon our ability to feel grateful for everything we have been given and all that we have experienced. We are taught that if we consistently dwell on what we don't have, we will never find satisfaction in what we do have. We will then spend our lives constantly wishing for more, without ever noticing the abundance right in front of us.

That said, blind insistence that we should always be satisfied with what we already have may prevent us from recognizing when we don't yet have what we want or need in our lives. Refusing to acknowledge feelings of dissatisfaction may cause us to miss critical messages about where we truly want to be. Without an awareness of where changes are needed, we can't take the necessary steps forward to ensure that we fulfill our soul's purpose.

How do we find a balance between our gratitude for what we already have and our discontent with the status quo? When gratitude feels elusive, start by asking yourself *why* you aren't satisfied with what you already have. Is it because you are comparing yourself to others? Are you stagnating in your current circumstances because making a change feels like an insurmountable endeavor? Is it because you have devoted your time to meeting the needs of others, without remembering to honor your own soul?

Or, is it because something stirring inside of you is telling you that you were meant for more than this? That you would choose a different path if you allowed yourself to consider the possibility? What would you do if you knew you could not fail? How would you live if it was your last day on earth? What would you choose for your life if your priorities flowed from your heart, instead of from your to-do list?

I certainly do feel blessed that I have a secure job position, particularly when so many others are struggling. I am thankful that I have the ability and the opportunity to help people in crisis, giving them tools and options that may keep them afloat or provide peace of mind. I'm grateful that I feel valuable and needed when clients call to ask for my guidance.

At the same time, I am all too aware that I have consistently sacrificed my physical and mental health while putting the needs of others above. I have inadvertently neglected my husband and children while I answered "one more" email, even though I would list them as my top priorities in life without a moment's hesitation. I can't even remember what I like to do in my free time because I leave myself no free time to fill with activities that make my heart sing.

My frustration with the manner in which I have allowed my work to take over my life is an important red flag that must not be brushed aside in the pursuit of gratitude. It tells me that I won't be truly satisfied until I find a way to bring some balance to my life. It teaches me that devoting all of my time and attention to my work prevents me from devoting my energy and love to my family, which is where I want to be. It warns me that continuously setting aside my needs will lead to burnout and compromise my health. It reminds me that I need to find a way to serve my clients while also ensuring that I am finding ways to fill my soul.

Gratitude fills us with positive emotions, allows us to appreciate good experiences, improves our health, and enhances our relationships. As we explore areas in which we might want to make changes in our lives, we can still express our gratitude with where we are and what we have, while simultaneously reaching for what we want to experience in the future. As author James Rohn said, "Learn how to be happy with what you already have while you pursue all that you want."

Count your blessings, and fill your heart with gratitude for what has already come into your life. Then, listen to the voice inside that says, "This is not enough." Encourage your soul to rise within you, and ask yourself what it is you truly want. Imagine the life you wish to live and contemplate how you would feel if you actually lived it. When you have allowed yourself to acknowledge your inner yearnings, you can take the first step on your path to your desired life, while expressing heartfelt gratitude for everything you've received and achieved along the way.

Bio

Karen Gabler is an attorney, intuitive coach, and psychic medium. She is also a published author and inspirational speaker. Karen is passionate about encouraging others to live their best lives. She provides clients with intuitive guidance regarding personal and business questions, facilitates connections with their loved ones in spirit, and conducts workshops on a variety of spiritual and personal development topics. Karen earned her Bachelor of Science in psychology and her Juris Doctorate from the University of Hawaii. She enjoys reading, horseback riding, and spending time with her husband and two children. You can find Karen at www.karengabler.com.

The Third Rail Powers Everything
By Kathryn Eriksen

As I stood in London's King's Cross Station, waiting for my train, I noticed one silent track. The train was stopped, shades pulled down, and only one person was attending to it. The contrast between it and the rest of the station was so stark that I had to investigate.

I walked over to where an older man was working and said, "Good morning." At first, he didn't hear me because of the background noise, so I tried again. He turned around, and his eyes met mine.

His face was lined with a roadmap of wrinkles, indicating a long life, but his blue eyes were as young as a boy's. Gripping a wrench in one hand, he reached in his back pocket for a towel. Wiping his brow, he answered in a low, gravelly voice that had seen its share of cigarettes and whiskey.

"Good morning! How can I help you?"

I smiled and said, "I was wondering what you were doing. You seem so content working."

He laughed and gestured to the electrical panel. "That's funny you noticed in all the chaos. I'm the guy behind the scenes who keeps the trains running."

"But you seem to enjoy it. What do you think about while working?"

He glanced up at the ceiling, contemplating his answer. He lowered his voice and leaned forward, as if sharing a valuable secret. Without thinking, I mirrored him and held my breath, waiting for his response.

"I think of electricity as the "third rail." It's energy you can't see that makes everything else possible." He motioned toward the station activity before going on. "When I stay connected to the energy running everything, I'm always on the right track."

I felt like he'd pulled back the curtain on the secret of how the world works. But I didn't have the instruction manual, merely a feeling that what he said was an essential piece to the puzzle of life.

As he awaited my response, I felt the tingle of *knowingness*, that indescribable sense to pay attention. Over the years, I'd learned to listen to this nudge and follow wherever it takes me.

This was one of those times.

"Could I buy you a cup of tea?"

Surprised, he nodded and set down his tools. He tidied his work area and nodded toward a door, away from the noise and crowds.

"You don't have to buy me a cup, but I can see you want to learn more about the third rail." His words were kind, as he opened the door for me.

We walked down a long hallway glowing from fluorescent lights, then entered the employee lounge. He filled a kettle, put it on the stove, then retrieved two cups and began preparing the tea. The silence was comfortable and relaxed. After the tea was ready, we sat down, and he spoke.

"I know you have questions about what I said earlier," he began, sipping his tea. "I'm 64 years old, and I've concluded that life is so much more than what we can see, hear, taste, touch, or smell."

I nodded for him to continue. When I felt the nudge to record him with my phone, he smiled slightly and sighed.

"Those contraptions are a blessing and a curse. The blessing is that we stay connected to the world, but we are cursed when we forget that the world lives inside of us."

"How does a cell phone relate to the third rail?"

He laughed and shrugged. "That's as good a place to start as any. When we only see the world through our five senses, our connection to the third rail is lost."

I shook my head, frustrated, while puzzling through his words. "You still haven't explained the third rail! In the train station, you said it was 'the energy that runs everything.' Now you're saying that we've lost our connection to it. How can we lose our connection to something we don't know about?"

"That, my dear, is the million-pound question! Think of how trains move—they're propelled by an invisible, higher energy." He used air quotes when he said the word higher. "The same is true for us—when connected to higher energy, or the third rail, we move forward on a different track from what the world tells us to do."

I nodded, smiled to show I understood, and asked one final question. "What do you call this energy that runs beneath, in, and through everything?"

He didn't hesitate. "Gratitude."

At my surprised expression, he continued. "Gratitude is our appreciation for the present moment. When I am grateful, the past is over, and the future has not yet arrived." He paused, took a deep breath, and added, "It's like that German guy said. I think his name is Eckhart—"

"Eckhart Tolle."

"Yes, Eckhart Tolle. That's it! He said, 'It is through gratitude for the present moment that the spiritual dimension of life opens up.'"

I nodded, wanting to hug him for the gift he shared. "So, gratitude is the third rail," I murmured, more to myself. He heard me, and added, "When you stay in gratitude for this moment, you're connected to a higher source of intelligence than you could ever have by yourself. With gratitude as your default setting, the tracks of your life won't ever seem pointless."

"If I stay connected to the third rail by being grateful, my life will change?"

"Now you're getting it! Gratitude is the energy that expands your attitude, beliefs, and actions. Remember the image of a train riding down the tracks, smooth as silk, connected to the third rail. That is your life in gratitude."

I hugged him, thanking him for his time. A light shone behind his blue eyes, and we both smiled our gratitude for these few moments of connection. We turned away, back to our lives, and I heard him shout, "Remember the third rail!" I raised my hand in acknowledgment and knew I would never be the same again.

Bio

Kathryn Eriksen is an Empowered Way coach, meditation and mindfulness teacher, author, and speaker. She shows women how to connect to the feminine side of money and peacefully create abundant wealth. Her passion is to raise the abundance vibration for women, so they step into their power and change the world. Learn more about Kathryn at www.EmpoweredWay.com. Her e-book, *Five Money Beliefs that Sabotage Your Success*, is available for free when you join her email list.

Smiley
By Kathryn Seymour

When I see someone, I automatically flash them a smile, as it is the easiest and frequently most overlooked way to share gratitude. Smiling activates muscles in your face that tell your brain to release endorphins—the feel-good ones. After all, smiling is a way to show people that you're happy, friendly, and confident, which helps lift spirits. The simple act of giving a smile also opens you to receive a smile in return, and most often than not, you always get a smile back. This is why my nickname is Smiley and I hope you will share your smile with others too.

My grandmother was an extremely positive lady and always said: "Everything is just lovely." Funny how a simple phrase can incite joy instantly. You can practice cultivating being grateful by using this phrase anytime, anywhere. Perhaps you find yourself sitting in traffic and becoming annoyed or impatient, try on a smile and say out loud, "Everything is just lovely." Notice how it feels to be grateful for the way things are instead of wishing how we want it to be.

I am grateful for all of my children, each one unique in their special place on earth—Kerrie, Gordon, Clint, Dave, Chris, Darren, and my youngest daughter, Allison. I am grateful that my daughter Allison survived; she was so tiny when born. Her father, Larry, raced to the hospital when I was in labor to deliver nine weeks early at three pounds, one ounce. She is my miracle baby who was meant to be here. A miracle means something that you wouldn't think would happen or seems impossible to happen does and surprises you. I am grateful this morning as I look out the window of Allison's home in White Rock beside the sea. We are here together, and I wish all my children could be in one place so I could share time with them all. They say that sometimes the shortest distance between people is a smile.

Carl is my neighbor, who is generous to help me run errands with his car, as I am not able to drive. His east coast Nova Scotia accent reminds me of my travels there. Back in the year 2000, I traveled from coast to coast across the USA and Canada on my Yamaha FJR 1300 with several friends. We dubbed it the "Y2K C2C" trip. Nova Scotia and the east coast was a beautiful part of my trip; the landscape incited a feeling in me as though I had arrived home, even though I was from the west coast. As I learned later on, there are many Seymours in Newfoundland, so perhaps there is some old connection from long ago that I could sense when I was there. I am grateful that I was able to have this traveling experience that has become a treasured memory to recall. When I hear Carl's accent, I smile fondly.

You never know how life will turn out—the twists and turns, the good the bad, the happy the sad—all make life thankful to be a part of. I am relaxed as I savor the simple pleasure of a good cup of coffee first thing in the morning. I awakened early today and watched the clouds drift by on the blue horizon. I anticipate the day ahead as I listen to soft music. My favorite song is Cristofori's *Dream*. The music of this song grabs me. It's like being mindful—you pay attention with your whole being savoring the beautiful music.

Bartolomeo di Francesco Cristofori invented the piano and what a beautiful dream of his that has brought such pleasure to the world with inventing piano music. This reminds of the elderly people in homes who are sad and lonely, some have Alzheimer's like me, and when they hear a song from their era, they light up and become full of joy again. There is a non-profit initiative that brings music to Alzheimer's patients called "The iPod Project." This makes me smile to see people happy, and I am grateful people are doing this work to spark joy in seniors. My late father played piano with a tailgate jazz band in Edmonton, and my mother played as well. Music was naturally a part of our family, and I am so grateful for it as it helped shaped my love for the joy of song.

Although I had a love for music, I would much rather enjoy the outdoors when I was a teenager. I had a horse when I was 15, and my motto was: "Just grab the mane and jump on!" I loved riding free in the pastures that surrounded our neighborhood, which were aplenty back in those days in Edmonton. I smile at these memories and also enjoy my time currently with walks around Mill Lake Park near my home. Watching the wildlife and water of the lake truly brings me happiness in the moment. I smile at other people walking by and rejoice in receiving a smile in return. It seems so simple, yet smiling at a stranger is often difficult for many people.

Recently, I celebrated my 76th birthday with my family, and received well wishes from friends alike. A new experience to travel somewhere made this birthday so much more special, as my travel opportunities are less frequent. I feel so grateful for the rich experience to explore somewhere new, try new foods, and take photos of where I have been. This is something we all can create in our lives by being a tourist locally. Experience enriches the brain and leaves a smile on my face.

As I create this story from my life's experiences, I want you to know that I've come to learn in my 76 years that the most beautiful things cannot be seen or even touched, they must be felt with a smiling heart.

Bio

Kathryn Seymour is a retired care-aid from Menno Hospital in Abbotsford, British Columbia, Canada, and avid smiling enthusiast. She derives her passion for life through cultivating daily gratitude lists and the simple practice of smiling. She is inspired by nature, music, traveling, and spending quality time with friends and family. It brings her heart joy to inspire other seniors who may be lonely or sad as their life changes with age. Kathryn is committed to donating $1 from every book sale to "The iPod Project" to help seniors with Alzheimer's and dementia reconnect with joy.

Dear MaMa
By Katie Elliott

God blessed me when He placed me into your loving arms. Your beautiful face was the image that I saw. You were my first love, and you will forever be. You have been my anchor in life. No matter the circumstance I find myself in, you are *always* there for me. You have given me the priceless gift of knowing there is one person in the world who loves me, just as I am. You are the bright light in the darkness that reassures me that I am never alone. And when I am worried or upset, you inspire me to put on my Superwoman cape and face the world with confidence.

You have shown me how to be loving, authentic, independent, honest, and feisty. Your actions have shown me the true meaning of "to thine own self be true." You do not follow others; instead, you lead. You are my role model and a courageous trailblazer. Even though there are challenges along the unbeaten path of life, you march on with fierce intensity. Your bravery has shown me how to venture off on the roads less traveled with courage. Because of you, I am the woman I am today.

When you enter a room, it brightens with your beautiful smile, big blue eyes, and your sassy attitude. You have never met a stranger in your life. No matter where you are, people are drawn to you. They like how they feel when they are in your presence. Our hearts are touched every time we hear your friends call you "Mother Mary." They love and respect you as we do. You are not only our mother, but also our best friend.

My all-time favorite TV show is *I Love Lucy*. We are lucky to have been raised by our own Lucy. The episode of Lucy and Ethel wrapping candy in the chocolate factory epitomizes who you are. You always had great intentions, but often unexpected results. We had to ride our bicycles to the grocery store in search of a relaxer or toner for hair fiascos. Being seven months pregnant, with a tornado warning, you decided to go to the grocery store. While you were shopping, the roof blew off. You parked your car wherever you wanted. If there wasn't a sign, you considered it a parking space. You believe that it is easier to ask forgiveness than it is to get permission. There are more stories than can be written.

You are one of the most honest people I know. You always told us that a *real* friend is someone who will tell you the truth, even when it hurts. When you see a friend or family member in pain, you become the voice of reason. You may ruffle some feathers along the way, but you always speak your truth. It may sting a little at the time, but you love us enough to tell us the truth. Your real friends understand and appreciate your sincerity. We have learned how to be the same kind of friend to others.

You have such a generous heart. You have blessed so many people with your kindness. If you see someone who is in real need, you come to their aid. People may not ask you for your help, but you are willing to offer what you can. You give money to a mother who struggles to feed her children. The children you sponsor in India receive a college education because of your life-long support. When a family does not have presents for Christmas, you provide for them. Innumerable lives have changed because of the random acts of kindness you have performed. You give freely and, if at all possible, anonymously.

Being the mother of six children has had to be the most rewarding and yet, challenging role in your lifetime. It is hard to imagine the devotion, sacrifice, patience, and selflessness it takes to love us like you do. We frequently pull you in six different directions at once, each of us vying for your time, attention, and approval. And yet you make us feel uniquely special. Each of us has believed at one time or another that we are your favorite child. Even so, you made sure that everything was fair and equally divided. You never wanted anyone to feel slighted.

As the matriarch of our family, you have taught your children and grandchildren invaluable lessons. You told us that it does not cost a thing to smile at someone or to say please and thank you. You told us that our smile might brighten someone's day. We extend our hand to help others in need, friends and strangers alike. You treat all people with dignity and respect, regardless of their status in life. It is second nature for us to be the same.

You have always been an extremely hard-worker. Working two to three part-time jobs was your norm. The money you earned throughout our childhood was for *us* and our future. You have blessed us with opportunities and privileges that otherwise would not have been possible. We have all needed your help at different times in our lives. When it was necessary, you have given us a hand up, not a handout. You have also sent us money in a card for no reason at all.

We attended college and graduated debt-free. We did not want to take typing in high school or get extra certifications in college, but you suggested that we do so if we wanted to continue our studies. Being able to fend and provide for ourselves was of utmost importance. Because of your guidance, we are self-sufficient, prosperous, and happy.

We are so blessed that God allowed us to be your children. We have loved and cherished you every day of our lives. Thank you, MaMa!

"A mother is she who can take the place of all others but whose place no one else can take." ~ Cardinal Meymillod

Bio

Katie Elliott: She is a contributing author of the international bestsellers, *Inspirations: 101 Uplifting Stories for Daily Happiness* and *Manifestations: True Stories of Bringing the Imagined into Reality*. Katie is also an academic tutor, providing individual and small group instruction to help students improve their educational performance while uplifting their self-esteem. She has been a teacher for over 30 years, including college, high school, and elementary students.

A Soul Realignment
By Katye Anna

Every day I wake up and say, "Thank you, thank you, thank you," for this opportunity to be alive on this planet.

While this is true today, it wasn't always. In 1987, I received what I call a *soul realignment*. A soul realignment is a sign to stop and reevaluate your life. Soul realignments come in numerous forms. Mine was a nervous breakdown. At the time, it seemed like I was never going to be happy again. A lot of people were surprised when I fell apart. Most people who knew me thought I was happy. Why would they think otherwise? I smiled. I went through the motions of life, even while inside, I was dying. No one knew the despair and sadness I was feeling inside.

One day something within me cracked, and I found it impossible to keep on pretending.

I went away to rehab for thirty days.

In this place of safety, the unraveling began.

I realized that I had lived my entire life without questioning why I did what I did. Like many people, I had been an unconscious creator. I had lived most of my life as a victim. At the time, I didn't know that my thoughts and emotions were creating the experiences of my life. Nor did I know that the power to change my life was within me all the time.

During my time in rehab, I began questioning everything. I purged years of sadness and shame. I began releasing old, outdated beliefs. After thirty days at rehab, I came home. I was unsure what the future held, but I was filled with gratitude that I was beginning to remember who I was—an incarnated soul.

During this time of awakening, my dreams began to guide me. Angels who had been my constant companions as a child began to guide my life once again. Many shifts occurred in my life during the next few years as the unraveling continued. As old, outdated beliefs were released, I grounded new beliefs.

At the age of 40, I went to college. I believed I would work in hospice or become a therapist. My personal healing continued, and I began to be guided by my soul and the world of spirit. I was going through a rebirth. It was a time of self-discovery. I began to walk in gratitude every day for my life. I began to take responsibility for my thoughts and emotions.

Six years after my soul realignment, I began working at the York House AIDS Hospice. This was a time of more awakenings and insights for me. It was during this time I realized that I could see things other people weren't seeing. The brave men and women who came there to die became my teachers. They would talk about seeing loved ones who had died. They saw angels, and so did I. I held space for their deathbed visions. I encouraged them to talk about their experiences. It was during this time that I coined the phrase *birthing into spirit*. I witnessed first-hand that physical death was a lot like childbirth. It was hard work. I think back to those days, and I can clearly see how my soul was guiding me. Even now, as I write, my soul leaps from my heart. I smile, beyond grateful, as I think back on my life.

What felt like the worst thing in the world that could happen was actually a blessing, for it led me onto the illuminated pathway of my soul. My soul became the guiding force in my life. Angels became my constant companions. My soul and the world of spirit guided my life and my work.

It was during this time I made the decision to teach people how to live consciously so they could die consciously. I became a Reiki Master and began giving healing sessions. I became known as the angel lady.

Thirty-three years have passed since my soul realignment. I have been blessed to be teaching about the journey of the soul for 26 years.

In 2013 I began writing transformational books. Many years earlier, I had been shown in my dreams that I would write books. I remember laughing, but I had come to trust my visions as soul guidance. I trusted that, if my soul wanted me to write books, my soul would make it happen. I sit here in gratitude, knowing that my books have touched the lives of many people.

Gratitude has become a way of life for me. Every day I walk in the gratitude that I know who I am and why I am here on this planet. With each new sunrise, I know I have the opportunity to bring forth the creative expression of my soul. At the end of the day, I reflect on what I achieved as well as what I could have done better. I end each day with gratitude for the gift of life.

As the teacher of soul, I seek to help people bring forth the creative power of their soul. Our souls seek to express themselves through our lives. The greatest expression of your soul is joy; therefore, seek to experience joy every day.

As I am writing this article, the world is currently going through an unraveling. Collectively we are going through a soul realignment.

Collectively we have come to a stop sign.

We are called to eradicate fear and to stay open to love. Practice gratitude every day. This will help to raise your vibration and the vibration of the planet.

Be gentle with yourself and with others as the unraveling and shifts continue. We are resourceful, resilient, and creative beings of love. We are called to come together in divine collaboration and the spirit of cooperation. Converge in love. Take *full* responsibility for your thoughts and your emotions. Understand that we can only succeed together. Practice gratitude and stay open to love.

Blessings, Katye Anna, Teacher of Soul

Bio

Katye Anna is the teacher of soul, a modern-day mystic, and spiritual teacher. She is an inspirational teacher, speaker, and author of nine books. Her gifts of travel and illuminated sight allow her to give first-hand descriptions of the world of spirit. Katye Anna teaches how to live a soul-inspired life. Through her books, speaking engagements, retreats, and classes, Katye Anna works with individuals, families, and organizations to provide the resources they need to successfully navigate the entire journey of the soul. Katye Anna holds an annual transformational retreat at Mago Retreat Center in Sedona, Arizona.
https://www.katyeanna.com

A Mother's Life Lesson
By Kayela Sorenson

Who I am today is not only my doing. The trials and experiences I lived through had a huge impact on me—friends I've made throughout the years, family hardships and growth, school and life-changing occurrences, relationships, and job experiences. Either you can let these events tear you down and bring out the worst in you, or you can learn from them, keep your head up high, and continue with life. I'll share with you one of the biggest trials I've experienced that had the biggest influence on me and shaped me into who I am today.

Imagine being born and adopted from a third world country, raised by a single American mother, who also adopted another sibling and tried to raise them to her best ability, but who also fought illness after illness, until the final illness took over and won. At only 17-years-old, growing up into this American lifestyle away from my home country—never had a father, and now without my mother—I was trying to take on this life by myself.

Ever since I was little, my mother had always been ill. Because of her health, she could only exert so much physical movement in a day until she needed to rest. The biggest moments began in 2008 when I was in the seventh grade. My mother got knee surgery that required her to spend months in the hospital and rehabilitation center trying to build up the strength and motions to walk again. During that time, my sister and I had to live with our aunt for a few months, since we were too young to live by ourselves. Learning to keep my home clean, do laundry, cook for myself, do homework, and so on—these were growing moments for me to become independent. I lived at my house on and off throughout the eighth and ninth grades, without always having my mother around.

Sophomore year came along, and I remember seeing my mother having a huge breakdown one night. The next day she went to the hospital, and I found out she had almost experienced kidney failure. This moment was a shock for my sister and me, as well as our whole family, thinking we had almost lost my mother. I wasn't ready for this.

My mother then spent five months in the hospital recovering from her accident. This time, my sister and I were able to live in our home by ourselves. Once again, I made my meals, did my laundry, completed errands, shopped for groceries, and kept up with school and homework. I was living like an adult. Finally, summer came along. My mother recovered from her incident, came back home, and life went on.

Junior year finally came. Everything was going fine until December 18, 2012. My acapella concert was that night. I was excited for all my family to be there. Everyone showed up except my mother and sister. I wondered why.

When I got home that night from the concert, I remember walking into the living room, seeing my mother and sister on the sofa. They had news for me. That night, December 18th, my mother was diagnosed with leukemia. I lost it and broke down in tears. We were all crying and hugging each other. I was only 16—I couldn't imagine losing my mother so soon. Just thinking about not having my mother around for my high school graduation, moving away for school, getting married, and having children made the tears keep flowing.

My mother decided she was going to go through chemotherapy. She wanted to do everything she could in order to stay around for my sister and me.

Everything was going smoothly during chemo for a while. My mother kept getting treatments and daily checkups at the hospitals. The last three months of my junior year until the end of my senior year was a different story. The cancer hit hard and spread.

On the morning of December 18, 2013, exactly one year from when she was diagnosed with leukemia, my mother passed away.

My mother was everything to me. She was a mother and a best friend. Through those six years of fighting to survive, my mother never gave up. She kept pushing through for my sister and me. We meant the world to her. Seeing my mother fighting and never giving up made me so grateful and even stronger. Grateful to be her daughter and grateful for her giving me the determination to fight for what I want in life and to succeed. I won't give up. Yes, I could have let this whole occurrence weaken me to give up on my future, but no. If my mother could push through, so could I.

I thank my mother for who I am today. Her life journey was only the beginning of shaping me into the strong, independent woman that I am today—Kayela Sorenson, only 23 years old. I live life with a faithful heart, and take care of myself and others. And when I am given work, I will work hard. Giving up is not in my vocabulary. Instead, it's gratitude that's on the top of my list. Gratitude for the life I was given that molded me into the person I am today.

Again, either you can let events in your life bring out the worst in you and give up, or you can take from it, learn from it, and run with it. Keep your head up high and live with passion and appreciation, and continue to thrive in this life. Push through and give it all you have with a joyful heart. You never know what blessings and revelations will fall right into your lap. And to know all this, I am grateful.

Bio

Kayela Sorenson is a leader, friend, and mentor when it comes to connection and creating community. Her life experiences blossomed her into the woman she is today. She enjoys sharing her life story about overcoming the challenges of facing the death of her mother, adoption life from a third world country, exploring both Latin and American cultures, and finding her birth mother through faith-based seeking only. Her passion is to inspire many women and sharing the importance of self-love and what it means to care for and nurture one's spirit, inward, and outward. You can reach Kayela at kayelasorenson@gmail.com.

Shower Of Gratitude
By KC Miller

It wasn't until I traveled to India that I understood gratitude on a deep, visceral level.

Gratitude has always been familiar to me; I've been a pretty happy-go-lucky person my whole life. I'm an optimist by nature! As a longtime student of *A Course in Miracles,* I consciously choose to be "miracle ready," which means choosing to be in a state of gratitude and readiness as a daily practice.

What I experienced in India was *visceral*. An adrenaline rush caused my heart rate to rise. I held my breath; it elongated into a sigh, followed by a deep and joyful cry. I felt gratitude in every pore of my body.

Imagine traveling over 30 hours—without much sleep—to the other side of the world, only to arrive at a modest ashram in Mulvu, India. We were assigned to a camp-like dorm room, outfitted with low metal cots and a packed down futon mattress.

The shower consisted of a simple pipe coming out the wall about two feet off the floor, with a blue plastic bucket in front of a rusty faucet. A dipper-like cup hung off the side of the bucket. Oh, yes—there was a small plastic stool on which to crouch while using what was known as "the bath bucket." It was apparent that warm, let alone hot, showers were not among the amenities. Luckily, I had entered the trip with a yogic attitude: Experience the sensations and choose not to suffer!

Modest and *humble* would be some of the more luxurious words to describe our accommodations. Yet, they were not any different than how the facilities were advertised. It was an ashram. We got what we signed up for.

Our days began with ritualistic gratitude, as early each morning, we attended morning worship known as Aarti, where flashes of light are offered to the divine in the form of lite oil held in a simple silver metal tray. Aarti is an expression of gratitude, prayers, and reverence to deities, elders, teachers, and the divine.

The Aarti ceremony is extremely symbolic. The tray holding the fire is waved in a circular fashion, in a clockwise manner, facing the altar. After every circle, when the Aarti tray has reached the bottom position, the person doing the ceremony waves it backward while remaining in the bottom. The idea here is that Aarti represents our daily activities, which revolve around the divine, the teachings we have chosen to live by, and our intention for the day. It is a spiritual discipline of keeping the divine at the center of all activities and reinforces the understanding that our worldly activities are secondary in importance.

This understanding is intended to give believers the strength to withstand unexpected grief, keep them humble, and remind them of the divine during happy moments. Apart from our earthly comings and goings, Aarti also represents one's self—signifying that we are like the lighted wick. Our internal light can chase away darkness when coupled with the daily practice of gratitude and thanksgiving.

It was my good fortune to have one of the senior assistants at the ashram explain to me the first day we were there that she uses the morning Aarti as a gratitude practice. During the light ceremony and morning chants, she counts her blessings as she sits in stillness, releasing any restless thoughts or judgment of any kind that she identifies as mental modifications in her mind. Immediately I adopted her understanding of this morning practice.

We share this ceremony with the local residents, who modeled the gesture of showing respect and gratitude to the divine and their teachers. At the end of the ritual, those gathered could choose to approach the altar, bow in reverence, and apply sacred ash to their forehead to leave an auspicious red mark.

Many of us followed suit, anointing our third eye with what I've come to call "the mark of gratitude!" As soon as the morning rites were complete, a dozen of the local men rushed away to prepare our organic, vegan breakfast. We recognized them first by the rice red dots and, after a couple of days, by their familiar and knowing smiles.

A graceful rhythm developed. Even though the tastes and texture of the food being prepared for us were foreign, the experience of their loving presence seemed to be filling the holes in many of our souls. I found myself weeping during the Aarti ceremony and often when the humble men carefully served us food harvested from their local fields and gardens, prepared by their hands and open hearts.

Each day included a physical Asana practice, followed by Yoga Nidra—a form of guided dhyana, or meditation. The main activity of the day was sitting erect for several hours as our teachers shared their wisdom around the Yoga Sutra scriptures and other epic Vedic stories.

Sounds pretty idyllic, doesn't it? It was, yet, all the sitting took a toll on my body; I began to get a craving for "real" coffee and a menu my stomach recognized. Plus, there's the homesick factor: wanting your bed, pillow, and a hot bath. I definitely hit a point where I was experiencing a lot of sensations, and my monkey mind began to run amuck, teetering between mild grumbling to simmering frustration.

It was five days into the immersion when I decided to skip the evening activity and go to my room for a little solitude and journaling. As I prepared to retire early that night, I sat on the plastic stool bracing myself for enough cold water to remove the grime of the day.

To my great surprise, hot water flowed from the pipe. It actually took me a few moments to register that the water was hot enough to scald me. After a quick adjustment, I began to shake—not from being chilly, rather, from deep humility. Gratitude coursed through my veins. I had never experienced the divine's embrace in this way. I wept.

The experience of extreme gratitude on such a deep, visceral level has not left me, and I pray it never will.

My gratitude practice is now forever rooted in the ritual of Aarti. I rise each morning and find my way to an altar—sometimes, it's in the meditation room at my home, and other times I mentally transport myself to the basement of the Holy Temple on the grounds of the ashrams. A candle is lit, chimes are rung, a chant is whispered—and gratitude courses through me.

My draw to India was the opportunity to study with a teacher who had an authentic lineage, who fully embraced the original yoga teachings which I have come to credit my personal and spiritual evolvement to—the Yoga Sutras. What I left with was how ordinary, yet grand, the experience of gratitude can be.

The embodiment of gratitude involved my humanness, humility, and a heartfelt belief that the divine intervened, warming me to my core when I needed it most.

Using poetic license, my translation of Yoga Sutra 1.21 encapsulates my experience: "For those who have an intense urge for spirit and wisdom, it sits next to them, waiting to shower over them. Reach out in grateful anticipation!"

Bio

KC Miller is the founder of a nationally-accredited college offering holistic health and wellness courses leading to transformational diplomas and degrees, and the owner of Spirit of Yoga in Tempe, Arizona. She has practiced yoga for over 30 years, is a part of the Yoga Teacher Training team at the Southwest Institute of Healing Arts, and loves teaching and blogging about practical ways to interpret and apply the Yoga Sutra. KC is a longtime student of A Course of Miracles and is contributing author to three other anthologies, including *Heaven Sent, Living Brave— Finishing Strong*, and *Entrepreneurial GRIT: A Hero's Journey*.

Grateful Time
By Kenneth I. Laws II

T his particular submission is written amidst the COVID-19 pandemic. I cannot begin to say how much my heart breaks for all those affected and lost due to this. I do think that the Universe is forcing all of us to become a little more grateful for all the little things—how and where we spend our time, who we spend it with, and what we do with it. This has also affected people close to me, as well as from a personal and business standpoint. In short, this has caused many to re-evaluate how time is spent, and to be grateful for how that time spent.

I am unsure why, but this has caused me to reflect on my life and all the choices, decisions, and actions made and the time spent making them. As I look back at all of it—and not only most, but all of it—I have to be grateful for every single thing that has occurred in my life. Every action, choice, decision, and mistake. Grateful for every moment. To define them as bad or good depends on one's perspective.

It has taken every single one of these actions to not only be where I am today but to be the person I am today. I am still a human being who will make mistakes, but I have to be grateful for them. I do believe they are, in fact, moments to not only learn from but grow from. I have to be grateful for the time given to me to make these mistakes and to grow from all of them. Time, in my opinion, is a man-made construct in which to place limitations on that which we can accomplish in a set time frame. Usually, the 24-hour period which defines a day. Although some of us do not live life by the man-made definitions of time, it still exists, especially in our workdays, our day to day activities, and time spent with our family and or loved ones.

Having said that, from someone who dislikes time and its constraints, there are certain things that we all need during the previously-stated 24-hour time period. *Need* might be a strong word, but things like who and where we choose to give and make time—things that are important on a daily basis, if you will. In other words, be grateful for the time you can spend and conscious of how it is spent.

As it relates to these predetermined times frames, I think, as humans, we should look at those time constraints, whether we subscribe to them or not, and determine what is most important during these times. It is a given that having fun, laughing, and doing things we enjoy is a part of this. Activities that bring us joy and support our passion or are therapeutic are most certainly a necessity.

Those who have yet to experience the exact limitation of time have a tendency to spend it with activities, self-preservation, and doing things from a selfish perspective. These things fill a temporary void that exists within all of us, but is still a necessary part of existence. Those are things that bring temporary satisfaction but quickly go away. Therein lies the need to do it again, but without consideration of another. This is not necessarily a fault, but a learned and taught behavior.

Those of us who have experienced the true limitations of time, be it through the death of a loved one, or even their death, tend to view time a bit differently—not only time but how it is spent. There is a certain finality that comes with that experience. We become grateful for each and every moment spent, how it is spent, and who it is spent with. As hard as it is, I wish all could experience the finality of time, and what comes after, which is an altered perspective of time and how it is spent and dedicated. It's a perspective that few get to experience at an early age and it gives one the ability to see it in a whole new light.

It begins with how we make time for not only ourselves but for others. It has a way of changing how and where we choose to dedicate our time. Yes, the dedication of time for ourselves is of utmost importance, but we begin to dedicate time to those who are important in our lives, like family and loved ones. We begin to place importance on making that time for those people, and not using all the time for our selfish needs. More importantly, we become extremely grateful for every moment spent.

The importance of how our time is dedicated can only be learned through experience. It can be told, it can be read, it can even be taught, but it's value never becomes relevant until we have experienced the finality of the time of another human being, especially a loved one. It's only then that we realize the value of time spent.

It is only through this experience that we are truly grateful for actually making time for others and not ourselves. This is not a flaw of any human, but something that has to be learned. I can only wish that I could teach all those I love the value of time spent.

May we all see what is going on around us and genuinely consider the time we spend and how we spend it. It's obvious that we never know when the finality of time will occur to someone you know or love. Be kind, be loving, and be grateful for every moment spent with those you love. More importantly, make and take the time to show them how much they matter.

Bio

Kenneth I. Laws II has been on a spiritual path after a series of life-altering events in 2013 and has spent his time trying to understand the unexplainable—his awakening. Through his search for answers, he has come to understand the true meaning of "oneness," as well as divine events designed to elevate the mind above the ego-driven, fear-based life. Kenneth has come to accept that part of his mission and gift is to write about love, forgiveness, and kindness. His contributions can be found in the books, *Inspirations: 101 Uplifting Stories for Daily Happiness*, and, *Manifestations: True Stories of Bringing the Imagined into Reality*.

Thank You In Advance, And So It Is
By Kim Purcell

Is your spouse driving you insane? Is your boss a micromanaging control freak? Are you losing patience with your family? Well, thoughts become things. Whether you think you will, or you think you won't, you're right. Wayne Dyer said, "If you change your thinking, you can change your life." Practicing gratitude can change your life for the better without changing anything else in your life. Being grateful for what we have invites a sense of peace and harmony with all that is.

It's easier to notice what's missing than appreciate what we have. Reframing to gratitude takes conscious effort. Rather than focus on what we lack, simply notice what *is* with gratefulness. Greet each new day with gratitude. Thank you, earth, beneath my feet. Thank you, air to breathe. Even through the clouds, thank you, sun; I know you're there. Thank you, rain, the garden needed you. Even if they're annoying, thank you, friends and family, for being there. Each moment, if we try, has something to appreciate. The shift happens when we stop complaining and start appreciating every living, breathing moment of our lives. That's not to say there will be smiles in grief. We experience loss, are wronged, and can often feel less than. Still, within the fabric of that, it is possible to leave space for more. We may never come to experience gratitude in the same feeling space as we experience the loss of a loved one, or physical disability or something less grave. But, to leave open that space of hope—that "hopening"—somewhere deep beneath the grief, there is growth. There is life. There is space to experience gratefulness if we allow it.

Recognizing the divine order of things, we open ourselves to expanded awareness, despite how dispirited by circumstance we are. Divine wisdom is always available to us. Deep in our soul is the whisper of what is true, divine insight, the voice of the higher self—although, it is harder to hear when we are mired in judgment, complaining, sadness, anger, or vengeance. We tame ingratitude by becoming mindful. Consciously practicing gratitude invites acceptance, and thereby, harmony with what is. Recognizing there is something greater always watching, guarding, guiding us through, we open the door to access that wisdom by stepping outside our personal experience, outside the ego (or "edging God out"). There is mastery with practice. Practice being that shirtless little boy stomping in the puddles and singing with the birds, even with a belly yearning for a meal.

Here's a simple challenge I learned from an acting coach years ago. Try saying yes to every question for a full day. I'm fickle, and it's hard. If a server asks, "Would you like Sprite?" say, "Yes," even if you want something different. All day long, let the answer be yes. It's interesting to witness as the actor and the audience, and is a challenge I still repeat. I modified a version of this challenge to improve my gratefulness. It may seem simple, but try it, and you might learn something about yourself. Every time you hear a compliment, say, "Thank you." Notice how often your answer may feel more self-deprecating.

"You're good at that."

"Not as good as MaryAlice."

"Hey, nice outfit."

"What, this old thing?"

"Your face is beautiful."

"Are you calling me fat?"

The key is to continue until you can actually receive the positive intent of the compliment. Even if you don't believe it, simply say thank you, and notice how it feels to receive the compliment. If it is especially hard to believe, try, "Aww, thank you." When you do receive the compliment as it was intended, feel it lift you up.

Dr. Joe Dispenza says the feeling creates the healing. Neuroscientists say that we can change our brains by changing our thoughts. As we imagine a new possibility and crystalize that potential reality in our mind, we actually create new circuitry in the brain to realize that potential. So, when we are grateful in advance, by envisioning what it will look like, feel like, and how we will act once we are in that particular state of abundance, we already set in motion the events to bring about what we want. Beyond gratitude for what is, we can practice gratitude in advance as a form of manifesting.

There's an ancient Toltec practice of putting intention into our relationships, called *The Medicine Bag*. I will share an abbreviated version that I've modified slightly to include gratitude. Select small stones or trinkets to represent each important relationship in your life and gather them together in a small pouch. Make sure to include a trinket for yourself. The practice is to work with each relationship, one by one.

181

Hold each trinket in your hand, holding the relationship in your awareness with your attention. Assess the state of the relationship. Is it where you would like it to be? Is there something you feel you need to say? Maybe an apology? A need to forgive? Are you easily annoyed by them or often impatient? Assess the relationship and take time to think about how you would like to see the relationship shift. Maybe you would like to be closer or more at peace. Envision yourself doing whatever would bring more of what you would like into the relationship. Before moving on to the next symbol, think of at least three things about that person for which you're grateful. It helps to give yourself plenty of time with the Medicine Bag, especially in the beginning. Sit with your medicine bag daily, if possible. And, notice your relationships begin to shift. Step outside of the relationship to witness it transform with gratitude and intention.

To reframe to a state of gratefulness is to enter one of the highest vibrations we know. We stay in that state with perspective, forgiveness, acceptance, and love.

We become what we think about. We change our world, from the inside out, with gratitude.

Bio

Kim Purcell is a wellness workshop facilitator and self-love coach. Married for 18 years, they have three thriving teenage children. Kim worked in publishing for 15 years, where she developed her passion for nutrition. Diagnosed with Crohn's/Colitis, Kim healed herself through food and nutrition. Her passion for healing the body is rivaled only by a passion for healing the whole soul self. For the past six years, Kim has been working with women and teen girls on their journeys toward mind, body, and spiritual wellness in Ponte Vedra Beach, Florida. She loves to help in any way she can. Find her on Facebook as Kim Droge Purcell or www.facebook.com/thrivetribekp. Email agehealthier@gmail.com or call 904.545.1327.

Life's Grout
by Kit Macy

I found out at an early age that I was Irish, and with that, came all the privileges of the luck of the Irish, or so I thought. But life has shown me, over and over again, that there's more to success in life than luck or genealogy. For me, it all begins with gratitude, which is what I call "life's grout." Grout is that pasty, sticky stuff between the tiles in your kitchen or shower that sort of, you know, holds things together. That's what gratitude is for me. It's like grout: pasty and sticky. It's meant to be functional, not ornamental.

I knew at an early age that my gender was a gift, and as the song says, "I enjoy being a girl." By that, I mean, for example, that I was spared some of the grueling outdoor chores, like yard work, that my brothers had to endure in the heat of the desert sun, while my limited tasks were relegated to the "easier" stuff, like dusting, inside the air-conditioned house.

As a child, I never understood "big picture" topics, such as how eating all my vegetables would help the starving children in China. Or, why women had to labor to give birth.

Because our family lived in an upper-middle-class neighborhood near the heart of the entertainment industry, everything in our family had to look good. Or nice. Or pretty. My parents both worked in "The Business," so appearances mattered. The upside to this was, I had the good fortune to land great jobs in high school. The motto of the day was, "It's who you know, not what you know." At that time, I assumed that's how the game was played and how life was done. It wasn't until I was a young adult and left Tinseltown for college that I began to realize, in real-time, the power and importance of gratitude. After all, when things come your way, there's nothing to compare your reality against, and you assume it's like that for everyone. I never wanted to leave home, but my folks thought it was for the best. Little did they know (or did they?) that sending me away to college was for more than only getting a bachelor's degree. It was for my Ph.D. degree in the school of life and the university of gratitude.

While I was away at school, I met lots of students who came from varied backgrounds, religions, and cultures. I met a girl in the dorm who loved to listen to the twang of Johnny Cash, and who slept with the window open in the middle of winter, so the snow piled up on the floor at night. I met a boy who chewed tobacco and spit it out when it piled up so far in his lower lip that he couldn't put his lips together. And I knew a girl who was so desperately homesick and out of balance, that she committed suicide. I also met a family with eight kids and no indoor plumbing. The mother had to haul water from the well to wash diapers and do laundry. It was what we called a "dirt farm." They literally lived off the dirt. They planted their crops and prayed for a harvest, fed their livestock, and built their house on the dirt. They gathered eggs, milked cows, and shocked wheat bundles, without fail because their existence depended on it. It was mindboggling to me to witness how "backward" this family was. I mean, really? We had recently put a man on the Moon in 1969, and they were still churning cream to make butter. I watched the cream rise to the top of the bucket of the fresh milk from the cow in the barn that they'd milked that morning. I tossed hay bales off the back of the wagon to feed the cattle and watched calves being born in the middle of subzero winter. It was too cold to make snow angels, and it reminded me of my mother defrosting the refrigerator, back in the sunny southwest. My "new normal" became being willing to consider the possibility that there were two ways of seeing things in life. I was beginning to have my eyes opened to the possibility that "these" people, who, through no fault of their own, had nothing—yet everything. The deep and genuine bonds of the family between the siblings and the respect they shared for each other, their parents, and their God, was something I had never experienced. It felt like I was living in a Willa Cather novel.

I do believe that, at some level, deep within my being, I experienced a sort of metamorphosis. I often felt like I was glazing over, almost like going into a mild state of shock with some of what I observed. I came away from college and the harshness of that life and those raw experiences, with an appreciation of what it takes to survive, if not thrive in the world without a swimming pool in the backyard. The visceral experience of having to perform the "hard chores" in bone-chilling wind and snow, whether or not you felt up to it, or to have real hunger pangs, captured my heart, mind, and attention. But the thing that lingers still is the revelation of how deeply ingrained my judgments were, along with my lack of gratitude for all that I had been given and gifted with as a child. And I never knew it. The lesson for me was clear.

So, when someone describes the Grand Canyon as "just a big hole in the ground," give it a minute, look again—at them and the Canyon, with awe, wonder, and gratitude. And say thank you.

Bio

Seeker of universal truth, planetary evolvement, and human empowerment. Email: kmacy64@gmail.com.

Irvin's Rock
By Kristi Blakeway

"Change your perception, change your life."

One of the simplest ways to increase happiness is to help others. When I begin to feel sorry for myself, or when I notice my stress level increasing, I make a conscious effort to help someone. This simple practice helps shift my perception, grounds me, and diminishes my worries.

Ten years ago, in an effort to help those who are less fortunate, I agreed to organize dinner service at a local homeless shelter one evening per week. As a high school counselor, it was easy to gather up like-minded students and staff who wanted to make a difference. We began what we thought was an act of giving.

Looking back, I am overcome with gratitude. I set out to help, but I ended up gaining more than I could have ever imagined. My first night in the shelter was a profound experience that shifted my life's work.

It was a rainy October evening in Vancouver. My students and I had dinner prepared, and together, we anxiously waited for the shuttle bus to arrive. In our community, those living on the streets are not able to walk to the shelter, as neighbors fear the idea of homeless people on their streets. Instead, a shuttle bus picks up passengers from local parks and drives them to the nightly shelter.

Just after 10:00 p.m., the bus arrived with eight guests. Irvin had the stereotypical image of a homeless man: unruly hair, unshaven, and ragged clothing. It was easy to judge Irvin by his appearance, but there was something soft amidst his rough exterior. Perhaps it was the way his bright blue eyes sparkled, or perhaps it was his gentle nature as he thanked us for dinner. I took the seat next to Irvin, and one of my students sat across the table. As we engaged in conversation, Irvin let us know it was his mom's birthday. I asked if he would like to use my phone to call her. He smiled and told me he could not call, as his mom had passed away years ago. I apologized, "I'm sorry—I guess you didn't get to speak to her then."

With wisdom, he smiled back, "Now I get to talk to her every day."

Irvin shared he had also lost two sisters. Assuming their deaths were recent, I asked what happened. Irvin's voice softened and he took us back to a horrific night over 50 years ago in Milwaukee when he was only six years old. Living in poverty, Irvin awoke to find his house on fire. He woke one sister who shared a room with him. He then ran across the hall to try and get to the room his other sisters shared. The fire blocked the entrance, so he ran to wake his mom. Irvin shared the memory of his mom running into the fire, trying to save her daughters. He then recalled the image of his mom emerging from the house burned, yet empty-handed. She whispered, "They are gone." In that moment, Irvin lost a three-year-old and an eight-year-old sister. Fifty years later, the pain was still as raw.

Trying to hold back my tears, I told Irvin he was a hero for saving two lives. He smiled in appreciation, but his face told me it was not enough. He politely excused himself to go for a cigarette, and I excused myself to wash the dishes. In that instant, Irvin taught me that homelessness is not caused by addiction, but rather by trauma and hurt.

At the end of the evening, the student who had heard Irvin's story told me he had struggled for months with the news of his parents' divorce. After hearing Irvin's story, he realized he still had two parents who loved him, and he needed to stop feeling sorry for himself, as his problems were minimal compared to Irvin's. I realized we were not only helping the homeless—they were helping us.

For the next year, we enjoyed our weekly visits with Irvin. His eyes would sparkle as he would speak of his adventures, and on a good night, he would break out in song. Tears would roll down his face as he would sing Eric Clapton's *Beautiful Tonight*. When he finished his dessert and left the table, he would always shout out with enthusiasm, "Cowboy up!" This simple expression symbolized Irvin's strength to stay positive and keep going.

One evening I asked Irvin what he would do if he won the lottery. Instantly, he shared that he would give the money to charity to thank those who have helped him. On our final night at the shelter, I gave Irvin a lottery ticket and told him I hoped his luck would change. Irvin reached in his pocket and told me he had a gift for me. Not knowing what to expect, I remember feeling nervous about what could possibly come from his pocket. When he unfolded his hand, he held out a small brown rock. He told me that the year before the shelter opened, he was living under a bridge. Middle school students had approached him with their teacher and offered him some cookies. With the cookies, they had also given him the rock and told him it was a friendship rock. They asked him to keep it in his pocket, and to remember each time he felt it, that the community cared. Irvin asked me to take the rock, and put it in my pocket, and remember that he cared too. Eight months later, Irvin passed away. His rock remains my favorite gift.

Next time you are feeling down or overwhelmed, I encourage you to reach out and help someone. This simple act will help shift your perception and remind you how much you have to be grateful for.

Bio

Kristi Blakeway is a school principal in Vancouver, British Columbia, where she lives with her husband and two sons. She is the bestselling author of *Beyond HELLO: Rekindling the Human Spirit One Conversation at a Time*. She is the founder of Beyond HELLO, a student-led initiative that helps the homeless reconnect with family. She is a TEDx speaker, Olympic torchbearer, and winner of the YWCA Women of Distinction Award for connecting community. Kristi encourages everyone to step outside their comfort zone, engage in soulful conversation, and connect with compassion. A storyteller at heart, she blogs regularly at www.beyondhello.org and www.hopefullearning.com.

Reflecting Gratitude
By Lindsey Sadowski

Never in my wildest dreams did I think that experiencing one of the biggest tragedies of my life would lead me to one of life's greatest lessons. That being the lesson of gratitude. At the age of twelve, I was one of those children who knew exactly what I wanted to be when I grew up, which was to pursue a career in sports medicine. I loved playing soccer, but more importantly, I loved helping people. My passion never wavered, and I went on to study athletic training. I could have chosen many paths to work in, but I decided to work for a hospital system that contracted me out to a high school. Not many people have the patience to deal with high school students, but something inside of me was guiding me to be there.

One day, in my athletic training room, this hefty young man walked in, whom I didn't recognize. We began to talk, and I quickly found out that he came from a home that was filled with drugs and alcohol. He resonated with me, as I have an older sibling who also chose a life like this. In my gut, I knew I was meant to help this young man, so I decided to get him involved in wrestling. He agreed, and it helped him turn his life around. In July of that year, I decided to take a short vacation before sports started again. When I returned home a few days later, I ended up being rushed to the ER feeling extreme pain throughout my entire body. The doctors ran many tests, but the results were coming up as normal. Nothing made sense until I received a text message around 6:00 a.m. It was one of my student aides, asking me if I had heard the news. I quickly wrote back, "No, what happened?" She wrote back that this young man had died of a heroin overdose. Within minutes the pain had released in my body. I did not know this at the time, but I found out he was in the same ER I was in when he died. Somehow, my body felt him die and released the pain after his passing. I was devastated, but at the same time, when I saw him in the casket, a sense of peace came over me.

Fast forward four months, and now I was in football season. It was just another day of practice when the football coach walked in. He had a look on his face, and I instantly knew something was wrong. He asked me about a particular student, so I told him he was under observation for a possible staph infection. The coach nervously told me that he was found dead at home. Within minutes I was questioned by the school administration as to what my protocol was for this child. I had done all the right care, and I had referred him to a physician for testing. Later that night, I turned on the news, and all over was coverage about his death. The school falsely reported that he died of a deadly staph infection. Days later, we received both testing and autopsy reports that confirmed he never had a staph infection. I was portrayed publicly as if I had done something wrong. I was humiliated and felt as if I was wearing a scarlet letter. The media never fixed the misinformation, so I was left with people thinking I did something to contribute to his death.

As time went on, I began to develop horrible pain in my shoulders and back, the inability to sleep, severe panic attacks, and anxiety lasting most of the day. I suffered this way for over two years without getting any sort of help. At this time in my life, I was extremely upset with God. I could not understand how something like this could happen to a person like me, who was only trying to do good in the world. I pleaded with God to lead me to where I could get help, and that's when the strangest thing happened to me. I was asked by a friend to participate in a meditation with a Peruvian shaman. I had no clue what a shaman was until I started doing research. I was scared out of my mind, so instead of going, I chickened out last minute. The shaman returned four months later, and I reluctantly went. Little did I know, that night was going to change my life forever.

I had the intention of healing the unnecessary guilt that I was holding on to, but instead, I was led to the root of my suffering. I went into a deep subconscious meditation, and it showed me that I was a wonderful person to all of those around me, but an absolute monster to myself through my inner thoughts and feelings. That energy put me into a negative state, thus causing me to attract negative circumstances. I was shown a profound tool that night—to face myself every day in the mirror and state out loud one positive attribute about myself or something I was grateful for. I cried many times because I felt like I was lying to myself. Even though it felt fake, I continued to do this gratitude practice every day, and after three months of doing it consecutively, some things began to shift in my life. People started asking what was different about me and began telling me how happy I looked. I still didn't feel great about myself, but the only thing that was different was my daily gratitude practice, which I still do every day. Through this practice, I met the love of my life, created a fabulous new career helping others change their lives, and became a spiritual speaker/teacher. Having gratitude for myself completely changed my life, and I will never stop doing it.

Bio

Lindsey Sadowski is a certified Neuro Emotional Technique practitioner, certified and licensed athletic trainer, and spiritual public speaker and teacher. She helps people release deep emotional trauma from their subconscious brain using Neuro Emotional Technique and helps them to retrain their brain to create new pathways of thinking so they can live a more optimal life. You can reach Lindsey through her website at www.toadalpositivity.com or call her office at 440-867-6416.

Love In The Time Of Corona
By Lindy Chaffin Start

Today is my forty-eighth birthday, and as I write this, I must tell you that finding a reason to love—to feel grateful—isn't easy. The times we find ourselves in feel more like a Michael Crichton book playing out chapter by chapter. Each day the plot thickens. The story changes. The hero runs up against setbacks, and the villain gains ground in making life miserable.

I can't speak to how we came to find ourselves here. Nor can I say that our response is right or wrong. We each are individuals with beliefs, understandings, and opinions.

What I do know is, if we are going to get through this, we must find love.

No, I don't mean romantic love or the hysteria-induced sex that's going to lead to our next largest generation, the "Coronials" (millennials subjected to forced quarantine due to coronavirus). I mean the love that emanates from God and the Universe, the true foundation of all we hold true. The love we connect to daily that fuels our passion to do good works, feeds our curiosity, and fills our souls.

In a time when everyone seems to be contrary to whom we have known them to be, when life is upheaved, when friends and neighbors seem to hoard instead of share—how are we to be grateful?

The truth is, nothing has changed. Our perceptions have been challenged. So, as with every new day, I will choose to begin with gratitude.

"God, Universe, guides, angels, and ancestors: thank you, thank you, thank you for this new day." It is with this phrase, prayer, intention that I start every new day. A clean slate filled with gratitude for the breath in my lungs, a comfortable bed to sleep in, food on the table, or in the freezer as times may dictate, and a beautiful daughter who gives me purpose outside of myself.

I wasn't always this way. The last 15 years have been the years that challenged me. They dared me to discover my true self. As painful and difficult as they have been, they have shown me what true gratitude is and how it can affect change in one's life.

With the birth of my daughter in 2007, my outlook and intention for living changed. I became a mom, nurturer, coach, caregiver, tutor, chauffeur, nurse (among many other things) and not only for my daughter. In those years, my parents also became ill, experiencing long hospital stays followed by physical therapy, home care, and hospice. I cared for, made difficult decisions for, and buried both of them.

Though I didn't have a real understanding of gratitude when my new journey began, over the years, I have grown to know it intimately. I have found gratitude to be my connection to God, the Universe, my guides, angels, and ancestors. It connects me to the unseen. It fills the nooks and crannies of my heart and soul like mortar in joints shoring up my spiritual foundation.

Gratitude is a multi-faceted tool, one you can harness to affect change in your life. Each day is a fresh, new beginning. Each day we wake up, but do we see the opportunity, or do we stifle it with worry, frustration, and carryover from the day before? It truly all depends on the things happening in our lives and on our perceptions. I have found that if I begin my day by acknowledging my gratitude to the source who created me and all my spiritual touchstones, my day goes smoothly.

Each day includes time outdoors, walking in gratitude. A long walk isn't necessary, but the location is critical. Listening to the birds chirping, feeling the cool breeze, or the warmth of the sun on my face reminds me how blessed I am to be free to move and be able to take in the magic that surrounds me. So, I begin with gratitude for these simple pleasures.

"Thank you for the birds that remind me of love, strength, and camaraderie. Thank you for the squirrels that remind me of the joy in being playful. Thank you for the path I walk on, the green trees and plants and grass. Thank you for the laughter of children, and the good-morning greetings from my neighbors. Thank you for the sun on my face, the gloves on my hands, the coffee fueling my movement."

To each person I pass on my journey, I extend my love and gratitude by wishing them a good day or asking God and the Universe to provide what they need most in that moment. I create mass positivity. Experiencing gratitude in this way, I can elevate my frequency in the Universe to connect me, and keep me connected, throughout my day.

But there are those days when finding that connection feels hopeless, when it feels as if the whole world is resting on my shoulders. It is on those days when gratitude is most important. When I'm angry, irritated, frustrated, sad, or grief-stricken, I look deep into myself to flesh out the source of my pain. I craft a list of those troublesome things, then find ways to be grateful for each one.

"Why am I hurting today?" the questioning begins. With each answer, another "Why?" until I truly understand the source of my pain. Once identified, I turn that pain on its head. I find ten things about the pain I am grateful for: the lesson it teaches, the person or thing who created it in me (P.S. the answer is always me), feeling the emotion that accompanies it, and how it caused me to work on myself.

The process isn't easy. The result is always the same—relief.

When I know and embrace gratitude, especially in unprecedented times like these, I am being true to myself, honoring God, the Universe, my guides, angels, and ancestors. I am the change I desire to see in the world.

Today I encourage you to do the same.

Bio

Entrepreneur coach and marketing maven, Lindy Chaffin Start, provides entrepreneurs with insight, strategy, and advice to help them identify their highest purpose and passion and achieve their business goals. She creates marketing strategy and creative as unique and authentic as their company that builds trust with their audience. You can reach Lindy via email lindychaffin@att.net or visit her website www.unstoppablestart.com

The Gratitude Paradox
By Lori Nielsen

Gratitude feels fantastic! Except when you are struggling to find it. In the grand scheme of things, you might have a great life. So why are you waking up feeling empty, lonely, or crummy in general? You already know how to do affirmations and meditations, but you are not snapping out of it, and you feel lost or isolated. People in their yoga pants and meditation rooms seem so far ahead of the game, which feeds your feelings of inadequacy. Why does something so beautiful and necessary for happiness feel so unattainable at times?

There is purpose in this process. The pain we experience in our lives is one of our greatest teachers. It shows up when we are ready for the next steps, although we rarely feel ready. We often feel blindsided and ask, "Why me?" The answer is, "Because it's time." It's time to grow. It is the reason we are here in the first place.

Our negative experiences are what create the contrast necessary for us to notice when things are good. Without the experience of negative emotion, we would cruise through our lives without recognizing the positive aspects, because they've become standard. Life would feel like a common, ho-hum experience, which would subsequently lead to a lack of gratitude altogether.

When our lives feel like they are in a phase of happiness, ease, and flow, we rarely do the internal work that allows us to grow. We tend to relax and enjoy, or even take for granted, the ease of our lives at that time. "If it ain't broke, don't fix it" seems to be a natural mental state for us when life is happily clicking along. Change is uncomfortable, so why introduce it when all is well? When life continues in this manner, the lack of conflict begins to go unnoticed. There is a new baseline of easy, day-to-day activity that has become typical and uncelebrated.

Then it happens. Something occurs in your life that rips the rug out from under you, and the downward spiral of worry, insomnia, and pain ensues. You feel like a helpless victim. It not only seems impossible to feel grateful at this low point, but it's also difficult to recognize that gratitude is even an option. Don't be fooled. This is a test, a crossroads, a new opportunity. This is your chance to grow. Free will allows you to choose your actions and your perspective. The beauty is that this is *your* experience, and you have the power to put whatever spin on it you choose, so choose wisely. I believe it is safe to say that nobody wants to feel miserable. Yet time and time again, I witness people choosing the misery path regularly through their negative thought processes. What you choose to focus on is what you receive in return. It becomes your reality. If you choose to focus on and complain about your circumstances, you will continue to experience those same circumstances. It is universal law. You are feeding the beast and giving it momentum. Challenges will arise, and it will always be your choice to either accept the challenge to find the gratitude and growth, or to crumble under pressure.

You must be patient and compassionate with yourself. It is critical to allow yourself to feel the pain you are in because it is here to teach you something. However, you have the choice to wallow in it, allowing it to ruin your daily life, or to find the things around you that are going well. Even better, find the positive aspects of experiencing the negative circumstances in which you have found yourself. What? I know that sounds unrealistic, but stick with me.

As much as we agonize through these negative experiences, they are a necessary evil for which we also need to be grateful. They push us out of our comfort zones, and while we kick and scream through all of it, we come out the other end of the experience changed.

I went through an extremely shocking and painful divorce. Miserable. It was also the best thing that ever happened to me. I had no idea I was a pleaser back in the day. I didn't recognize most of my partner's toxic behavior. I attempted to please *more* to fix it! I didn't know I was hiding inside myself, staying small, trying to keep the peace. This crushing experience painfully cracked my soul wide open to the point where I thought I would never heal. Almost six years later, here I am writing about gratitude, coaching others, and helping *them* heal. What a hideous yet beautiful experience! I hated every minute of it. I love the outcome. It uncomfortably squeezed, molded, and shaped me into who I am today, and doggone it, I like myself!

Negativity, pain, and suffering are the best damn teachers I've ever encountered. They mercilessly blast you in the face with what you need to heal to go forward in life. Therefore, as counterintuitive as it sounds, befriend your negative circumstances. Befriend your pain. Ask it, "What are you here to teach me?" Know that it is not the enemy. It has shown up to grow you. Know that you are on the cusp of leveling up once again. Say thank you, dig in, and be ready for the greatness that is you. Allow it. Embrace it. Learn what you need to heal, then heal it! Then watch your current life shift into the life you desire, the life you wouldn't have appreciated if darkness had never introduced itself.

Thank you for the contrast. Thank you for the expanded perspective. Thank you for the push. I'm certain I would have never jumped into that dark pool of total uncertainty because I was also blind to its existence. I've learned and grown so much, and for that, I am eternally grateful.

Bio

Lori Nielsen is an empowerment adviser and energetic healer. She assists individuals with reclaiming their personal power through an internal process of healing soul wounds. Her mission is to teach individuals how to live their lives from the inside out with unconditional self-love, releasing all self-imposed limitations. Her experience is that once one identifies and reclaims their soul power, their light, they acquire the ability to stand unwaveringly in their power during challenging circumstances. One must own their light before they can securely hold their light, and then all things are possible. You can reach Lori at OwnYourLight.org.

Gratitude
By Maggie Morris

Oh, gratitude, gratitude, gratitude,
Where are you?
Are you with the in me morning?
Yes, I'm here.
Are you with me in the darkness?
Yes, I'm here.
Are you with me when I'm happy?
Yes, I'm here.
Are you with me in the sadness?
Yes, I'm here.

I find you in my soul
Deep within
Always there
The music of my soul
You feed me.

By definition, gratitude is the "quality of being thankful," but creating a lifestyle of gratitude truly creates it by definition.

I have found that learning to live a life of gratitude typically takes effort on my part. I needed to retrain the learned mindset created by my environment, circumstances, and life choices because it was not always built of gratitude. Our world does not teach or inspire gratitude naturally; we must cultivate it by our intention.

Every day when I wake up, I have a choice when it comes to living a life of gratitude. I can choose gratitude or not, it is genuinely that simple.

Does the environment in which I live make that choice, or do I choose gratitude regardless of my circumstance? Do I allow my circumstance to make that choice, or do I choose gratitude in all circumstances?

It is my belief that the choice is always mine to make and mine alone.

It is my belief that the amount of my gratitude directly impacts every aspect and circumstance in my life. In any and every life circumstance, we can choose gratitude or negativity. Both options are always available.

Last year I put that to the test. I was experiencing a negative mindset without much gratitude for life itself. One day I read, "The greater your state of gratitude, the faster you attract things to be grateful for." I thought, could this actually work? I decided to give it a try with a simple 30-day gratitude journaling challenge. At the beginning of the challenge, my entries were simple sentences or point form things I was thankful for. By the end of the challenge, I noticed that my entries were in greater detail—sometimes pages long. That got me thinking! Maybe changing my mindset does change whether I feel negative or positive. This challenge seemed to do that. I found my negative attitude had begun to shift to one of looking for gratitude.

I then decided to incorporate gratitude mantras. I would do these mantra exercises morning and night. In the morning, I would, with gratitude, thank my creator for waking me up. I would speak thankfulness for health, my children, my dog, the sun, my senses, the home I woke up in, and the list goes on. In the evening, I would express gratitude that I did my best in this day and that is all that is expected of me. I would release myself from the guilt of mistakes or unfinished tasks and again end my day as I started—with gratitude for my day, my breath, my life. Life is a treasured gift!

As a death doula, I regularly visit with the dying, and have consistently found that there is no greater teacher about gratitude in life than the dying. Those facing death have figured out the things in life that matter most and those that don't. High on that list are love and gratitude.

During my gratitude shift, I found that my natural way of thinking had begun to change. It was easier and easier for me to express gratitude and genuinely feel my life change. I no longer needed to look for things to be thankful for; it had become natural for me. I noticed less and less negativity filling my thoughts. I found joy in the simplicity of life itself. Gratitude had taught me an important life lesson about what truly matters. It's not about how much money I have (although money is great), it's not about my career, my social status, or things I acquire, it's about appreciation. Appreciation for life itself! For me, listening to birds sing fills my heart with gratitude. Walking in nature fills my heart with gratitude. Nature itself has the ability to give us eyes to see the raw beauty in our existence and teach us gratitude.

Does that mean I am in a constant state of gratitude when trauma hits my life? Is life all butterflies and buttercups? Absolutely not! I am human, after all. That being said, though, I truly believe that in all of life's traumas (even in death), we can find gratitude when we have eyes to see it. My granny used to say, "A spoonful of honey makes the medicine go down." I believe a life of gratitude makes life's medicine go down better.

Gratitude is available for everyone, but it is not free. It costs you your negativity. Just as light and darkness cannot reside together in the same place at the same time, neither can gratitude and negativity.

I challenge each of you reading this chapter to put gratitude to the test. Allow gratitude to change your mindset. Allow living in gratitude to change your life. Gratitude is contagious—the more you have, the more you see. Try it for a day, a week, a month, a year, or a lifetime. You will see that your life will never be the same.

Life is a precious gift; one we rarely appreciate fully. Let today be the shift for you. Choose a life lived fully in gratitude for everything, every moment, and everyone. Gratitude for the beauty of life itself. Simple gratitude. Shift the perspective in our world with gratitude. The world doesn't owe us anything; we owe it our gratitude for everything. Be the change! Start with gratitude!

And remember, the more you are in a state of gratitude, the more you attract things to be grateful for. Or, like the Rumi quote, "Wear gratitude like a cloak, and it will feed every corner of your life."

Namaste.

Bio

Maggie is an authentic, caring, sensitive soul with a passion for nurturing others with her soul love. Maggie lives her gifts of service to humanity through her generosity and her ability to ignite the flame in others to see their limitless possibilities. Maggie uses her intuition and connection with spirit to be an example of strength and courage to all she meets. As a life coach, mindfulness mentor, meditation facilitator, and death doula, Maggie continues to pursue her passions as well as help those she connects with to find healing. You can reach Maggie through her website at www.whispersofwisdom.ca.

On Guilt, Grief and Gratitude
By Marci Zeisel Rosenberg

Early afternoon sunlight filters through the gently swaying branches of two 40-foot tall evergreen trees in my backyard. Hidden within these branches, birds tweet their staccato songs. An owl's methodic hoot can be heard from a distant tree. In clay pots along a wooden fence separating my property from the neighbor's, seeds of summer squash, watermelon, carrots and cucumbers are doing their magic under the rich, warm soil. An occasional breeze carries the hypnotic aroma of orange and lemon blossoms. It's springtime in Arizona. It's also day 31 of my at-home isolation during this reality-altering coronavirus pandemic.

My backyard is my sanctuary—a safe place to lose myself when reading a book on the comfort of a well-loved wooden bench swing. Or, to enjoy a nap under the evergreens on a blanket spread over the soft grass. Planting a vegetable garden was joyful work, and tending to it every day gives me purpose and the hope that someday, in the not-too-distant future, food from this garden will be shared in celebration with friends.

Unlike the privacy offered by my backyard, the yard in the front provides opportunities for social-distance contact. Nearly every evening at sunset, I mix a Margarita and sit on the shaded front porch, waving at neighbors as they walk or bike along this quiet, residential street. More people are out now than ever before. Occasionally, someone will stop to chat, sometimes about the beautiful spring weather, but more often, the topic is pandemic-related—what grocery store has eggs, who they know that has the virus, when this will be over, and how life will be different when it is.

Having more leisure time has a downside for me—guilt. I've questioned whether it's selfish to find joy and relief in this slowed-down pace, in my comfortable home, with a nature sanctuary for escape, and food in my refrigerator while millions of people in my own city, state, country and around the world are sick and dying, or working with the sick and dying, or grieving the sick and dying. And I wonder how do I reconcile the feelings of guilt that I am secure and healthy, as are those I love when so many people are suffering in pain, fear, despair, homelessness, abuse, sickness and fatigue from being a victim or on the front lines in this war on the world?

Survivor's guilt is a recognized response to trauma, even though it's not always rational. And what is this global pandemic if not a traumatic event? Some suggestions I found online for coping with this type of trauma have been helpful to me. Accept and allow the feelings that surface. Okay. I'm recognizing how I feel—not resisting it. Take time to process the guilt, grief, fear, and loss that accompany a traumatic event. Yeah, I'm working on this; it's not an easy process. Being patient with myself helps. After all, this is brand new territory, for all of us. Do activities that feel good. Some things that are working for me include: taking a long walk or bike ride around my neighborhood every day, watering my garden and sitting outside, and taking a hot soak with bath salts at the end of the day. I'm feeling the guilt dissipate. Yet, the grief, fear and loss I'm feeling because of the pandemic are sticky. Not easily remedied by a hot bath, a nap under the evergreens, or a good Margarita.

I grieve for all the people who are suffering. I fear the unknowns in post-pandemic life. And I feel a loss of optimism. To counter the weight of these emotions, I realize that I must count my blessings every day and give attention to what I have now:

- Good health
- A roof over my head and food in my fridge
- Meaningful work
- Caring neighbors, family and friends
- FaceTime
- Facebook
- Zoom
- Netflix
- My bicycle
- A mask and gloves for when I need to use them

As the western sky is painted with orange and purple brushstrokes of the setting sun on this 31st day of my at-home isolation, I look forward to post-pandemic life:

- Holding my grandson
- Hugging my son, daughter and son-in-law
- Playing with my friends
- Going to a club to hear live music
- Attending the theater
- Dining out

And as I look out my backyard, I imagine the day when friends and family will gather around picnic tables to laugh and celebrate the simple joy of being together. It will happen. And it will be good…even better than before.

Bio

Marci Zeisel Rosenberg lives in a friendly, historic neighborhood near downtown Phoenix. She continues to enjoy a long career in urban planning, public policy and community engagement. As soon as it's safe, Marci will fly to Alaska to see her daughter, son-in-law and baby grandson. This is Marci's third contribution to a book published by As You Wish Publishing, and not her last. Connect with her on Facebook and at MarciZRosenberg@gmail.com.

Gratitude As An Act Of Self Love
By Maria McGonigal

"The Soul Loves the Truth" is the Soul Coaching® motto, and as a Soul Coaching® Trainer, I was asked to look with complete honesty at what gratitude meant to me. *The Grateful Soul* conjured in me lofty thoughts of nobility and grace. My heart expanded with a desire to express these elegant qualities, but other landscapes were calling the wild horses of my imagination.

Growing up, I was accused of displaying a sense of entitlement and never healed from feeling there was something wrong with me. I was seen as not being grateful for what life provided me. I believed I was an ungrateful person and acted like one.

It wasn't until the 90s, in my early 30s, that I revisited this wounded story through the "Gratitude Experiment," which was an email chain inviting everyone to practice gratitude. It spread like a virus around the world. The Gratitude Experiment revolutionized my life.

I learned to be grateful for everything: the food I ate, the walks I took, the husband I chose, my parents, grandparents, ancient ancestors I'll never know, the stars, dark nights, sorrows, and beauty, the tailor and the mailman, the teacher and the scientist, the musician and the artist, the wanderer, and the dreamer. I was so grateful to realize that so many humans contribute and provide the means for me to have such a comfortable and extraordinary life. I was profoundly affected by this novel idea. It was like feeling a tangible connection with every human being.

It was a realization that no matter how distant, we could trace the connection from ourselves to the monk sitting in meditation in the Himalayas. We then walk through life, embracing everyone and everything with a magnified appreciation of life itself. Experiencing gratitude allowed me to perceive life from an expanded space where everyone and everything was included, except me.

I learned that I didn't know how to be thanked by others or receive praise. When someone expressed gratitude to me, I would come up with a story where I was no longer the protagonist. I was unable to receive. Believing that I was an ungrateful person wounded me. If I was ungrateful, then how could I receive gratitude?

I feel privileged to have found Soul Coaching®, which enabled me to face and masterfully integrate my woundedness and my shadow. I could re-write my stories and give them a different meaning. It empowered me to know that my life isn't frozen in some distant past. I have complete freedom to create a brand new and beautiful life, based on new beliefs. This is only one of many remarkable tools that Soul Coaching® offers. I began healing aspects of myself that brought me shame and guilt and disempowered me.

I also stumbled upon the philosophy that we embody multiple archetypes: the Child, the Mother, the Victim, the Narcissist, the Teacher, the Perfectionist, the Warrior, the Judge, the Whore, and so on. Each archetype revealed an aspect of myself that, although potentially out of balance, had a specific purpose and role. Each archetype stepped forward, informing and guiding when needed most. When seen with intuitive eyes, archetypes can reveal dimensions of reality previously hidden, and enlighten us on how to face a challenge from an empowered perspective. Archetypes are equally important. Through the archetypal dimension, I can exist beyond the paradigm of good and evil and embrace all aspects of myself. I can honor each one of these archetypes as drops of rain falling into the ocean of my very existence.

My teachings integrated this expanded awareness with a desire to liberate others from the chains of judgment, shame, guilt, and disempowerment. I would share with my students, "The soul is not looking for a fairy tale ending, the soul wants to have as many experiences as possible. We are here to feel and integrate the full spectrum of emotions and patterns." You don't look at a rainbow and say, "Hey, let's erase the color blue. I don't like it." Just like a resplendent rainbow, we encompass all the colors. We are learning how to exercise compassion, love, and accept the full expression of our humanity.

This realization couldn't be more poignant than now as we face the coronavirus pandemic. We are being forced to accept that we are all connected—that we are indeed one. What hurts us hurts the world. When we choose to see and forgive ourselves, likewise, we will see others through the lens of forgiveness. A deep and profound sense of gratitude for everyone and everything arises. From this place of acceptance and love, we make choices that take into account the wholeness of humanity instead of our selfish needs. An understanding that each of us holds unique and precious nuggets of wisdom essential for the whole to thrive. Our priority, if we want to survive as a species, requires acknowledging one another's treasures.

This journey's reward is gratefulness toward myself, including the treasures I carry within my heart. Gratitude then becomes an act of self-love, an urge from the evolutionary nature of life itself, calling us to be the highest version of ourselves we can be, for the sake of humanity and planet Earth.

Bio

Maria McGonigal is a Soul Coaching® Master Practitioner, and Trainer praised for her keen intuition and profound wisdom. Maria's teaching style is direct, dissecting, not suitable for the faint of heart, yet full of heart. Maria assists you in finding missing pieces, energetic or physical, to connect you with your soul. Be ready for profound, lasting transformation, which demands a willingness to acknowledge what is lurking in the shadow and holding you back. Maria's deepest desire is to create a safe, sacred space for you to discover the most glorious and magnificent version of yourself. You can reach Maria at www.mariamcgonigal.com.

A Grandmother's Love: Grandma Jackie
By Megan Oldenstadt

"I don't want to live anymore. I've done everything I've wanted to do in my life. I've had a good life," she said. "Why can't I just die?" We'd had this conversation countless times before, but it was apparent from the desperation in her voice that she spent the lucid parts of her days dwelling on it. "We love you, Grandma. We want you here," I'd say, "but it's okay if you need to go." "This is no way to live," she'd say as she drifted away.

Officially diagnosed with Lewy body dementia and legally deemed incapacitated by the courts, her son was now in charge of her medical decisions. She was constantly paralyzed by hallucinations of snipers in the trees, or being stolen from and physically beaten by the assisted-living caregivers. She would show us her imagined bruises and insist we get her out of there. We watched her slowly slip away, crippled by anxiety, worry, and constantly crossing the line between a nightmare-like hallucination and the one where we, her family, still existed. Moving her away from my grandfather, where they shared a spacious and well-heated apartment in a luxury assisted-living facility, into a memory care home was one of the hardest decisions. She needed 24-hour, one-on-one care and, although scarcely weighing 90 pounds, she was becoming increasingly more volatile as her cognitive reasoning deteriorated. Less than five months later, she unexpectedly passed away early one morning, alone except for the other residents and the on-site caregiver.

217

Grandma was an amazing woman, albeit complicated, conflicted, and quite private. She was warm, loving, and creative—known for her fiber arts, photography, sewing, and constant artistic pursuits. She was family-oriented, hosting regular meals and holiday gatherings, but for reasons I'll never fully know, she was estranged from a majority of her siblings. Caring for both her mother and mother-in-law in their final years of life, she more often than not sacrificed for those she loved. Married to my grandfather for 63 ½ years, she put up with a lot, considering his authoritarian disposition, strong will, and endless teasing, but they chose to ride the ups and downs together. They raised three rebellious, extremely creative sons and had the joy of knowing six grandchildren (of whom I was the only granddaughter), as well as two great-grandchildren.

I had the profound joy of living near my grandmother until I left home in my early 20s. Our relationship was one I don't think many people get to experience, especially with a grandparent. My parents both worked full-time, so she was often my primary caregiver. I spent time before and after school walking to and from her house throughout my elementary years. After my parents moved us to the family farm in a different state when I was eleven, my grandparents built a house next door to our new house, following us in the move a year later to enjoy their retirement years in the countryside. All through middle school, high school, and some college, I saw her daily after school or on weekends. We enjoyed each other's company and would spend time visiting or going to art and craft shows, museums, shopping, baking, or cooking together. We were close, not only as kin, but as friends.

We witnessed each other's experiences for the 37 years our lives overlapped, timeless in the language of our hearts although two quarter-centuries apart in age. Not to idealize the woman, she was flawed as every one of us is. She was private and scarcely talked about her first marriage, which resulted in a son (and is speculated to have been abusive and forced due to the morals of the time), or her strict religious upbringing, only sharing a few stories about her childhood.

None of that mattered, though. Grandma was warm, soft, and kind. She saw me in this life as no one else has. The love was endless. When I was young and stayed over at her house (which I often did), she would pamper me with bubble baths and go as far as to heat the bed and warm the towels. She would wash my long dark hair in the utility room sink, layering a bed of towels on top of the washer/dryer so I could comfortably lie on them. She brushed my long hair until it shone, and once she revived a trend from her childhood by tying my straight hair up in rags—resulting in a head full of corkscrew-tight ringlets (like the 1930s actress Shirley Temple). I would shadow her in the kitchen, in the garden, doing yard work, or cleaning the house. Never will scrubbing the sink or washing windows be as fun as it was with her.

Where we truly connected was in her art studio. No matter where she lived, she always had an art space. Although we also had a designated art room in my home, it was never as magical as doing art alongside Grandma Jackie. I don't know a lot of other grandmothers with a table saw, band saw, workbench, and tool cabinet. Art was our love language; from the days she buckled me into the highchair to finger paint, playing under her loom as she wove, or teaching me to dye the yarn that she had spun, we didn't need words to know how truly special our moments together were.

Grandma carved a life-long gift into my heart by allowing me to boundlessly express my creative side. I learned to enjoy the process of creating more than the final product. I like to believe by providing and encouraging art in my life, she reconnected and healed parts of her wounded inner child. Although she seemed to lose some of her connection to her creative expression as she aged, Grandma Jackie will always and forever be my torchlight of creativity, unwavering love, and a beacon of endless gratitude for the gift in knowing a soul such as hers.

Bio

Megan Oldenstadt is a writer, visual artist, public speaker, freelance bookkeeper, and consultant. Her life was interrupted in 2011 with the diagnosis of an invisible illness, which forced learning a new way of living. With the hope that what she has learned over the past decade navigating chronic illness will help others, she shares her exploration, discovery, and journey back to health on the online platform www.wrestlingdaisies.com. She lives in western Montana at the base of a beautiful mountain range, entertained daily by her two lively golden retrievers and two curious orange cats. You can reach Megan at www.meganoldenstadt.com.

A Grandmother's Love: Grandma Kay
By Megan Oldenstadt

T enacious: the adjective I would choose to describe my grandmother over any other descriptor. I don't imagine it's a word often used for what otherwise would be known as a loving, creative, elegant, and gentle woman, yet it's fitting nonetheless.

Born in the early 1920s and the oldest of five children (the births spanning 17 years), my grandmother Mary Kathleen, called Kay, didn't have a choice in becoming tenacious. With the economic necessity of the time, she learned how to be practical, frugal, and resourceful. The importance of education was deeply instilled in her household from an early age, and she pursued it with a fierceness that few women of her generation expressed. She learned how to cook, sew and repair essentials such as clothing, and care for her younger siblings. Kay graduated high school and went on to college, where she obtained Bachelor of Science and Master's degrees in home economics, and in the 1970s, completed a doctorate in sociology. It wasn't until well into my adult years that I learned she wanted to be an architect, but that wasn't an accessible profession for women at the time.

Tenacity was at the root of the story of how she met my grandfather and then courageously boarded a train shortly after their marriage, leaving her east coast life behind to move across the country to a small college town where they began their life together. After creating a home, a family, and boldly pursuing a career teaching college, she is now a lifetime member of her sorority, a charter member in women's organizations, was a 4-H Club leader, and has participated in the same book club for the past 60 years.

One of Kay's milestone accomplishments in the 1960s was to design and oversee the building and interior decoration of her family's home in the modern style of the time. She challenged the rules of motherhood as well by taking a teaching position away from home and leaving her youngest daughter in the care of her husband. My grandmother relied on her tenacity at the unexpected loss of my grandfather just as their retirement years were within reach. She unwaveringly showed up when my younger brother was born prematurely, making sure my two-year-old self was well taken care of, moving in and staying with my family for several months.

Many of my childhood memories of Grandma revolve around Christmas when we would spend the day together in our pajamas opening gifts, followed by the traditional family Christmas breakfast menu she started in the 1940s and continues to this day.

After marrying my step-grandfather, Grandma Kay moved back to my town when I was in the third grade, bringing her tenacity as my piano teacher, competitive afterschool go-fish or slapjack card player, and as volunteer docent of an art history education program that she introduced into my school.

A lady of refinement, my grandmother was always impeccably put together, making and wearing the gowns, dresses, and professional suits of her creation, hosting dinner parties, and attending events such as the theater, symphony, orchestra, and social dancing clubs. After retiring from the university educator's life, she found her creative outlet and passion through quilting. What started as a hobby disassembling thrift store clothing soon became an intense exploration of the craft. This led to becoming an expert teacher and lecturer, developing a fierce passion for collecting and restoring antique quilts, and amassing hundreds of breathtaking hand-quilted masterpieces of her own creation.

My step-grandfather endlessly supported her pursuit of all things thread and fabric, often reading out loud to her during her many hours hunched over a quilting frame meticulously and perfectly stitching. Once when on a deadline, she even utilized his medical doctor-trained surgical suturing skills by talking him into assisting with the quilting. I'm suspect that his skills were not up to par with her high standards, as I don't recall him helping more than that one time. Quilting became her life, color her language, and fabric her obsession. Grandma shared the love and adventure with her daughters and instilled in me, her only granddaughter, a passion for the craft.

While I was in middle school and this new hobby of hers was gaining speed, she came to visit my family, who had recently moved to a new state. Wanting to light the spark in me, Grandma Kay set out to enable me to become a master quilter, gifting me a lovely antique Singer® featherweight sewing machine. We then ventured to a local boutique fabric store to purchase the supplies I'd need to get started. She helped me wash and iron the fabric, pick out a pattern, cut out, and sew my first sampler project. We have had over 30 years of sewing together, and although my attention to detail and mastery for the craft have never quite met her professor standards, what it has offered to me is even more valuable. The tangible lesson of fully stepping into a passion, by witnessing someone I love take the time and have the patience to hone a craft and master a skill. My tenacious grandmother was confident in her abilities, skilled in her acquired techniques, and proud of her creations. She owned her strengths, never letting someone else tell her she couldn't do something or stand in her way (well, other than that whole architect thing).

Grandma hasn't been able to quilt as much in this last decade of life. But her passion for the craft has not waivered. She has outlived two amazing husbands, cumulatively married for over 55 years, and is the mother of three immensely creative, capable, and independent women. She's been a loyal friend, a step-mother, and a doting grandmother. I'm deeply grateful for the gift of spending a good part of my adult life living with and enjoying the company of my tenacious Grandma Kay. What I have learned from her will forever color the way I live my life, stitching our journey together always.

Acknowledgment: What an immense gift in this lifetime— two unconditionally loving, supportive, and creative grandmothers. Thank you to my friends and family for the support, guidance, and encouragement. To all of the mentors, teachers, healers, makers, artists, and way-showers I've met along the way, I take each of your gifts with me always. To my furry family members, both present and past, who selflessly share their exuberance for life and endless love. A special thank you to the most constant woman in my life, Mother Nature, who, by example, shows that peace is always available, and in quietly observing, joy can be found.

A Grateful Soul through Loss
By Michelle Ryan

A dear friend of mine has passed. We were women on similar paths. When she became ill this summer, I immediately felt the devastating impact this would have on her family, and realized the depth of the quiet treasure that she was. When I was called out of the country during my daughter's pregnancy, this friend created a women's circle for my daughter, so that she would know my friends were there to be called on while I was gone. My friend had supported me, and given me love and guidance, through times when my female friends filled a void. As an adult daughter without her mother, I identified with her children intensely and felt what a deep loss this would be for them. She had spoken to me of the hopes she had for her future that would not come. The most precious was of being a grandmother, and she expressed sadness as she accepted that if her children were graced with children, she would not be there, and would miss these moments. The aspect of grief that teaches us to be grateful and honor our relationships, before the inevitable loss, was significant in this moment of her illness for both of us.

Many layers of healing rained on me as I participated in the conscious dying process my friend had orchestrated and asked for. When she decided to end her treatment, she went home, and space was created in the living room for her care. The feeling of sanctuary was palpable. The community responded with meal deliveries and loving visits. The artwork she found nourishment and strength in hung from the mantel. The music she cherished played in the background. The prayer circle brought a hand-knitted afghan to keep her warm and beautiful. The fire in the fireplace framed the hearth and heart. Life slowed to her speed.

She had a depth like Mother Earth and such a thoughtful response time to life, and she had always reminded me of the turtle. She picked the turtle medicine card with her pastor.

She requested that, during the time of her spirit movement, three days of vigil be sat for the long goodbye for her loving husband and three children. This was a practice she had studied and utilized around her father's death several years before. Comfortable chairs surrounded the bedside for her final visits and laid the circle of energy for those of us who sat vigil following her passing. When that time came, we all spoke of how nurturing this experience was for each of us, giving us new images and experiences of death. Her grace in accepting her illness and mortality—in doing her work toward completion—laid a fertile path for us to follow and rest in as we felt our sadness and appreciation for all she was to us and said goodbye.

During the sleep, after she left her body, I had a powerful dream and woke up at the same time that she had stopped breathing 24 hours before. I felt anxious and concerned and began meditating and sending energy to the vigil holders, before falling back into a deep rest. When I woke a second time, I began to tend to the day, picking up the guest room for a friend who was coming to pay her respects. The guest room is also my grandchildren's room, and as I picked up one of their books from the floor, strong energy and weakness shook me. I remembered my mother had spoken to me in a dream hours before, and she had written the name of this book on a wisdom list.

I believe in the power of fairy and folk tales, and this one had been a favorite to read with my daughters, and most recently, with my second granddaughter. She requested it each day at nap time. She loved to chant the words of the characters with me and recreate parts of the story; it was clearly her favorite and spoke to her on many levels, as fairy tales do. They address our deepest fears and are multi-faceted in our consciousness. Today, I marveled at how the story spoke in my dream.

In the dream, my mother was the age she was when she died. I was my current age. We were having a conversation, woman to woman, about our learning and experiences. I felt the kinship of adult female relationships happening between us, and it was so special to feel. Then she handed me a note with three lessons she was learning. While I can't remember the first two, I remember the third.

"Like the fairy tale," it said.

Astonished, I said to my mother, "You know that's Avery's favorite book."

She shook her head with sadness. "No, I do not know, because I have not been here."

Truth and reality, spirituality and magic, all collided, bringing acceptance and healing for me. This dream connected to the power of motherly love, and of a mother seeing and knowing her child and protecting her—important themes in the fairy tale. Weaving together my friend's death, my mother's visit in my dream, and this spiritual literature,

I was nourished. My friend had the gift of seeing others. She felt and shared my experience as a daughter longing for her mother and filled a space for me. She knows, and I know, we are all connected in spirit, and sad in the loss of these bodies. She knew how to bring ease and support in accepting the loss, and the inspiration of connection, community, and one breath, together. Our helpers and friends are all around, loving us as we need.

Thank you, dear friend.

Bio

Michelle Ryan is a mother, a grandmother, and a retired school teacher with a master of arts degree from CU Boulder in Multi-Cultural and Social Diversity Education specializing in Special Education and English as a Second Language. She has traveled with several nonprofits to Central Asia, supporting people to people connections and self-esteem work. Michelle has thirty years' experience volunteering on the boards of three humanitarian organizations. She has facilitated women's retreats and loves being with women. She currently lives with her husband, a beekeeper, on a farm in Boulder County and spends her time listening to the Universe and creating.

Legacy Of Tears
By Nicole Newsom-James

The tears are streaming from my eyes while I am cooking. I'd just cut up some peppers and forgot when I went to wipe the tears and touched my eyes. They are stinging now, but that's not why I am crying. I am crying because I'm reminded of my uncle's death. You see, the tragedy is that my uncle committed suicide. When he did so, he not only killed himself, he destroyed a piece of our family, and left a gaping hole in our hearts. Like my mother and brother, I have never been able to recover completely from his death. I wipe the tears away because I want to tell you that he was a beautiful person, not that he was a good-looking man, even though he was. My uncle was an adventurous soul. I remember him riding motorcycles and trying to get me and my brother to ride them too. I remember, as a teenager, he put me on a huge Harley cruiser. I was to ride down the road, turn it around, and come back. I was able to ride in a straight line down the road, but as I tried to turn, there wasn't enough room, and I laid it down. He picked it up for me and asked if I was alright. That was the kind of man he was. My uncle was a mechanic, he collected artwork—mostly Windberg prints—and he was a craftsman and loved working with his hands. He crafted beautiful stained glass lamps and scenic pictures.

Somehow life overcame him. At work, he had a new boss who undermined him. His girlfriend was flighty, but he loved her deeply. They would often break up and then get back together again. He saw something in her that the rest of

229

the family could not because they fought a lot. He had lost his daughter in a heartbreaking custody battle and had not seen her since his ex-wife spirited her away. We later found out that right before his death, he was having financial troubles, and his pride kept him from asking for help. So one night, he took a shotgun and blew off his head. Days later, my mother found him. They were extremely close. It was devastating for us because that is the last memory we will ever have of him. I miss my uncle. Yet, because of how he chose to end his life, the family has never spoken about him again. It was too painful. We all felt responsible for his death. We should have known what he was going through, and we should have stopped it from happening. I not only lost my uncle that day, but I also lost all the memories too. It has been 35 years since my uncle's death, and it feels as if it was yesterday. My continuous tears make me realize how the heart remembers our loved ones. It somehow keeps them safe. So how can I be writing about this tragedy, when I am supposed to be writing about gratitude?

Well, let me tell you that I know what it feels like to lose a romantic love that you cannot imagine a life without. I know what it's like to lose a career you spent your whole life building, and, in a moment, with circumstances beyond your control, you've lost it. In those dark moments, I know what it is like to imagine ending my life. I am sad to say that thought has occurred to me more than once in my lifetime. When it happens, I always think of my uncle. I think about what a beautiful person he was and that if only he could have remembered that, he would not have taken his life. I think of my mother, who was devastated at the loss of a brother she treasured. I think about my grandmother, who lost her child in her lifetime. And then I know I would never put my family through that again. So I cry. I go to sleep. I wake up. Go to work. And, ultimately, I choose a new way of being. I imagine and create a new life that I do not want to leave. I change the way I react to things, and I let go of what does not work, including people who do not support who I am and what I desire. I choose to embrace what brings me passion and makes me smile. Then I think of how grateful I am for my uncle's life, and I will never forget the legacy of what he taught me through his untimely death.

Never give up on yourself; you are too precious. Instead, give up the things that don't serve you in your life, and from the darkness, you can become reborn, come into a new light, and bloom.

Bio

Nicole Newsom-James is an educator, designer, and heart-centered realtor. Her studies include healing the body by studying the spirit. She combines both eastern and western philosophy and techniques that remove energetic blocks from her clients' lives and environments. Nicole also works with real estate agents to positively change the energies of the properties they want to sell. Her passion is to guide her clients through the storms of life through education, by designing a supportive environment, and guiding them to locate their dream home. You may reach Nicole at 918-443-0592 or via her website www.newsomjames.com.

Always Go With Love
By Noella Vincent

Love and gratitude go hand-in-hand to me. How can you feel gratitude without feeling love? How can you feel love without being grateful? When I was about five years old, I would watch my mom and dad working in adjoining home offices. I knew their work was about helping people. I wanted to help people. I created an office space for myself, complete with a chalkboard. What was I going to do to help people? I wrote on the chalkboard, "Always go with love." As a child, I was always choosing love. Having this phrase reinforced that. That was my business, helping others go with love.

That phrase seemed to be always what I needed. Something I had for myself. It has stuck with me as the years passed through both good and bad. Through multiple moves, I would always write it on my bathroom mirror and other places around my room to remind me to go with love. When I was feeling down or less than love, I would see the phrase, and it would remind me that love is wherever I am. I am love. I don't always feel it, but even when I don't feel it, I am still love.

Is going with love always easy? It hasn't always been easy for me, and I still have times where I have to remind myself to take a breath, think about what is going on, and then ask myself, "How do I go forward in this with love?" It is when things are the darkest that we need to turn to love the most.

Life can be messy. Over the last several years, I have been dealing with a chronic medical condition. There were stretches that I would be in the ER multiple times in a week. It was easy to lie there feeling down and defeated. And then I would think, "Is this love?" I would look around at all the things I had to be grateful for: medical staff helping me, supportive family, my animals offering unconditional love, and good friends to make me laugh. At that point, even when the medical staff were doing painful procedures on me, I would find ways to make them laugh to make their job a little bit easier. That is what I consider going with love.

Love can bring tears. When you have a friend that you love so much and something great happens to them, it can bring happy tears. Or, when you love something so much, and you have to say goodbye, it can make you cry. Love doesn't always feel good, like when you watch someone close go through a hard time. Being there for them and crying with them is going with love.

Love is a feeling. It is happiness, joy, compassion, gratefulness, and more all mixed together. It is a feeling that comes over you and feels warm inside.

Love can make you do things. It can bring out your passion. That passion can give you the ability to do things you did not know you could do. It can be the driving force to accomplish the seemingly impossible.

Love can bring out your compassion. It can help you feel so deeply for another person that it hurts. Love can motivate you to serve others in life-altering ways. One of my big loves is animals. I have been volunteering at a veterinarian clinic since I was eleven. I was told I was too young and to come back when I was 16. I persisted till they let me observe and, in a short amount of time, was truly volunteering. It is my goal to become a vet, so I can help animals and alleviate some of their suffering. People tell me all the time how hard becoming a vet is. My love drives me where that does not stop me.

Love can be terrifying, and that is okay. Some people love rollercoasters even though they are terrified of them. They still ride them because they love the feeling riding them gives them—the rush, the thrill, the joy. Ask yourself is this hurtful or harmful to me? If it is, you might want to rethink if it is truly love.

So how do you go with love? The first step is to know you *are* love. To do that, you have to know that you are worthy of love. To go with love, ask yourself: does this person bring me love? This situation? This relationship? This work? If not, you may need to change those things in your life. You can still feel compassion, but you shouldn't stay in circumstances that you don't feel love in.

Try to always do, pick, and be what love is. Let your actions be actions of love. Actions include words. Try to use words from a place of love. Pick what love is. This could be when you are shopping, daily choices, relationships, or any choices you make. Being love is simply being the person you think defines love. Ask yourself, "Is this me being love?" When you find yourself not being love, don't beat yourself up. Use it as an opportunity to learn and grow to keep presenting yourself as your highest possible expression of love in that moment.

As you embrace going with love in all aspects of your life, the more you will experience the feeling of love, and then you will have something to be truly grateful for. Always go with love!

Bio

Noella Vincent is a 17-year-old high school senior at the time of this writing. She has already experienced more challenges than most people do in a lifetime. Through it all, she has stayed true to "Always going with love." It is her mission to bring more love into the world. Her ultimate goal is to become a critical care vet to share that love with animals. You can join her on her mission of spreading love at www.alwaysgowithlove.com.

Gratefulness As A Way of Being
By Patricia Walls

What does the word "grateful" mean to you? In my previous career, I taught courses in EmoTrance and Energy Emotional Freedom Technique (EFT) that were developed by Silvia Hartmann. One of the exercises was to give the students a list of ten words that they were to submit with their definitions of those words. I found it interesting that almost no one had the same definitions.

One of the words given was love. Would you ever think that there would be anyone who would consider love to be a negative word? There are, though. How about the word gratefulness?

In our existence, our experiences create our responses to all things. Consider that for a moment, please. What has been your experience with love? What has given you cause to be grateful in your life?

What could be negative about gratefulness? Did you know that gratefulness contributes to a healthy heart? And, that a healthy heart contributes to overall health? Have you ever truly taken stock of your surroundings, and what there might be to prompt the feeling of gratefulness? There were a lot of questions in that, weren't there? I like questions. Questions cause one to ponder. Pondering causes one to think outside the box. Pondering creates an expansion of imagination. I like it immensely.

My belief is that all of life is an experience. It is why we came into this physical existence at this or any time. I have witnessed that, as emotional beings, human beings are easily influenced. There are few that I have seen being single-minded and resistant to change. In that way, I believe that you can influence someone who is in a constant state of negativity by having them look for what is good in their life and focus on gratefulness for that.

We come into this physical incarnation with a pre-planned blueprint of sorts. Everything is pre-determined, down to the millisecond of our time here. Even the seemingly simple experience of a smile exchanged between two people in a crowded restaurant. Perhaps it was determined that one of those recipients had experienced something that was devastating or heart-wrenching. That smile is what gave them hope and a bit of light. It was a pre-determined agreement to provide support at a critical space in time. Much like when one is down in emotions and calls out to their creator, God, angels, or guides for help and hope, and then suddenly feels better. Pre-determined. Nothing is by chance. We are such amazingly magical creators that we pre-planned our helpers, rescuers, and even our challengers. How amazing are we? How does that make you feel to know how powerful and in charge, you are?

Most Americans were taught that prayer occurs at specific times, such as a meal, bedtime, time of crisis, or group worship service. Yes, I said prayer. Few of us were taught that gratefulness is a prayer. Would you think that our God/creator would rather have you constantly pray for more, or a prayer of gratefulness for your blessings? Which would you, as a human being respond to favorably, "You're doing a great job, God," or "Why haven't you answered my prayer for a million dollars?"

Let me share a story. I am of an earth-based way of knowing and honoring. When you honor life, you naturally feel grateful for it. Speaking for myself, everything is a prayer. Gratefulness is a form of prayer. I am in prayer 24/7/365.

To give an example, when I cook, I am in prayer. I am thinking of the beings who gave their lives for our nourishment and health. When I say beings, I am referring to everything from the ingredients of the meal, to the gas that creates the fire, to the metal in the pots that the food is prepared in, and even to the materials that bring the electricity and water into my home. What about those humans who invented all those pots, ways of bringing electricity and water into my home, and the appliances? And, the humans who took those schematics and made the specific water systems and electrical towers/connectors, pipes, stove, and pots that I use? And the ones who marketed it, boxed it, sold it, delivered it? Have you ever considered how many beings' energies are in the one pot that you cook in? Now expand that to everything that it takes to prepare one meal. Gratefulness for the humans, plants, animals, stones, metals, air, sun, moon, everything. A lot of us never consider how much goes into one thing and how many lives were sacrificed or energy given for that thing. I consider all of it.

And that was the gratefulness of the ability to prepare a healthy meal. I didn't mention the food/ingredients. The food that you ingest has also gone through numerous hands, transformations, and energies, and emotions are induced into it. My apologies, I have gotten off track again. That is another story: the emotions.

All that to say, when I am preparing food, I am thinking of all those things. I am in gratefulness for all those things that are available to me so that I might have nourishment and share that nourishment with my family and friends. Gratefulness is, to me, the highest form of prayer.

When we sit down to eat, I ask my husband to offer a blessing for the food. After a time, he asked why I never offer the blessing. Before he asked, I had never considered that my way of being in prayer might be different from his. His teaching was to bless the food when everyone sits down to eat. My way is to pray/bless the food as I purchase and prepare it. It was a good reminder, and I was grateful for that moment of knowing. So, you see, the meals that I serve are blessed by the grateful heart of the masculine and the feminine.

What and how are you grateful?

Bio

Patricia Walls is an intuitive alchemist. Through her psychic gifts and natural gift of language of light communication, she works with all life to assist in healing, balance, and expansion. Her training began some 40 years ago in shamanism and evolved through learning, practicing, and teaching many different alternative healing modalities. She has served as an international speaker, teacher, artist, author, women's retreat leader, healing facilitator, and mentor. She continues her earth traditions by working with the elemental and animal world in making ceremonial drums, tools, and art. Her websites include PatriciaWalls.net, GalacticFrequenciesofLight.com, and WiseWombyn.com.

Aging Gratefully: The Key to
Aging Gracefully
By Paula Meyer

Watching someone slowly die before your eyes is one of the most painful things to witness. My husband Gary passed on June 1, 2018, after a long battle with cancer. He didn't have much time to "age gracefully," in fact, the cancer made sure it wasn't graceful at all. At least, not physically. In the short time that was left, he showed me how to "age gratefully," and when you can age gratefully, regardless of what your body shows you, what life shows you, or what your experiences show you, that is how you age gracefully!

Here are the key lessons that I learned watching Gary age prematurely and die at the young age of 62:

When he was diagnosed with throat cancer:

He did not wallow in pity or victimhood. Because of his 30-plus years on his spiritual journey, he knew he was responsible for his body's illness. Instead, he looked within and determined what emotions caused his illness. He blessed and thanked the cancer for bringing this to his attention so that he could continue to evolve his thinking and being. He was a way-shower for me about the power of expression, and what the consequences are when we choose not to express our voice out of fear or unworthiness.

He opted for non-traditional therapy that was still somewhat based on traditional methods. He understood that because of the severity of the cancer, he had to have one foot firmly planted in the modern medical world, while the other foot was anchored in the spiritual world. Even though he believed he had the power within to heal himself, he knew the best outcome for his highest good would require both worlds. And while the end result wasn't the healing he had hoped for, he was gifted with a little more time to learn what he needed to learn.

When it became clear that he was not going to live much longer:

He made the best of each day he had. He could have left it to me to handle all his feedings and medications, but he was independent to the end. He even created a contraption out of wood and heavy wire that would hold the feeding tube hands-free so that he could feed himself. Just that little bit of independence allowed him to feel in control of his illness.

He wanted to serve his body as best he could because he was so grateful for the service his body had provided him throughout his life. In retrospect, he was consciously loving and honoring his body through the illness in a truly compassionate way.

He prepared cards and gifts for friends he was unable to see. His last act of love for me was having his brother send a card with an owl (my totem) for our anniversary that came a few months later. Rather than write the message for him, his brother included Gary's handwritten note. Such a graceful exit.

Two days before he passed:

He awoke full of energy after having been unconscious for a few days. He tried to stand up and immediately fell as his legs could no longer support his emaciated body. He sustained some minor scratches and bruises, and when we got him back in his chair, he began speaking with the voice of a young teenage boy.

His first question was: "Is the tumor gone?" And when I looked and said no, he matter-of-factly continued talking like it was no big deal.

I realized the power of the spirit as he stayed conscious in this younger version of himself, full of energy for the next 26 hours straight. He showed no signs of pain where the cancer was and fully moved that part of his body like it was completely healed.

He was constantly doing a ritual that looked like he was tying and untying things and stretching this "string" away from his body while looking at it with one eye like he was assessing how best to apply it to whatever he was attaching it to. Then he performed another ritual with me and then his brother, where he had me put my hands together, like in prayer with the fingers pointing toward him, and then he tied these strings around my hands. As I questioned him about why he was doing this, I finally coaxed out of him that he was connecting us so that we would always be together.

I truly felt that these 26 hours were a gift from his spirit, just for us. It was so amazing to be speaking to him in this way. A reminder of his youthful and energetic spirit and a comforting way of showing us that he *is* spirit and will always be with us. He wanted us to know that he was okay, that his body was simply a garment he used for this lifetime and did not define his true spiritual nature.

What I've learned through this experience:

Life is filled with endless opportunities to learn and grow. Many of these opportunities come from the challenges, tragedies, and breakdowns that we experience throughout our lives. There are so many things to be grateful for, even in the face of devastating loss.

When we ask ourselves, "What is this loss teaching me," we make a divine choice to see the bigger picture. We open our hearts to understanding and acceptance. In opening our hearts in this way, we affirm our self-love, and then we can light the way for others.

Have you ever gazed upon an elderly person who is so full of love and kindness and think to yourself, I hope I can age as gracefully? Some of us will have a shorter time on this planet and won't have the luxury of physically aging gracefully. Yet we can still age *gratefully* by enjoying every day and expressing love, gratitude, and kindness. And when we can do that, no matter our exit date, we age gracefully!

Bio

Paula Meyer recently retired from a position as an events director for a *New York Times* best-selling author. She has more than 30 years' experience as an event/workshop/meeting planner and as a procurement/contracting specialist, and 12 years in author/speaker management. After recently becoming a widow at 54, Paula's goal is to help other widows get back in the game of life and realize there is still so much to learn and love with the time we have left. Paula travels internationally and lives in Washington, Colorado, and Florida. For information on her travels, events, and grief retreats, go to www.gpeventworx.com.

Gratitude As A Path To Healing
By Rhonda Lee

Several years back, I encountered a health scare. My symptoms were quite severe at the time, and my body stayed in a state of anxiety and physical trauma. My mental and emotional states were not any better due to the panic attacks brought on by the health issue. Largely, I was exhausted and depressed, desperately seeking help from my doctor. I frequently ended up having to beg for lab work to be done to try to get to the bottom of my issue. I begged for relief from my symptoms for something that I already knew was wrong. Simply put, I was suffering tremendously with no relief in sight, and could not get my doctor or any doctor to run the labs that I knew I needed. It was a terrifying and traumatic experience. No one could help me, and unfortunately, this was not my first time being in this sort of position.

With each passing week, my condition continued to worsen. I had already taken the lead and tried an exhaustive list of therapies, supplementation, and any other healing modality I could think of to provide relief from my symptoms. Daily, I would research to see what else I could do. I meditated. I visualized. I practiced laughter yoga and did any other activity that I could find that would distract me mentally from my suffering. Many days I could not get out of bed. As my condition prolonged, I started suffering from tremendous anxiety attacks all day long. They would come out of nowhere, and I could not even breathe through them. I would break out in a cold sweat, become light-headed, and then came the tears. Lots of tears! Of course, the next thing to be affected was my sleep. The stress and anxiety made it difficult for me to fall asleep, much less sleep through the night.

One day I decided that I needed to revisit an old trick that I had used in the past to lift my spirits. After trying every therapy I could think of, I decided to fall back on gratitude as a source of relief from my agony. Drawing from previous experience as a self-professed gratitude junkie at one point in my life, I got back to work using this amazing mental state as a tool for my healing. If this worked so well for me in the past, then it should certainly do something for me at my current point of suffering. Previously, I was so sold on this practice that at one point, I even used window chalk to print the word gratitude in all capital letters across the back window of my car so I would always see this huge reminder everywhere I went. I even created a piece of jewelry with the word gratitude etched on a sterling silver cuff to keep me always reminded to use this powerful force. If this shifted my mental state before, it *had* to help me now—I just knew it.

At night I would settle into bed, and I would immediately start a mental list of anything that I could think of that would induce the feeling of gratitude. Not only did I list each thing that I was grateful for, but I took the time to truly feel the emotion of gratitude for every single thing on my list. I would do this nightly as I fell asleep. When I woke up multiple times a night, I would immediately start right back into the gratitude practice. Over and over again, I would start listing any and everything I could think of that I was grateful for, along with taking a moment to truly feel the gratitude.

Sometimes I would have to list the same thing repeatedly when I could no longer think of anything else. I truly concentrated deeply so that I could stay in a mental state of gratitude. I would do this all night long until I drifted back off to sleep. It didn't matter how many times I had to fall back on this gratitude practice. I committed to staying with it endlessly.

I became so comfortable using my gratitude practice to help me sleep at night, that it was a natural progression for me to start using it during my waking hours as well. One day, I spontaneously started using my gratitude practice during an anxiety attack. It was an effortless progression from my nighttime routine, so I decided to follow the flow. Instantly, I found tremendous relief, and my mood became so uplifted that I could stop the anxiety and allow my body to catch up with any symptom that was present. This proved to be the next pivotal point in my healing. A lot of things started to rapidly shift, and it was like I was drawing total healing toward me. Things previously outside my control started to change. Finally, I was able to get a nurse who saw and understood my symptoms to push the doctor to run the labs I had been begging for. It was like the force of gratitude started opening pathways for me. I kept at this practice without ceasing. It became much larger than I could explain and multiplied upon itself. The more frequently I held the state of gratitude, the better I felt, and more healing opportunities came my way.

The result of this season of my life was that I achieved total healing physically, mentally, and emotionally. I do believe that my gratitude practice created numerous pathways for me to overcome my health issue. I feel that it changed me on a cellular level in every possible way.

Gratitude was the force that soothed my spirits, calmed my physical body, and ultimately allowed me to find the healing I needed within myself.

Bio

Rhonda Lee, M.Ed., is the creator of Spirit Mist Smokeless Smudge, a Reiki master, and a laughter yoga leader. As a keynote speaker, she has delivered programs concentrating on stress release, healthy living concepts, and the power of laugher as a healing tool from New York City to Los Angeles. One of Rhonda's many passions is teaching others to feel empowered by taking control of their personal and surrounding energies through various modalities. She enjoys deep laughter, too many gemstones, endless adventure with family, and is completely owned by her three spoiled-rotten fur children: Buddha, Scarlett, and Oliver. Find out more at: www.infusionoflife.com.

Grateful To Be Able To Forgive
By Rina Escalante

"Tell the story of the mountain you climbed. Your words could become a page in someone else's survival guide."
~ Morgan Harper Nichols

I always knew whatever I was going through was for a reason. I never doubted it, and I accepted it because I knew the answers would eventually reveal themselves. The saying "God only gives His toughest battles to His strongest soldiers," always rang true for me.

Power comes from within.

In thinking about what I am grateful for, I had to go into my memory bank for when I *felt* that I had become an adult. Not a legal adult of 18 who can vote, but an adult *woman* who made conscious decisions that would impact not only herself, but also the children she bore from a marriage she was too young for, wasn't prepared for, and probably shouldn't have happened, but it did. This isn't going to be a story of regret, because living in regret is ridiculous, as I have come to learn on this life journey. We are unable to go back in history to change our decisions, experiences, verbal diarrhea that has been spewed at us, or what we've retorted in response. I was once told, "Words are like garbage, once you throw them out, you can't get them back."

Regret is pointless—you can't change the past, you can only learn from it.

I was only 19 years old when I married the father of my daughters. I had never been intimate with a man prior to him.

My first experience wasn't what I'd call "consensual," but in the early 80s, we weren't educated about what date rape was, nor were women who came forward about it even looked at as victims. I was 18 at the time, twelve days before I turned 19. In those days, it was more like the woman was blamed for that type of violation by the community, authorities, and even her family. I was extremely insecure, and I turned to the only person I felt I could trust. She took me to the only place she knew that wouldn't judge me, Planned Parenthood, so I went. They did what they do with new patients, and I was sent off with birth control pills. I was afraid and didn't volunteer information.

I don't think I was taking those pills for more than three months before I carelessly left them out, and they were found. Less than a year later, I found myself married to this person. Within the first year, he thought it would be acceptable to throw me around, but I was feisty and fought back, so that ended before it started. The relationship was verbally and emotionally abusive, and he was unfaithful. Thankfully, we spent a lot of time at my father-in-law's nurturing and welcoming home, watching our nephew grow up, watching baseball, sharing meals, family celebrations, or simply enjoying each other's company. I loved his father and my brother-in-law. They were loving, supporting in-laws, and I learned much from them. I only have fond memories of those visits.

After the girls were born, I used to take them to visit with their paternal grandmother, and she would tell me stories about my husband's childhood and how she handled discipline specifically related to him. She did educate me about certain moments in his childhood that were probably traumatic for him. Unbeknownst to her, those discussions ultimately helped me understand the "whys," which helped me to eventually forgive him.

Childhood trauma affects who you become as an adult; positive and negative experiences will manifest themselves.

There were two eventual marriage separations, which made divorce imminent. It came as a great shock to most friends and family, because our personal issues were never discussed publicly. Our divorce and child custody dispute lasted two contentious years. It was eventually agreed upon that child visits would be held at a location that was supervised. After a certain amount of time, the visits ended. The girls' father said he was not comfortable at the center, so he eventually stopped visiting his daughters.

Children need both parents to thrive and become well-functioning adults; girls need their daddies.

The visitations ended when the girls were two and four years old. I needed to help our daughters move on, and I needed to help myself move on, or I feared I would become a bitter, angry woman, which was not an option. I had always felt God in my heart, and I knew I had to forgive my husband for abandoning the girls, and for the actions he had imposed on me. I remembered all the things his mother had told me about his specific traumatic childhood that he had no control over. I thought and prayed intensely about everything.

"Forgive yourself for not knowing what you didn't know before you learned it." ~ Maya Angelou

I knew what I had to do, I had to forgive him. I had to do it for myself, I had to do it for the girls, and I had to do it for our mental health. If every time I looked at their little faces and I saw him, what good would it do if I felt anger towards their father? I would eventually let it out on them, right? So, it was up to me to stop the cycle of ignorance! I went to parenting classes, individual therapy, and we participated in family therapy sessions. On weekends we would spend time together learning things at museums, book stores, going for long drives exploring, they attended different types of camps, the Boys and Girls Club, played soccer, and I would take them to the golf range with me to shoot balls—anything that was family-oriented. They needed to know they were loved, that's all that mattered. We lived in gratefulness.

"We must develop the capacity to forgive. He who is devoid of the power to forgive is devoid of the power to love."
~ Martin Luther King, Jr.

Bio

Rina Escalante is a first-generation Salvadorian-American from the San Francisco Mission District. She's a multi-stroke and cancer survivor; she wholeheartedly believes that if you surround yourself with positive energy, you can make anything possible! She shares her life experiences in her storytelling with the intention and hope that the reader will feel inspired and know that they are not alone on their journey. This is her second collaborative book. You can contact Rina at rinaesca@gmail.com.

My Precious Ones
By Rollie Allaire

My Soul has been grateful for a number of reasons throughout my lifetime. But the part that warms my heart the most is having become a mother.

I have been blessed to have been pregnant three times. I was blessed to have two living sons, while their sister connects with us in the spirit world. I lost my first child through a miscarriage. Although I did not meet her, she was an essential part of my life. She changed my life forever.

I never physically knew if she was a boy or a girl, but I have always believed we have spirits that surround us. My oldest son, Michael, shared one day that he met his older sister. I know that he had the ability to see spirits because when his grandfather passed away when he was only two years old, he asked why everyone was sad when we gathered at his grandfather's after his passing. We shared that Grampa was gone. My son shared that Grampa was sitting over in the corner watching us. So when he shared he met his sister, I believed him.

We decided to name her, Melissa Leanne, which would have been her name had she joined us on this plane. For a long time, he talked about her. As an adult, he would probably think we are crazy now, but I appreciated the conversations we had.

Melissa Leanne was conceived at a difficult time in my life. I had been suffering from Anorexia and Bulimia since I was a teenager. I managed to hide it well, or so I thought, until I saw my doctor who threatened to have me hospitalized if I didn't maintain a minimum weight. As much as I didn't want to be at that weight, I did what I could to maintain that minimum weight.

I was able to keep my secret for many years later. Then I met a dentist who questioned Bulimia because of the enamel damage to my teeth that was consistent with Bulimia. I denied it and didn't go back to a dentist for many years later. I was afraid that he might share his findings with my doctor.

In late 1993, I became pregnant with Melissa Leanne. Her father and I were excited that we would have a baby. During this time, I continued to suffer from Bulimia. Anorexia was a little more challenging because everyone was noticing me eating and commenting on how I was now eating for two. I could hide the Bulimia by using morning sickness as an excuse.

As much as I was excited to become a mom, gaining weight was extremely stressful for me. I was watching my tummy get a little bigger as it protruded past my hip bones that were sticking out. I just kept eating in front of others, then secretly purging.

In November 1993, my doctor informed me that I had miscarried and I would need to abort the fetus. He referred me to our local baby doctor. They scheduled me for D&C. This doctor tried to make me feel better, but had no idea that I was experiencing Anorexia and Bulimia. He indicated that I probably did not have enough fat on me to maintain the pregnancy.

I spoke about it to my family doctor who shared that it was certainly a possibility. We talked about what I was doing and agreed that I was still above the weight that he said I needed to maintain, and provided that I maintained that weight, there would be no hospitalization.

Despite all my guilt, I returned to my regular patterns and habits, until I became pregnant a second time. Every ounce of my being dreaded gaining weight. Hearing that the fetus was not viable was all that I was reliving in my head during that pregnancy.

I forced myself to eat every day despite that I was vomiting every time I did. I was fearful of the same thing happening to Michael, yet I wasn't doing it intentionally like with Melissa Leanne. With Melissa Leanne, I didn't change any of the behaviors.

I wasn't gaining weight because of the morning sickness. I even struggled to get to work. The doctor prescribed me medication to prevent me from vomiting. I took that medication for my entire pregnancy with Michael. Every time I would stop, the morning sickness would start again.

I was grateful for the lessons that I learned through my first pregnancy. It was what I needed to survive my second and third pregnancies. As much as I dreaded the weight gain, becoming a mom was the best thing that ever happened to me.

Although things went well with the pregnancy, there were complications with the delivery. Michael went into distress and they had taken me in for an emergency C-section. The moment I laid eyes on him, I was more in love than I ever had been in my life. I knew I loved him while I was pregnant, but I loved him even more in person.

After Michael was born, I was able to stay away from those destructive patterns. I began nursing and needed to be sure I had enough to nourish him. Then I had to make sure that I had the strength to take care of him.

What Michael said to me about his conversation with his sister was that she loved me and was lucky to have me as a mom. That warmed my heart.

I'm grateful that he had that ability to see others from beyond. As crazy as he may think this all is now as an adult, I still remember. I remember the encounters that he had with his grandfather. He knew things that no one shared with him about his interactions with his grandpa. And when you would ask him how he knew, he would tell us it was Grampa.

I am grateful for the love of my children that helped me learn to care for myself. To help keep me alive. A mother's love truly is like no other.

Bio

Rollie Allaire is an experienced holistic life and wellness coach who combines years of clinical psychotherapy skills with Chakra work, Crystal Reiki, ThetaHealing, Akashic Records readings and clearings, Meditation, Ho'oponopono, Qi Gong, Moon Medicine teachings and looking at life through the Medicine Wheel in the form of Life & Wellness to facilitate her clients' journeys to wellness. She has recently opened Bridging the Gap Wellness Center in her community where she works with other practitioners to provide their services within their small Northeastern Ontario community. She is a proud and loving mother of two adult boys, a wife and daughter. You can find Rollie at her website www.rollieallaire.ca

Self-Love: I Am Enough. You Are Enough.
By Rollie Allaire

I woke up one morning, unable to get out of bed. Putting one foot down on the floor was the biggest challenge there was. I didn't know if I would make it through another day, and frankly, nor did I want to.

In December 2014, the last straw had broken this camel's back. I have always been a survivor. I was tough, and I could handle anything that was thrown at me, despite having anxiety from a very early age.

Life for me started out in a dysfunctional home with parents who loved me and tried their best at the time. I learned later in years that my relationship with my grandmother was one of the tools in my strategies to develop resiliency.

My first sexual experience resulted in a trip to the hospital because the condom had broken. My boyfriend at the time came home, and his mother took me to the hospital, where I was prescribed the morning-after pill. I survived being raped by three different people that I knew and trusted, as a late teen and in my early 20s.

I coped through much of my trauma with an eating disorder that I was able to mask behind my unconventional eating patterns. I'm extremely intolerant of foods with smells, textures, and taste, which in itself is a challenge.

Domestic violence was a pattern in two long-term relationships that I was able to escape from physically unscathed. As I worked with others in these situations, I am able to say how fortunate I was to get out and not remain in these relationships.

I lost my first child through a miscarriage, most likely caused by malnutrition because of my eating disorder.

These are only a few of my "major life events" that contributed to my resiliency. When December 2014 came around, and I couldn't get out of bed, I didn't know if I was ever going to have a normal life again.

As I was struggling with the feelings of incompetence as a parent to a teenage addict, unbeknownst to me, my husband was having an affair. I've always been strong and independent—the person everyone could count on. Not in that moment. My identity as a mother and wife was stripped from me. I became suicidal and couldn't function.

I knew that I couldn't handle it by myself, so I had a few appointments with a mental health professional. I reached out to my doctor and started on antidepressants. The medication helped. The sessions helped. I knew the things that I needed to do. And on the surface, I was fine, but I truly didn't address those issues.

I was "managing life." For the most part, I was able to manage day to day. But it was all over when I lost my job. I struggled with my identity as a parent, as a spouse, and now professionally. I was devastated.

I reached out to a mental health professional again, and this time, I was even referred to a psychiatrist. I know that if all of these things happened one at a time, I would have been resilient enough to handle one thing at a time. Before I was able to finish dealing with one thing, the next thing happened, compounding my issues, and when this final straw landed, that was it for me.

And so, my healing journey with gratitude began. It wasn't that quick, but looking back, it was the best part of my healing. This is where my healing journey truly began. I attributed my healing journey to when I was 14, and my family was mandated to family counseling. I needed to face the reality that my life would never be the same. All those traumas came flooding back, compounded by all the things that had been happening in the last couple of years.

The first three months that the psychiatrist had me off, I completely understood and worked through the things that were coming up. I knew that I wasn't ready to start working full-time, but I believed I was ready for part-time. I even applied for a part-time position, until I went to see him. He didn't think I was ready for any work. Off I went to connect a little deeper with myself, not by choice. When the end of those three months was over, I knew that I needed more time. I was finally feeling good enough to tackle those much bigger issues.

During those three months, I worked even deeper with gratitude. I was able to deepen my relationship with myself. I expanded my spirituality. I have continued to expand through to today. After that time, I started a business. This business has evolved to working with women. When someone asks me what I do, I say, "I'm a life-changer." I help women live the best version of themselves.

I've been able to do that in many ways. My biggest accomplishment is hosting my third annual Women Inspiring Women Conference. Leading into my 2020 Conference in March, I was contacted by a women's business organization that informed me that I was nominated for the Changemaker Entrepreneur of the Year.

This is award recognizes a social entrepreneur who has roots in creating social change. The social enterprise is designed to make money, but the primary goal will always be to create positive social impact. I still am not sure who nominated me, because who I thought had nominated me said it wasn't them. I didn't win this year, but it was a great honor to have been nominated.

Although my life has been challenging, I am grateful for all of my experiences that have led me to this moment in my life. My life experiences have allowed me to know and understand the challenges that my clients have faced or are facing. We can overcome these "roadblocks." They don't need to define us. Whenever I start to feel down on myself or about situations around me, I start with my feelings of gratitude. And take things one day at a time.

Self-Love: I Am Enough. You Are Enough. This is the theme for my 2021 Women Inspiring Women Conference. I am so grateful and inspired by the women I meet along this journey. I grow a little more with each encounter.

Bio

Rollie is grateful for the client who, despite my "mask of happiness," was able to intuitively know what I needed that day. "I don't know what's going on, but this hug is for you. I know you need it." Rollie is extremely grateful for all the women who have come into her life as mentors, clients, students, friends, family, coaches, speakers, guests, and vendors. Especially those who shared a little piece of themselves as they grew to become the people they are right now in this moment. Gratitude is the greatest gift you can offer yourself.

The Turning Point
By Rose Bourassa

My turning point happened when my 25-year-old son died tragically in late 2014. What I knew of death and dying at that time was nothing compared to what I learned after his passing. Through the sorrow and pain of losing a child, I was in for an amazing awakening into life after death.

A close friend of mine has always been intuitive. She was studying mediumship, and she had an Akashic records reading every year to track her spiritual progress. In 2014, her reading was scheduled for mid-December. I had never been to a medium or had a reading. I knew of them, but that was it—until the night my friend called to ask if I was open to hearing what had transpired in her reading. My son had come through with a message.

What an amazing conversation we had! I was intrigued and needed more!

Thus, began my journey.

For the first year after his death, we went to a different mediumship demonstration every month.

At every event we went to, he came through with a treasured message of love from the other side. At first, there was disbelief, but then I realized it was not a coincidence every time.

By the end of that year, I was signing up for classes. There was definitely more to this, and I wanted to understand how and why. I yearned to learn this magic of speaking to the dead.

My mind and heart were open to the new belief. With the reality that I could speak to spirits, came the revelation that things happening around me my whole life had been caused by spirits. For years I would smell freshly-baked bread and long for a tub of butter to spread on that smell. I soon discovered that the aroma was Heaven-sent. In life, my father had worked for a bakery as the breadman. He was sending me a little hello from Heaven.

After losing my son, I was lost. I learned about messages from Heaven and began to understand and look forward to them.

Signs from my son are amazing to this day. This kid has spirit talent! He calls my name in the night. He makes the car radio connect via Bluetooth to my phone, always playing his favorite songs. Lights at home flicker. He walks the hallway at night—the dogs staring intently at the corner of the room as though someone is there.

The more I learned about signs from Heaven, the more I acknowledged them and found peace and comfort in them. I began to thank the spirits who sent them. I thanked the master spirit for awakening my "Spidey-senses."

My studies continue, and my group of likeminded friends increases. How wonderful to have a network of people to call friends—people to lean on, encourage, and be encouraged by. I am coming into my individual light. I am learning my strengths and weaknesses. It is a pretty special feeling.

My friend, Linda, and I taught high school confirmation classes at our church. One of the lessons focused on music and its meaning in today's world. We explored the lyrics and our perception of the meaning of each song. The most powerful song was *I Can Only Imagine* by the group Mercy Me. The song spoke of what the writer envisioned it would be like to meet his maker.

That song held a special meaning to us. With this song, we knew we had reached our students' souls that night. They understood God in a new light.

Sadly, Linda's health declined over the years. During the last weeks of her life, I visited her in the hospital every day. Often on the way, *I Can Only Imagine* would suddenly come on the radio. Coincidence? No. I knew spirit was getting me ready to say goodbye to my dear friend.

At the hospital, friends and family came and went saying their final goodbyes. Her brother and I stepped out to discuss the next steps. Out of nowhere, I heard my son tell me to "Get back to her room now!" At this same time, her brother received a call about her declining condition.

Back in her room, we stood watch, silently praying.

Linda and I had once envisioned what the afterlife would be like. I no longer wondered. I had learned so much, and it was all good.

The room filled fast with spirits of those gone before her. I could feel each one arrive. The love they felt for her was so intense that I momentarily left the room to cry my heart out in the hallway. I was overwhelmed. Spirit was teaching me about love.

Her eyes darted back and forth under her eyelids. She was seeing her parents and was overjoyed they had come to escort her home. Her eyes darted from one person to the next. I became so in tune with her; I felt her telling me that everything was so much more beautiful than imagined.

Her breathing became labored—her time was near. We continued to watch, pray, and wait. The moment her breathing stopped, *I Can Only Imagine* magically began to play from my cellphone. Everyone in the room sang from their hearts and the depths of their souls as she transitioned.

Losing my son changed my view of life after death. I am a soul in human form with lessons to learn, among them gratitude, thankfulness, and love.

Gratitude for the friend who started me on the journey and walks it with me daily. Thankful for those in my life who help me learn new things and reach new heights. Grateful for the understanding and knowledge learned before I walked into the room to watch my dear friend transition. Thankful to her for allowing me to be a part of her transition and for the experience of being on this side while being able to see the other.

Bio

Rose Bourassa is working procurement specialist employed with a mid-size contract for the manufacturing of hair and skin care products. She is currently preparing for a second career as an evidential medium and proprietor of a spiritual center. She is a wife, mother, grandmother, student, teacher, and volunteer. To keep sharp, she strives to learn something new every day—hopefully something to help keep up with grandkids—even when they have to dumb it down! You can reach Rose via email at Remnick@aol.com.

Gratitude
By Roxane Gaudet

Have you ever stopped and asked yourself, "What is gratitude?" Dictionary.com defines it as: "The quality of being thankful."

My definition of gratitude is the *feeling* of being thankful, grateful, appreciative. It is a positive feeling deep inside. It is a choice that I make every day. It is taking everyday happenings and turning them into blessings! It is also realizing that not all happenings or events are seen as positive. Sometimes it takes a devastating occurrence to open our eyes and hearts to gratitude. If there was no darkness, we would not know light. If there was no sickness, we would not know health. If there was no sadness, how could we know happiness? You are probably familiar with these teachings. Not that many years ago, I learned exactly what they meant.

As a young teenager dealing with all the insecurities of puberty and growing up, I encountered what would be a devastating happening in my life. Spending time at my grandmother's during summer vacation was new to me, as was spending time with my little-known cousins. Add to that my cousins' friends. After several minutes of them talking and hanging out, one boy looked me straight in the eye and said, "Damn, you are really ugly," emphasizing the really. Having been raised to be polite and non-confrontational, I said nothing. And neither did anyone else—no one.

Years went by, and I turned into a woman with somewhat good self-esteem. Through new friendships, I discovered Reiki and the chakras. I was hooked! Doing research and receiving Reiki treatments opened a Pandora's box of memories, feelings, and emotions. And by far, the most potent memory was of being told that I was "really ugly" by that boy. The pain of rejection and being abandoned by my cousins was still so powerful that I knew I had to find a way to heal. First, I had to find it in my heart to forgive them. I would meditate, focusing on my heart chakra while sending them love over and over again. Then one day, my heart said, "Thank you." Thank you? To a boy who made my fragile teenage ego come crashing down? Yes, I wholeheartedly thanked him for permitting me to learn that beauty is only skin deep! His comment had been based solely on his opinion of my looks, nothing else. My intellect, my emotions, my humor, and my spirituality were never considered when he made that judgment of me. I was so much more!

Gratitude made itself known to me on that day. I liked that feeling inside me, knowing that blessings are everywhere, albeit sometimes hidden. It would take patience and repetition to find blessings in unlikely situations. Gratitude is a positive habit that needs to be acquired one step at a time. It was easy to feel gratitude when life was good, but finding that inner feeling when life was not so good was different and much more difficult to master. I was practicing meditation, grounding work, chakra healing, and Reiki, along with angel work and visualization at the time. I was writing three things that I was thankful for every night before going to bed, but I wanted something more. That's when what I call "grateful chakras" was born!

At night or in the morning, I would sit or lie comfortably, but preferably with my bare feet touching the ground. I would ground myself as a tree with far-reaching roots going to meet Mother Earth. Her energy would then be guided upwards through my body and would fly to the Heavens above. Then, I concentrated on my root chakra, but instead of balancing and harmonizing it, I would thank it. Thank you, root chakra, for allowing me to stand strong and stable!

Then the sacral chakra. Thank you, sacral chakra, for my comfort with my sexuality, my relationships, and my power for making choices!

Thank you, solar plexus chakra, for my ability to be my authentic self and live with vitality and responsibility!

Then I arrive at the heart chakra. Thank you, heart chakra, for filling me with compassion, affection, and unconditional love! As well as helping me to forgive others and myself for mistakes or bad choices.

Then there is a mini-chakra snuggled in there between the heart and throat chakras. There are many mini chakras, but this is the only one that I concentrate on. Thank you, mini-chakra of gratitude, for life and for opening the energy path between my heart, my throat, and my mind!

Thank you, throat chakra, for the ability to be creative and able to communicate my projects and thoughts, as well as the ability to be receptive to others' communication!

Thank you, third eye chakra, for my intuition, my insight, and my connection to wisdom, along with the ability to see both the inner and outer worlds!

And then comes the crown chakra. I thank you, crown chakra, for connecting me to the Universal life force, for enlightenment, and for permitting me to know my higher self!

Then I harness the incredible healing energy of the Universe and guide it back down through my body, acknowledging each chakra on the way down, and let the energy descend once again to Mother Earth, grounding me.

Thank you, life!

So, what is gratitude? For me, gratitude is my inner being, my *way* of being.

It is growth, attitude, a full heart, and acceptance. Pure and simple. God bless.

Bio

Roxane, also known as Roxy or Rox, is still figuring out exactly what it is that she is meant to do! Her healing modalities include Level II Reiki, aromatherapy, gratitude chakras, rejuvenating facial massage, Indian head massage, some acupressure, and listening. Yes, listening! Vision Boards are of interest, as well as completing a course in SoulCollage. She may be reached at roxgroy@hotmail.com or by call or text at 705-498-7539. Let's chat!

Dear Death
By Sara Hamblin

Dear Death,

Thank you. Thank you for the lessons I didn't know I needed to learn. Thank you for leading me to spend countless days and weeks in the dark night of my soul. Because of you, I'm strong, and I know myself intimately. Thank you for using loss to teach me about life. You showed me the fragility and sacredness of the human spirit. By looking you in the eyes as my loved ones took their last breaths, you gave me a new lease on life. You taught me about mercy when someone's pain and suffering was in my hands. You taught me to stand up and speak for those who couldn't. In my darkest days and in the deafening silence of grief, you showed me compassion through those around me. You taught me endurance when I wasn't sure how I could keep going. You awakened the voice that was sleeping within me, and you made me listen to it. You empowered me to break the chains I had placed on myself. You taught me to admire my courage as I stepped into the unknown, into a new life that was honest and true to me. Thank you for showing me the path home. It was inside me all along.

Becoming grateful for the lessons that you taught me has been a long road. For longer than a decade, I resisted. I ran. I tried everything I could to escape the truth that you were trying to teach me. When I stood in stillness and let my fears surround me, I started to change my relationship with you and with myself. At that point in my life, you and your close companion, loss, had ripped away every shred of the life that I'd known.

By the time I was 27, you'd taken both of my parents through alcoholism. My dad died first in 2009 and left us reeling. A month after my mom passed away in January 2017, I started losing my husband—through divorce. Empty, hopeless, and lost, I grabbed what dignity and belongings I had left and moved away from the state that had been my home since I was two years old. Everything and everyone I knew was in Oklahoma, but I thought being a stranger would help me start again. So, I left for Denver.

Denver was a place where I already felt at home. I'd traveled there dozens of times for work over the previous few years, and I always missed it when I left. I felt untethered every time I visited. The newness of the city stripped away all my barriers because it held no reminders of my past. Something deep inside of me kept telling me I was meant to be there. As soon as I knew I was getting a divorce, I decided that's where I was going. But I failed to realize that bringing all my possessions to a new town for a fresh start didn't mean that I would get to leave my emotional baggage behind.

I know now that no matter where one goes, one's shadows follow. One evening shortly after moving in, I sat broke, alone, and heartbroken in my new apartment. I realized that I needed to confront everything I'd been running from. And for the first time in my life, I allowed myself to feel the pain I'd been avoiding. You taught me about the inexplicable grief that happens after life-changing loss. About the sleepless nights one spends wondering what went wrong and what one could have done differently to change the outcome. Over a few months, I'd started a new job, lost my mom, lost my marriage, moved three times— and I was living in a new state, where I knew almost no one. Was I crazy for following a voice within me that kept saying this was the right thing to do?

Through the turmoil, I kept returning to the same thought: how lucky I was to get to live this life. As each day began, I would watch the sunrise through my balcony window, in awe of the striking pinks and oranges over the mountains. I was emotionally exhausted, but there was a big part of my soul that was at peace. One day, while I was driving, I reached the top of a small hill. As a magnificent view of the Rockies expanded across my windshield, my breath caught in my throat, and I found myself in an unexpected moment of gratitude. Moments like these reminded me that I was right where I was supposed to be— and how lucky I was to live this life.

I've continued to look for these moments. I've learned to be grateful for the struggles because they've given me strength. I've found beauty in working through times of pain because they've brought growth. I've honored myself for overcoming insurmountable odds when everything in my life pointed to destruction and failure. And I've learned to appreciate every moment that I thought would break me down because I've always found myself thriving on the other side.

Everything I have is because of you, Death, and the losses I've experienced. If my mom were still alive, I wouldn't have left Oklahoma. If I were still married, I wouldn't have moved to where my soul was calling me to be. If I'd stayed in Oklahoma, I wouldn't have met an incredible group of friends who are all working on their shadows and collectively raising the consciousness of humanity. I'm grateful for everything I went through because it's the reason for everything I now have. I get to live an incredible life every day—because I find beauty and opportunity everywhere. I find my inspiration in everything around me. And I continue to seek experiences that make me realize how lucky I am to live this life.

Thank you from the bottom of my healing heart,

Sara

Bio

Sara is an energy worker, channeler, and Reiki Master. She helps individuals work through energetic blocks that have occurred in their bodies due to emotional trauma and other life events. She is able to accomplish this through her training and personal experience in using energy work to heal from grief on a physical and subconscious level. Her purpose is to help people heal on a soul level so they can live life fully. You can reach Sara at sara@moonworks.energy or at www.moonworks.energy.

Taking Things For Granted
By Sarah Gabler

"You don't know how much something means to you until it is taken away." Isn't that the truth? When we experience what it's like to have our most important or favorite things taken away, we realize how much we take what we have for granted.

With the ongoing COVID-19 virus, all Californians are on a statewide order to stay inside. With everyone in quarantine to prevent the spread of the coronavirus, everything I'm used to has been taken away. It's difficult, but it is also teaching me a lot about being grateful for what truly matters.

Most kids complain about school. At first, I was frustrated by random things that happen at school each day. I would get so angry at my classmates when they were making noise and keeping me from focusing on my work, and I would wish for silence. I would get annoyed when my teachers would give me multiple homework assignments, and wished for free time. Don't even get me started on waking up at 5:30 in the morning for "zero period" physical education!

Now, I need to stay home from school entirely. I am still happy that I don't need to get up quite so early, but it's hard to get motivated to exercise without my P.E. teacher's input. When I need help, I don't have the luxury of going to my teachers and asking them my questions in the moment. Instead, I have to email my teachers with any questions and wait for their answers. I must work by myself without my peers, and honestly, I would rather be in the classroom with my peers again. I realized how much I was taking my education for granted, and it never occurred to me that it could be taken away.

At the beginning of my school year, my Play Production class held auditions for parts in our upcoming musical, "The Little Mermaid Jr." I auditioned for the role of Ursula, certain that this was the only part for me. Unfortunately, I didn't get the part and instead was cast in the role of Andrina, one of Ariel's sisters. Although I did my best in my role during rehearsals, I was still sad that I missed out on the part I genuinely wanted. With schools being closed, it looks like we won't have any musical at all. My last musical of my last year at my beloved middle school isn't going to happen, and I will never get it back. Now, I wish I could go back to my rehearsals and sing my heart out as Andrina. I'm learning why it is important to be happy and grateful for any part given to me and to enjoy every part of the process of putting together a show, because you never know if it will be the last show you get to do.

I'm also learning to be grateful for my food. I am the pickiest eater on the planet and am not a fan of many foods. Before the coronavirus shutdown happened, I always complained about whether I liked what we were having for dinner, and often asked for my favorite pasta instead of whatever my parents were making. My dad and I recently went to the store, and I had no idea what it would look like. I heard that supplies and food were running low, but this was beyond what I had expected. There were no paper goods, no canned food, and few dinner options. My heart sank as I walked through the aisles and found that all my favorite foods were out of stock. No tortellini, no ravioli, no burgers—I was shocked! I spent half an hour wandering the store, hoping that I had missed something, and maybe, just maybe, there would be at least one more of something I like. Nope! I learned that I had to accept that not everything is going to be there for me whenever I want it. I had to be grateful for the food I did have, and let go of being sad about the food I didn't have.

I also used to hate running errands. I love spending time with my family, but did it actually have to be errands? When my parents asked me to get ready to run errands, I complained because I loved to simply relax in my room. Now that I am forced to stay inside, and I can't go anywhere, I wish that we could run errands again so I could get outside for a while.

Being grateful can be one of our most powerful tools in life. It is especially important to feel gratitude even when everything is going well, instead of only when things are taken away. I realize now that although I thought I was practicing gratitude by talking to myself every morning and every night when I recapped my day, I wasn't truly aware of how much I took for granted. I would think about what I was grateful for that day and focus on the opportunities given to me. Still, I didn't fully realize all of the little blessings in my life, until life as I knew it dramatically changed.

It is important not only to be grateful for the big things, but also for the little things that come across your path. This can be the love of your family or a smile that lifted your spirits when you were feeling sad. It can be a meal you enjoyed, or the sound of another person's voice, or the ability to move your body. It can be an opportunity to get an education or participate in an activity. Gratitude can open up your mind to the world, and it will help you look at your life differently than you did before. Even when the world seems perfectly fine at the moment, remember to be grateful for what you have and what you receive every single day.

Bio

Sarah Gabler is 13 years old and will be in ninth grade. She loves playing with her family and traveling to new places. She enjoys acting, singing, dancing, and horseback riding. When she grows up, she intends to be a motivational speaker or work in fashion design. She loves empowering people, even if they don't reciprocate! She began exploring spiritual teachings and soul empowerment concepts when she was ten years old and believes it has made her a better person today. It also has motivated her to find ways to help others on their journey to live their best lives.

An Eye For Gratitude
By Sharyn Madison

It was December, and the night before the opening of the medical conference in Orlando. Privileged to be a speaker, I decided to iron the travel wrinkles out of my blouse using the resort's iron and ironing board. Moments later, with the job done and the iron cooled, I began to wind up the cord when I noticed a push button on the iron.

"Oh, it's retractable. Hey, Sis, have you ever used one of these?" As my sister looked on, I pushed the button, and the cord came to life. Whipping up from the floor, it whacked me right in the eye. What are the chances? Right in my eye?

That hurt. It felt like there was broken glass in my eye with small, shattered pieces of shard cutting my eyeball and my lid with every blink. "No blinking!" I tried to tell my eye. It didn't want to stay open, but it didn't want to stay closed either.

We noticed a mark on my eyelid like a bruise. My eyelid must have closed before the cord hit full-on. Our eye winkers are something to behold, aren't they? Mine blinked before my brain knew what was happening. What kind of amazing machine can do that? Together my family and I talked about all the reasons to be thankful. It could have been worse.

It was nearing midnight, so I decided not to call for emergency responders until the next morning. They assured me then my eye appeared to be okay.

I walked to the conference with a removable eye patch, and the presentation went on without a hitch. After the conference, I went to an eye doctor in Florida who simply recommended I see my eye doctor when I got back to New York. I enlisted lots of prayers, Reiki healing, and all the self-care I could think of. I felt a deep sense of gratitude for so many caring friends.

In the meantime, I knew from experience that something good can come out of every challenge, so I wondered how it would all turn out. It strengthens my faith to keep track of what comes on the other side of a challenge, experiences I call my faith builders. January was around the corner, so one way to stay positive was to make my first intention for the new year a positive one: "I can see clearly with both of my healed eyes."

Sadly, that faith took a hit at my appointment with the New York eye doctor. By then, there was no eye pain, but the blurry vision remained. The doctor said, "There is nothing more we can do. There is a permanent scar on your cornea in the shape of the prong from the plug of that cord."

What? I have to live with blurred vision? Do you know what it's like to try to see when you need washer fluid on a mud-spattered windshield? Or what it's like trying to see through the dense fog? My eyes wanted my brain to fix that smudge on my eye.

Two months into the saga, my blurred vision got worse. I was not too keen on driving, so I chose my trips carefully. It happened to be a New York snowy day, so I pondered whether to venture out or not, but I decided to get on the road for the 44-mile trip to Cornell to pick up medicine for my Chihuahua, Mochie. The longer I drove, the effort to see bothered me more and more. To make matters worse, I lost an hour because my GPS stopped working. It had started up fine, then simply stopped. I shook my head in exasperation. I said to myself, "I can't live with this eye smear anymore."

Fed up with the situation, on the way home, I stopped at the Eye Center, the office of the well-known New York expert ophthalmologist, Dr. Ferguson. My chances were slim to get an appointment any time soon, but I was desperate. It couldn't hurt to ask.

Perhaps it was my forlorn look or my distraught tone that perked up sympathy when I asked, "Is there anything you can do, special glasses, medication? Is there any kind of help for this eye? Could I make an appointment to see Dr. Ferguson?"

The manager said, "She just happens to be here. Give me a minute." Five minutes later, the manager came back and said, "Your timing is perfect. She will see you right now."

Right now? What? That's a miracle! What angel disabled my GPS to get me here at the perfect time? Feelings surfaced in that space of gratitude, among them a relief that I decided to make the drive that day. It was the frustration of that trip that led to the spontaneous stop at the Eye Center.

The doctor came in. Eye drops, lights, and an analysis later, she said, "With another test for confirmation to be sure, I believe I know what's wrong here. I can fix this."

"You can fix this?" That flushed out pure gratitude right there! She explained the injury and the procedure for repair. Next, the surgery was scheduled, and I was on my way. "By the way," she said, "if you want, I can take care of the small cataract in your other eye."

I didn't even know I had one. Remember my intention? "I can see clearly with *both* of my healed eyes." Spirit knew before I did.

Looking back, I am grateful for my intuition. How did we get this one right? Spirit says, "Receive the gifts as they come." I am grateful for the gifts and the miracles of this faith builder. I plan to stay in the flow by keeping up my spiritual practices and by watching for more of the sacred with my new, clearer vision.

Bio

Sharyn Madison, MS, SCT, RM is a certified Reiki master teacher, practitioner, speaker, and author of the book, *Spirit Speaks*. She owned a large wellness center for many years, where she developed an extensive intuitive Reiki practice. She teaches about all things Reiki, including holistic care, intuition, meditation, spirit communication, and animal communication. She is passionate about the healing possibilities of both energy medicine and connections with our spirit allies. Sharyn wants healing techniques and conversations to help us all reach our highest potential. Contact information: sharynmadison.com and slemadison@yahoo.com.

Live Your Purpose
By Sherri Elliott-Yeary

*"Life's challenges are not supposed to paralyze you;
they're supposed to help you discover who you are." ~*
Bernice Johnson Reagon

D o you long for a life filled with joy? More time for yourself? Would you like to take better care of your health, reduce stress, and create additional balance in your life?

You're in good company. Quite a few of my clients and girlfriends have often shared that they spend so much time working they no longer have the energy or interest to invest in soul-sustaining relationships. As a result, these soul-nourishing relationships start to deteriorate, and we lose this critical connection.

As women, we often try to fill the holes deep inside of us with overspending, overeating, or overmedicating as we continue to drive ourselves to an even higher level of success, yet we are disappointed the emptiness remains. Could it be that our lives, our purpose for being here, are no longer connected to our job titles, where we live, or the car we drive? Many of us, myself included, can get too caught up in the stuff we think is important and fail to protect and cherish what is most important to us.

Like so many others, I was busy trying to survive my life, I had no soul left to appreciate it. I was trying to have it all, all at once, and I was paying the price.

If you desire a life filled with purpose and joy, you must let go of toxic relationships, friendships, guilt, and other self-imposed burdens. Only then will you experience a life of joy and gratitude.

Taking the risk to follow our hearts gives us energy for our future and breathes life into our dreams. By stopping and asking ourselves if what we are doing is leading us toward an inspiring future or away from it, we gain the opportunity to reclaim a life of purpose and joy. These are some of the hardest questions for some of us because it takes courage and faith to follow our heart's desire.

These questions can alter the trajectory of your life in an instant because as soon as you realize you're headed in the wrong direction, you have the power to make a new choice, a choice that can deliver the life you desire.

I personally need to remind myself to stop struggling long enough to smell the roses. As a reminder, I carry a piece of paper in my wallet that states, *"Haste will take the place of peace and grace if you are not proactively choosing how to live your life every day."*

By clearing space in my life to be still and listen, I can hear the messages of serenity, hope, and gratitude. Only I can make the right choice in the moment that allows me to sincerely live a life of purpose in alignment with my true heart's calling.

"Grace is the voice that calls us to change and then gives us the power to pull it off." ~ Max Lucado

I have been asked by a lot of my clients, "Do other people genuinely experience moments of grace?" I believe the actual question is, "What do people who experience moments of grace do afterward?"

Many of my clients who experience grace in their lives, don't recognize it or take the time to appreciate it truly. Instead, they brush it aside, write it off, keep quiet about it for fear it may leave and never come back if they honestly embrace it. Others I work with share their moments of grace freely, so people everywhere may be inspired by them and learn from their experiences. I feel that those of us who freely do so are helping heal the world.

It's time to come out of the dark. Now is the time to wave our hands, tell our stories, to shout our truth, to reveal our innermost experiences, and let those experiences raise eyebrows and questions that help us turn toward God for answers.

Only the brave vulnerably share their stories of pain, loss, and disappointment, for it's in these spiritual moments that sacred truths are made real for everyone who hears them. It's how our culture advances and how we evolve; the failure to live those truths causes civilizations to become extinct.

I can think of numerous instances that God has used to touch my life with His grace; one of them is through my girlfriends. They have loved and supported me through the loss of a child, divorce, job change, my daughter's addiction, starting a business, and writing my first book, *Ties to Tattoos: Turning Generational Differences into a Competitive Advantage.* We only have one precious life to live, and I am fortunate to live a life surrounded by women who lift me up.

For me, the definition of grace is the bounty of the relationships I have been blessed with in my life. I have come to believe my life is guided by a powerful and divine force. When I choose to align myself with this force, the best and most advantageous path unfolds before me.

I have learned there are no coincidences. Every event I experience, and every person I meet has been intentionally put in my path to help raise my level of consciousness. When we awaken to this fundamental truth, life becomes a true adventure—a spiritual adventure.

I truly believe that, more than anything else, my commitment to live a spiritually-based life has been the source of my external success. The more I surrender my will to God, the less I've had to worry about how to achieve my goals and live my purpose. Instead, the path finds me. Grace leads me to the exact events and experiences I need at precisely the right time.

Bio

Sherri Elliott-Yeary is a storyteller and a lover of words. She shares personal stories that lift our spirits, open our hearts, and offer us ways to create greater meaning in our lives. The driving force of her life and her work is the deep desire to live a life of meaning while growing spiritually and serving others. Sherri's coaching, speaking, and teachings are based on her personal journey and explore how, as individuals, we can come together and co-create a deeper sense of meaning in the world. To learn more about Sherri, visit: www.generationalguru.com, or contact her at 469-971-3663.

The Power Of Gratitude
By Sherri Elliott-Yeary

*"We tend to forget that happiness doesn't come as a result
of getting something we don't have, but rather of
recognizing and appreciating what we do have."* ~
Fredrick Koenig

For as long as I could remember, ever since I was a small child, I was mesmerized by butterflies. I love how they appear to float effortlessly and look so delicate and beautiful. As a butterfly emerges from its cocoon, it struggles and strains to free itself. This struggle is essential to strengthen its wings and shrink its body. Otherwise, the butterfly's wings would be weak, its distended body ungainly, and it would never be able to fly gracefully.

Butterflies everywhere that endure this struggle are rewarded with the glorious adventure of exploration, flying from blossom to blossom.

As women, we are constantly emerging from our cocoons—struggling and straining to become free, strong, and beautiful. Growth of any kind cannot occur without enduring some pain and discomfort. And with the lesson of the butterfly, we must acknowledge that cocoons don't fly.

I have tried on numerous occasions to move through this process quickly because it's painful, but without the experience we miss out on the rewards. As a child who grew up in a dysfunctional home where neglect and abuse were a daily norm, I felt like I was a survivor by the age of 12. When

I was adopted by the Ford family, they showed me what true love and belonging meant. They gave a troubled 12-year-old girl a chance to grow up normal, no longer worried about where she would sleep.

I had my daughter at a young age, and by the time she was nine years old, we moved from Canada to Dallas, Texas. When she was in her first year of college, she moved away from home. I missed her, but I knew this was a journey both of us had to experience.

Within six months of being away at school, Khirsten had lost a lot of weight—probably 40 pounds—and had developed bad acne. I was clueless to what was actually going on; I thought she wasn't eating enough. When asked, her response was that she had been studying a lot and did not remember to eat. I believed her. She gave me the answer she knew I wanted to hear—everything was okay.

Soon after, I discovered she had been using methamphetamines (meth) for almost a year. She was introduced to meth by a "friend" at school who told her that it would give her extra energy to study and help her lose weight.

Fast forward a few months, I received a call from Khirsten's apartment manager advising me her apartment was under surveillance by the Drug Enforcement Agency. I was shocked and terrified all at the same time.

When I tried to talk with Khirsten about her addiction, she would clam up. In fact, she threw me out of her apartment—the one I was paying for—while she skipped her classes. I eventually took her car away so she could not hurt herself or anyone else, since she was letting her boyfriend (aka "drug dealer") use the car to deliver drugs!

Prior to Khirsten going to college, I made the decision to leave my corporate role, started a human resource consulting practice, and started writing my first book, *Ties to Tattoos: Turning Generational Differences into a Competitive Advantage.* I was so scared, unable to sleep or eat with the fear my phone would ring with the news that Khirsten had been arrested, or worse, that she had overdosed or was dead.

My brother Terry was visiting from Canada and we took Khirsten on a trip to San Antonio. She was awfully thin, and the intensity of her need for a fix became evident, which resulted in uncontrollable fits of rage at times.

Terry and I were both concerned she was so far gone that neither of us could reach her. At this point, she had been fired by my client for using in the bathroom while at work, and she regularly hurled drug test kits at me from across the room because, as she assured me, she wasn't using anymore. Since Khirsten was no longer a minor, I couldn't commit her to treatment, and she certainly wasn't willing to go voluntarily.

When we dropped her off at her apartment, we noticed her door had been smashed in, and her place had been destroyed. The drug dealer had broken in and stolen everything she owned, including the car I had just given back to her with her pit bull, Mia!

In that moment, I hit my bottom—never mind her bottom—and informed her that if she didn't go to treatment,

I would no longer pay to support her while watching her destroy herself.

The day I left my only child, at age twenty-one, in a treatment center in Calgary, Canada, I told her how much I loved her, but I also made it crystal clear if she walked out of treatment, she was on her own. The good news is this was January, and it was frigid cold outside, so I thought she might factor that in.

I was barely able to keep my consulting business afloat while trying to survive Khirsten's addiction. I understood there were things I could change and things I couldn't, but the quality of my life would always depend, not on external circumstances, but my inner strength. Thankfully, I was referred to Al-Anon, a program for families of alcoholics/addicts, and it is in those rooms that I found peace through connection.

Out of our journey from her addiction, I learned the value of life and to appreciate and cherish the everyday moments of peace and joy.

My daughter's journey with her addiction is not over, but she is fighting to stay clean, and for that, I am forever grateful.

Bio

Sherri Elliott-Yeary is a storyteller and a lover of words. She shares personal stories that lift our spirits, open our hearts, and offer us ways to create greater meaning in our lives. The driving force of her life and her work is the deep desire to live a life of meaning while growing spiritually and serving others. Sherri's coaching, speaking, and teachings are based on her personal journey and explore how, as individuals, we can come together and co-create a deeper sense of meaning in the world. To learn more about Sherri, visit: www.generationalguru.com, or contact her at 469-971-3663.

Better Or Bitter: The Choice Is Yours
By Sherri Elliott-Yeary

"You have to find what sparks a light in you so that you, in your own way, can illuminate the world." ~ Oprah Winfrey

If you have ever been used, abused, deceived, misunderstood, forgotten, cheated on, or taken advantage of, you know what it's like to be burned. Most of us have had some of these painful experiences in our lives at one time or another.

When I was twelve years old, my great uncle, Neil, who has since passed away, molested me. He stole my childhood innocence and left me unable to be comfortable in a man's presence until I opened up and worked through it with a trauma counselor later in life.

Why do we hurt ourselves long after the offender has left? Why is it that we turn anger inward and continue to inflict pain on ourselves? Why do we overeat, hoping it will make us feel better when it only leaves us overweight and unhealthy? Why do we overspend, buying things we don't need to numb the pain?

I have tried all the above: I shopped—and never wore most of what I bought—to fill that void, until twenty years ago when I realized I was 150 pounds overweight and in debt.

As a result of overeating, I created insulation around myself so that men would not be attracted to me; it made me feel safe and protected.

I knew if I was going to free myself from my childhood trauma, I needed to take matters into my own hands and seek help.

Help came in many forms over the years—I read self-help books, worked with a therapist, and attended a multitude of workshops. Honestly, the best healing work came from a place deep inside myself, once I was able and willing to acknowledge I had a problem.

Because of the healing work I did, I can now look back at the hurtful actions I inflicted on myself and put them in my past. I am no longer a helpless, chubby young girl. I now have tools and resources, through my relationship with God and the power of His word, to help me close the wounds of the past.

Over eight years ago, I felt like I was staring into a dark abyss. To the outside world, my life looked great. I was married to the man of my dreams, or so I thought, had a successful career as an author and motivational speaker, and was living an amazing life traveling the world doing what I love.

On the inside, my marriage was crumbling. I still remember that ache in my stomach as he told me he wanted a divorce, and we had to sell our home because he was behind on payments—and, oh yeah, I was no longer welcome at our dental practice because my presence during the divorce was too uncomfortable for him.

I wondered if my heart would ever heal. I wanted to know if my life would ever get back to "normal."

One day early in my separation, a close friend reached out for some career advice, and in my heartache and stress, I yelled at her. Seeing the pain and shock in her eyes as I projected my pain onto her woke me up.

In that moment, I decided that I would do whatever it took to heal my heart. I would dig into the pain and mystery of this maze called "getting divorced" and find my way through it. I vowed I would use this experience not as an ending point in my life, but as a critical turning point that would help me find my purpose, my worth, and my calling.

The decision I made to do what it takes to *thrive* and not simply *survive* my divorce has been a guiding principle for me ever since.

I dedicated myself to intensive and thorough personal leadership and transformation studies. I trained with some of the world's foremost transformational teachers and became a certified life coach. I was intent on living a Zen life that included embracing my sensuality, and started my blog series, *Zensual Gal*. I wanted to reconnect to the sensual side of myself I had long overlooked as a result of my divorce.

I am currently working on the final edits of my latest book, *69 of My Dirtiest Secrets*. This book has been in the making for seven years and is now ready to be shared with the world. It has taken me a long time to publicly write and share on this sensitive topic as a survivor.

Of course, it hasn't always been a bed of roses. I have my moments of doubt and fear, but I have learned the tools I can apply with confidence to help me break out of my comfort zone. I feel the fulfillment that comes with creating a life and business that reflects what I feel my life's purpose truly is—to empower others to see and express their highest potential.

Looking back, I see that my divorce was indeed a turning point. I do feel grateful for it now because it launched me on a journey to discover the woman that I was truly meant to become.

In my work today and through my businesses, I am committed to passing on the wisdom I have learned to others. I work with some amazing and inspiring clients. I feel blessed and honored to be with them on their path.

If you're ready to learn how to transform your divorce challenge into a life-transforming opportunity, this is for you. If you're ready to stop surviving and start *thriving*, I would be delighted to support you!

Bio

Sherri Elliott-Yeary is a storyteller and a lover of words. She shares personal stories that lift our spirits, open our hearts, and offer us ways to create greater meaning in our lives. The driving force of her life and her work is the deep desire to live a life of meaning while growing spiritually and serving others. Sherri's coaching, speaking and training are based on her personal journey and explores how, as individuals, we can come together and co-create a deeper sense of meaning in the world. To learn more about Sherri, visit: www.generationalguru.com or contact her at 469-971-3663.

My Saving Grace
By Suzanne Harmony

Gratitude is what keeps me here. If you're anything like me, you understand the frustrations of being one of those persons who has an undiagnosed ailment. Sometimes you get plunked into the category of being a hypochondriac, but the pain is real and you know it. Sometimes it's beyond imaginable.

What is my saving grace?

Gratitude.

For years I was encouraged to document the pain. What brings it on? What am I eating? How am I sleeping? What's happening in the world around me? Wow! What an amazing tool to bring a suffering person into a dark, deep depression. It was wonderfully successful, so, when I noticed that pattern, I stopped it.

What did I do to replace it?

I began my gratitude journal, and that saved me. I began at the end of each day to write down at least three things that I was grateful for—three simple things, even at the end of a miserable, unbearable, unbelievably painful migraine day. Yes, I am a migraine sufferer. Occasionally things got worse than only the migraines. Some pain varied and fell into the category of fibromyalgia. When I applied my gratitude practice, it helped. I realized that I became calm. It didn't necessarily take away the pain, but it took away my deep awareness of it. I became serene. I became peaceful in that pain. I became aware of my blessings. It also helped me to sleep better. I became less focused on my pain and more aware that I'm here as a mother, a grandmother, a lover, a friend, a sister, and an aunt, and I had a purpose greater than to exist in pain. Wow! What a saving grace.

This was the beginning of my healing journey. Gratitude reignited my passion and expanded my purpose—as a healer, ironically. I am a Reiki Master, an all-sentient (psychic) and medium, an angel intuitive, and a spiritual guide. I was practicing all of these glorious modalities and going through life feeling somewhat confused, when I asked myself:

"If I'm blessed with these beautiful gifts, why am I suffering? What is the purpose of this physical pain?"

I believe it was to find gratitude. I learned that it was to live in a soulful way knowing that we are here as spiritual beings living a human life, and as human beings to experience a spiritual life. Gratitude, and the fulfillment that it brings, was my spiritual reminder that we're soulful beings. Our soulful purpose is to move forward even when this human body challenges us. This is what I learned through gratitude. Yes, we're here as teachers—teachers to help people expand and teachers to help others to learn and grow. Sometimes we're the experiment to find our soulful, peaceful place in gratitude.

I believe that we come to this great, beautiful earth to live our lives as human beings with a soul purpose, finding our spiritual strengths, and living mental, emotional, physical, and spiritual lives to blend it all and find harmony from chaos. Through gratitude, we can get there. Gratitude saved my life, and it continues to.

Upon waking, I say, "Thank you," and I am grateful to live another day with all the blessings that this day has to offer. I look to my left, and I am grateful that Mario is alive and well, and he will also share in another blessed day with me. Then, my dog licks my hand, and I am grateful that she is also here to bring us so much joy and loyal companionship. My meditation is also blessed with gratitude as I welcome the insights that this practice brings me; this is magnified with my prayer practice that follows. Yoga allows me to slowly, methodically, and spiritually connect to my soul, and for this, I am also grateful. This routine serves me well, and in turn, I am of great service to others. This is a form of self-care and gratitude which serves the highest good of all. Gratitude allows me to be my best self.

Gratitude blesses me with:

Peace
Clarity
Joy
Relief
Generosity
Calmness
Bliss
Creativity
Awareness
Selflessness
Serenity
Enthusiasm
Confidence
Grace
Harmony
Peaceful Sleep

Expressing gratitude doesn't have to be a formal affair. Choosing to be happy and excited for the day ahead is an expression of gratitude. Simply being kind to yourself and to those around you is another expression of gratitude. Of course, "Thank you," always helps too. Noticing the beauty around you and acknowledging the improvements in your life with a simple smile shows gratitude. Smiling instantly raises your vibration, and it is extremely contagious. Smile at someone—I guarantee that person will smile back, and your spirits will be lifted. Singing is equally as gratifying, uplifting, and magical. We're all too familiar with the amusement of an "earworm."

There are multitudes of journals and pens available in which you can jot down your gratitude. This is the choice for me because I love to write. I love journals and fancy pens, and expressing my gratitude is such a relief. (One of my daughters has already "claimed" my journals when I die. I love my children.) Sending cards, letters, notes, texts, e-mails, messages of appreciation, or "I'm thinking of you," are also wonderful ways to show gratitude.

Gratitude is also expressed through acts of kindness, such as:

Helping a neighbor
Volunteering
Paying it forward
Donating to a charity
Mentoring
Replacing the toilet paper
Putting the toilet lid down
Doing the dishes without being asked to do them
Being on time

Keeping your room clean
Recycling
Ride-sharing
Self-care

You'll discover that sincere gratitude is a gift that you give yourself. You'll realize that as you acknowledge all that you are thankful for, your spirit becomes enlightened, and you begin to attract the spirit and souls of similar energy into your life. Your life will improve. The more gratitude that you express, the more you have to be thankful for! It's that simple.

Thank you.

Bio

Suzanne is an international bestselling author, a Reiki Master, an all-sentient (psychic) and medium, an angel intuitive, and an Emotional Freedom Technique (EFT) coach. Her passionate purpose is to empower others to strive, thrive, and recover through forgiveness and shared wisdom. Her two books, *Leap of Faith: From Fear to Fulfillment*, and *Because I Didn't Tell*, (pen-name I. Katchastarr) demonstrate her dedication to helping turn tragedy to triumph. She shares this enthusiasm with numerous authors in two other collaborative books with As You Wish Publishing, and a solo book as well. Fun time is spent with her grandchildren. You can reach Suzanne at HarmonyHelps.ca.

Apartment 509
By Suzanne Rochon

When gratitude is a daily practice, it is difficult, if not virtually impossible, to choose one story to write about. As I look back on what I consider to be a relatively cherished and good life, every day holds a story of gratitude. While I could write about all of the wonderful things I have experienced, accomplished, or acquired over a half-century, the practice of gratitude has led me to an expanded understanding of what this means to me. I am incredibly thankful for all that I have in my life and for the people I love and who love me, however, the measure of deep gratitude as I have come to understand it is whether one can recognize, accept, and hold the inherent value of the moment despite what life delivers. A line in a poem called *The Invitation*, by Oriah Mountain Dreamer has long resonated with me: "I want to know if you can see beauty even when it is not pretty every day. And if you can source your own life from its presence."

My story of gratitude is about seeing the magic in the most difficult of human experiences.

I grew up with an aunt who was more like the sister I never had. Over the years, we remained close, even during moments when time or priorities didn't permit the regularity of contact I would have liked. When I occasionally visited her small apartment in a senior's complex, the visits were short and always pleasant as we caught up on the mundane. Over time, as her disease progressed and with new, increasingly serious diagnoses, a long, healthy, and vibrant

298

life was not the hand she would be dealt. Naturally, because of proximity and of our relationship, she reached out to me as she became less independent, and required more support.

Thankfully, life afforded me the ability to spend more time with her, helping out as I could.

As the winter of 2018 had frozen to its harshest reality, so had her medical conditions. What began as occasional support when she wasn't feeling well rapidly progressed to daily requirements. As a determined and strong-willed person, it was challenging for her to ask for help, so when she did, it was a sure indication that she could no longer manage on her own.

Respecting her fervent desire to remain in her home as long as possible, I knew I would be called to provide progressive care and eventually, palliative care. This was not an obligation; it was a conscious decision grounded in deep gratitude for the trust I had been afforded to accompany the walk on the sacred path back to one's maker. Knowing how potentially difficult the coming weeks or maybe even months would be as I juggled work, family, and this new unknown role, I decided to enter into the commitment with curiosity and openness. I made the conscious choice to be present to what the moment offered and to be a witness to the experience.

As the walls of her life closed in, the walls of Apartment 509 formed the container for all that needed to be said, heard, felt, seen, observed, and experienced. People came and went, some to say hello after many years, some to say goodbye, some to say thank you for the memories, some to say I love you, some to say I forgive you, some to be forgiven, some whose curiosity won over their common sense, some whose private conversations have yet to be revealed, and one who had enough love and courage in his heart to break free from the chains which had estranged him.

In the dialectical busyness of maintaining a sense of normalcy while preparing for one's final dance, I noticed how routines are crucial to the illusion of control over one's life, how television can numb and distract from reality, how filters are quickly forgotten when longevity isn't considered, how memories become a beacon of light in a sea of suffering, how laughter can lighten the spirit, how saying nothing is just as powerful as saying something, how rifts can be mended when tomorrow isn't guaranteed, how natural it is to be vulnerable when you have nothing to lose, how the tears we shed make room for more to come, how the line between selflessness and selfishness is easily blurred, and how frail the human mind is as it succumbs to the inevitable. I was *blessed* to have witnessed the realization of one's impermanence, the fear of facing the unknown, the pain of impending loss, a mother's undying love for her adult child's well-being amidst her fear and suffering, the unique coping mechanisms humans employ to protect themselves from pain and discomfort, the resiliency of the human spirit, the importance of lifelong friendships, the innocence of childhood in the face of endings, and beginnings which could have never been imagined. This is what I am eternally grateful for.

Being the witness rather than the actor in the play of life affords the benefit of space between stimulus and response, which is fertile ground for gratitude. I have come to realize that gratitude is available to me, irrespective of the external event, as long as I allow presence to permeate my experience.

Under the blue blanket with the satin edge with your one and only at your side as the near darkest hour of the night came to take you, I held a deep sense of gratitude for the gift you had given me that only a mother could understand. Thank you.

Bio

Suzanne Rochon is the creator of Imagine Life Solutions Counseling and Psychotherapy. As a registered social worker, she is in awe of the resiliency of the human spirit and feels immensely blessed to accompany other souls on their journey back to the self. With a background in holistic health practices, she is able to blend eastern and western approaches in her practice. Suzanne enjoys a loving partnership with Joel, and is grateful beyond measure for her three sons, Max, Alex, and Jonah. You can reach Suzanne at www.imaginelifesolutions.ca

You Are The Path. The Path Is You!
By Tammy Hopkins

Why do we not cultivate and express gratitude every day? Perhaps the fast pace and multiple distractions of life have made it all too easy for us to forget how important gratitude is. We make statements on social media when we remember to be grateful or if we want to find happiness through gratitude. This is fine on the exterior, during those moments in life when all is going well. At those moments, it simply feels good to give thanks for our blessings.

How do you tell someone to be grateful when they have been diagnosed with cancer or a life-threatening disease, betrayed by a partner, lost a wife, husband, or child, or lost their home? How about someone who has been raped, lost their freedom, or lost their job? How do we find gratitude when so much pain, fear, anger, and loss are present? These feelings are overwhelming, and they can break us.

It's challenging to look for blessings during our suffering. We often look for a quick fix to take away the pain and confusion.

Countless self-help coaches have emerged, claiming to know the secrets—to fix your life, read this book, do that yoga, meditate, eat well, or try an herbal remedy. All these quick fixes may alleviate the pain, but can we truly change?

Sustainable change involves more than awareness and action; it involves recognition, love, and risk. We can't run away from our lives, no matter how hard we try. It is scary to face yourself, your fears, your emotions. It takes courage to make choices that will heal the pain each situation has presented. The practice of gratitude provides healing. Gratitude opens our hearts. It is a skill that we need to practice daily and cultivate over time.

It's a challenge when we experience conflicting emotions. It's difficult to be simultaneously miserable and grateful.

However, it is nearly impossible to feel fear, negativity, worry, and pain when we are engaged in gratitude. Gratitude lives in the state of love—love for oneself and love for life's journey. This is a process you learn over time. It is a daily practice to slow down and pay attention to yourself, to heal, forgive, and accept. It is a time to reflect and to let go.

In my work, I offer professional support and guidance to hundreds of people each year. I encourage them to step into their power, to get what they need and want out of relationships, and to heal themselves. I fully understand that the answers come from the essence of pure love and gratitude.

I used to lie down at night thinking about all the things I might not be doing right with my life and all the things I was missing out on. I struggled with setting boundaries and frequently returned to relationships that did not serve me well. I was discouraged, disconnected, and had a diminished sense of self. The ongoing struggle to live an authentic life consumed me. I experienced the pain of wanting to do life differently but not knowing how.

I now know what it's like to be on the other side of this longing, to have the freedom to express my feelings without self-imposed barriers, to have a life where I wake up feeling as though there are not enough hours in the day to experience all the amazing things surrounding me.

I can engage with a magical force field that encompasses me, all of me. Being able to share it with you is of utmost importance.

I now go to bed at night thinking about how blessed and grateful I am, and I think about how I can give back by serving others. Best of all, I have space in my mind, love in my heart, and wholeness in my entire being. It feels so powerful to remember who I am and what a gift I am! I am love.

As a result of my journey through Ancestral Regression Therapy (ART), I now live fully in passionate joy. I communicate better in my relationships. I can experience true intimacy. I can be vulnerable and fully clear. And I have time for nourishing self-care, which inspires me to pursue a life being more aware, grateful, and purposeful.

Through ART, I have learned to navigate and experience a way of life that has transformed the way I relate to others and myself. I can help open this gateway so you, too, can experience the realm of the true light of love.

I want this kind of life for everyone. That's why I do this work! I want to help you remember who you are, without the entanglements from the past. Through our shared journey in ART, I can help you set yourself free and rise to your highest potential.

No matter what is going on in the world, some attuned people will see you when you dare to shine brightly. This is why I became a spiritual empowerment coach. I love helping my clients create true, authentic, badass relationships in which they can hold strong and healthy boundaries with self and with others while creating a life they love!

I believe our power exists when we ride the wave of divine energy in every moment.

I will support you as we tap into your highest divine self, empowering you to embody this wave and energizing the flow toward your true spirit.

Find freedom from self-imposed barriers and self-hate! Find freedom from ancient, painful stories so you can finally leave behind the old you. Your purpose on Planet Earth and in this boundless existence is to evolve, to transform, to experience your radical aliveness, and to awaken to your true nature.

Step into the life you have always wanted or into the relationship you know you want and deserve. We are each greater than we might have been led to believe. Let's connect. Let's embrace. Let's create.

In gratitude to the spirit.

Bio

Tammy Hopkins is an empath, medium, Reiki practitioner, hypnotherapist, healer, and spiritual empowerment coach who bridges the gap between human and spirit. Since birth, Tammy has been an apprentice of what she calls spirit, otherwise known as energy, the Universe, God, Buddha, and so on—a power that is greater than us. By using her perceptive skills of clairsentience, clairvoyance, clairaudience, clairscent, clairgustance, clairtangency, clairempathy, and channeling, she can feel, see, hear, smell, taste, touch, and channel as she interprets energy and messages from spirit. Tammy is the founder of Ancestral Regression Therapy (ART). You can reach Tammy at www.mayahana.com.

Two Worlds Of Gratitude
By Tara Ijai

I grew up an all-American girl. My younger brother and sister and I were raised in a small town in upstate New York. It had a population of about 3,000 people, and the mayor was the barber. It was an extremely rural community with no diversity. Many people who lived there worked at the prison, like my father, or had small dairy farms. There was a lot of history, and people lived there for generations. My father had moved us from another small town when I was in the sixth grade, for his job, and to be honest, I never felt like we fit in. We were "newbies," and it seemed like everyone knew each other or was related to each other. Upstate New York never fit my mischievous side, my rebellious side, and definitely didn't allow me to seek all of the wonders of the world. Maybe from working in a prison environment, my family always erred on the side of caution or even a little fear. I remember asking my mom once if we could go to New York City, and she said, "Oh, you don't want to go to the city. It's dangerous!" I lived in upstate New York for 24 years and still never visited the city.

When I got the opportunity in 1996 to move to Phoenix, Arizona, I couldn't wait! I wanted something different. When I moved here, I couldn't believe all of the different types of people—my first best friends were Vietnamese. I met every kind of ethnicity, race, and whatever label you want to put on people, and they were fascinating! It wasn't long after that that I was introduced to people of the Muslim faith. I needed to know more, and the more I studied, the more it spoke to me. I had never been a religious person per se, but I would definitely say I was always a deep thinker or soul searching. Someone said once that we are all looking to fill our "God spot." Those words always stuck with me.

After studying Islam and meeting some amazing spiritual mentors, I took the shahada, or testimony of faith. I embraced Islam in its entirety, which meant I chose to wear the headscarf. How little did I know that a 40-inch square piece of cloth on your head would make you foreign, political, and "othered" all at the same time. I chose the headscarf to be identified as a Muslim woman. How naïve was I to believe that the world would see me through my usual filter? How ironic that this new lifestyle that gave me so much joy and light would appear dark, foreign, and scary to others around me. I was 26 years old when I embraced Islam, and I can assure you my parents thought and perhaps hoped it was a phase. I converted two months prior to 9/11. Yup, I always had a gift with timing. My father called me from New York in tears moments after the first plane hit in absolute fear, pleading with me to remove my headscarf. He was completely terrified of what would happen to me. I told him that I had made this decision, and how could I simply set it aside because life had suddenly gotten difficult? I would be lying if I said I wasn't afraid, but I chose this.

When I reflect 19 years later upon those decisions in my life, this series of events, it occurs to me that, although I was tested at great lengths many times, I am grateful. I'm grateful for the unique experiences and nuances that I have been privy to by placing that 40-inch square piece of cloth on my head. I now understand there is a thinly-veiled line between being feared or not, understood or not, foreign or not. I may have never had the privilege of having someone lean directly over me and ask my husband if I "spoke English" without ever acknowledging my existence, or commenting on how fluent my English is when I speak to someone I have met. It is only through this journey from an "all-American white girl" that I could ever begin to understand the slightest of microaggressions that happen to people of different races, religion, and sexual orientation each and every day. The experiences were not all negative. It is ironic that by covering up my head, my mind has expanded, and I have met some of the most beautiful and diverse people. I began to meet people who came from places that I had never even heard about, and they shared stories of their journeys. I learned about another world that I didn't know existed, and it was beautiful. I met families that had fled wars and were so kind and gentle you would never have known unless you were in a space to connect with them. I saw humanity so much differently.

At times I felt like I was a soul caught between two different worlds. Too American to be the "right" kind of Muslim, and yet too Muslim to now be an all-American girl. Maybe it was this incessant conversation inside my head that allowed me to feel gratitude once again as I finally realized it wasn't about people or the box they placed me in, it was about me and the need to place myself in a box. I didn't need to merge two ideas of who I think the world thought I was and instead, I could just be me in all of the divine ways I show up. Maybe that 40-inch square cloth was a catalyst that propelled me into being my best me by placing me into situations that would have forever been unknown. Maybe it took me all of that to realize that I am the most epic kind of all-American girl—one at peace within and strong as hell—and I definitely think it's high time to visit New York City.

Bio

Tara Ijai is a love rebel who rebels against hate and negativity. She helps spread love in the world using her heart-shaped sunglasses as a tool and reminder to make the world a better place. Her passion is connecting with people one smile and conversation at a time. You can reach Tara at www.myloveglasses.com.

Gratitude, From The Guides
By AJ Cavanagh and Thomas Workman

For the past several years, we have channeled a group of non-physical beings we simply call "the Guides." The divine messages and insights they share with us have been profound and life-changing. We are honored and grateful to deliver their messages about the divine nature of the universe with the world.

Many of their messages focus on the subject of joy. The reason is simple—most humans are not living as joyfully as they could be. Joy, the Guides explain, is our divine right. When we experience joy, we also experience a higher vibration, which tunes us to expanded consciousness and awareness. In short, when we are in joy, we are at our very best.

Gratitude is also a high vibrational frequency. So, it is not surprising that the topic of gratitude comes up often in our conversations about joy. Our Guides state that gratitude is a vital ingredient of a life lived in joy. What the Guides have taught us about how we tune to gratitude, however, has forever changed the way we think about and practice it.

There are a lot of mixed messages about gratitude today. In the west, gratitude is often seen as a social norm or courtesy while also layered with religious and spiritual expectations. This makes gratitude often feel like a moral obligation rather than a natural response to the acknowledgment of blessings in our daily lives. We learn from early childhood that we should always express gratitude, especially if we hope to receive more. But sometimes, the sincerity of our gratitude becomes less important than our expression of it.

The Guides discuss gratitude quite differently:

Gratitude is the acknowledgment of a gift you have personally received. You can appreciate many things that are not yours, but gratitude is for those gifts from divine that are specifically for you. Gratefulness is thankfulness, yes. But it is more because it is the realization of the positive things that are happening for your benefit alone. It is a step on the pathway to joy. You choose to discover gratitude daily.

The Guides have revealed four points to the aspect of gratitude:

Gratitude is a Thought That We Choose

The Guides tell us that divine source does not see gratitude as an emotion or an emotional response. While we often describe gratitude as a feeling, the Guides describe it as a thought. Gratitude is the conscious recognition that we have received something of worth. In other words, the vibration of gratitude is not the result of the gift, but the realization that we have been given something of value to us. The difference is subtle, but critical, and explains why some can feel immense gratitude for the smallest of things, while others seem ungrateful for incredible blessings.

The key is in what we consider to be a gift. The Guides use the word "gift" intentionally. A gift is something given to us without payment. There is no obligation for us to reciprocate or compensate for a gift. You cannot earn a gift, and you owe nothing for it. Real gifts can only be accepted or ignored.

But first, these gifts have to be recognized or brought into our consciousness. The Guides explain that our most foundational beliefs shape our recognition of gifts. The way that we see our lives, ourselves, and our world determines whether we recognize a thing, event, or person's action as a gift or as a warning, obligation, challenge, or test. Seeing the gift is more than having positive attitudes or thoughts about the things around us. Our beliefs about giving and receiving, worthiness, obligation, and fairness all come to play in our recognition. The good news is that our thoughts and beliefs are a choice—and like all choices, we can change them when they do not serve us. When we struggle with gratitude, there is great opportunity to consider our thoughts and beliefs about who we are, the kind of world we wish to create, and how we want to live.

Gratitude is Separate from Appreciation

Before gratitude, there is a broader experience of appreciation. Appreciation is also a thought. We experience appreciation when we recognize and acknowledge the positive aspects of a thing, event, or person. A simple example is the recognition of something (or someone's) beauty.

Our Guides remind us that beauty is in the eye of the beholder, and that is exactly true about the things we appreciate. What we consider to be positive is always based on our perspective. One person may appreciate the practicality of a house's design or style when others describe it as bland, or appreciate someone's sense of humor even when others grimace. Therefore, appreciation is less about the object and is far more about our perceptual focus. What is critical is recognizing how our perception is focused. Are we quick to see the flaws and limitations, or do we first see the positive aspects? Appreciation is also a choice—and one that truly affects our level of vibration every day.

With this understanding of appreciation, it is clear why the relationship between appreciation and gratitude matters. The Guides tell us that it is only when we appreciate all things, including the things that are not ours, that we can then experience gratitude for the gifts given specifically for our benefit.

Abraham, another group of non-physical entities channeled by Esther Hicks, suggests a daily practice of creating a list of the positive aspects of the people, places, situations, or events taking place around you. They call it "rampages of appreciation." Our Guides made a point about that practice with the question: How is the first thought you have as you perceive your world serving you? What perception would serve you better?

Appreciation always serves us well, because the more we find to appreciate, the more we see all of our many gifts. The result of practicing appreciation has for us revolutionized our sense of abundance and joy. The world is full of beautiful things to appreciate.

Gratitude is a Response to Divine Love

Perhaps the most important teaching from the Guides about gratitude is that the gifts we receive are evidence of how deeply and thoroughly loved we are by divine source, or creator, or God, or however you conceive the center of all that is. That love, in a nutshell, has only one intention—our greatest and highest good.

It doesn't always seem like many of the things that show up in our lives, from illness to financial challenges, to traffic or the endless array of things that we can worry about, are gifts that intend our greatest and highest good. It often feels quite the opposite. But the premise that the Guides return us to is that there is only love. In other words, we must know that love powers all universal energy. There is no equal force of hate, no power in malice, no divine plan to punish or destroy us. The universe only expands, and only love can create. Love for the creation, in all of its diverse form, is the exact nature of the divine source.

And so, the job we lose might be the best gift we receive, as in time, we realize it opened up the opportunity to pick up our dream again. The house offer that falls through may also be the gift that takes years for us to realize its benefit to us, or the illness that forces you to stretch your trust or confront your fear may be the blessing we have needed. Ultimately, we recognize everything as a blessing because we know that the nature of the universe is love.

Several years ago, we discovered a piece of land with a home on it that seemed the ideal place for our residence and spiritual center, Camp Joy Ranch. The location, near the mountains north of Phoenix, seemed perfect. The house sat on a small hill, and though it needed a great deal of renovation, we saw its potential. For weeks, we kept jumping over the many hurdles to making a winning offer, convinced that this was where our dreams would materialize. But on the day that we planned to make our offer, we learned the property had sold.

To say we were disappointed was an understatement. We lamented the lost opportunity and the dashing of our dreams, not quite sure what the divine had in mind for us. We could not imagine that divine source was only starting to prepare our true gift. We needed to realize that "no" to the property was not a "no" to the dream itself unless it was not the dream that would lead to our greatest and highest good. So, we continued to visualize Camp Joy Ranch, whenever and wherever it would manifest.

Approximately two months later, we found a much better property with a newly renovated home, and upon our inspection, we both knew that this property was the real gift. Not surprisingly, our offer was accepted, and the sale proceeded in record speed without a single bump along the road. The home and spiritual center we have today is more than we could have imagined and is something we express gratitude for almost every day. It is truly the perfect gift.

The lesson for us is to trust the love of the universe and exclaim "this or something better" whenever we articulate our desires, knowing that the divine always has the best in mind for us.

One of the ways to keep ourselves in gratitude is with a game we call "Evidence of Well-Being." We start the day, reminding ourselves that we are beloved creations of divine love. We set our intention to see, throughout the day, the many gifts of people, places, and events that the universe has set for our best good. As the day progresses, we go about our lives. Often in bed, when we're about to fall asleep, we reflect on the evidence we collected, both large and small, the things that brought us well-being. It may merely be the telephone call or text from a friend that made us smile, the great conversation with a coworker that made our day easier, the train that came on time, or the beauty of the setting sun. All of it is evidence that our well-being is the intention of our divine source.

Gratitude is a Spiritual Practice That Benefits the Entire Universe

The Guides have told us that the vibration of gratitude alone leads to an expansion of our everyday consciousness. It serves to bring into our lives more of the things that bring us joy. And as we experience joy, we add joy to the universal consciousness. Our vibration of gratitude adds to the bright light that enables joy in all realms and helps expand creation itself.

The practice of gratitude, therefore, is a practice of creation. It is a spiritual practice benefiting both the divine and us.

Gratefulness remains the natural consequence of our knowledge that the universe is always taking care of us. That knowledge grounds us when we are anxious. It gives us perspective when we have fear. We have the power to refocus our everyday problems or perplexing circumstances. Most importantly, gratefulness helps us allow in new opportunities and find the wonder of life itself. The Guides tell us that gratitude is a choice we make daily. For us, that choice is always one that enriches our lives and brings many blessings.

Bio

AJ Cavanagh and Thomas Workman are intuitive channels, authors, and Joy Practitioners™. They are the founders of Camp Joy Ranch, a spiritual center in Phoenix, Arizona. Together they channel "the Guides"—a collection of non-physical beings from various spiritual realms who wish to help all humans expand their joy in body, mind, and spirit. Through the Guides, AJ and Tom offer joy coaching sessions for individuals and groups and lead workshops and circles on a variety of spiritual practices. You can sign up for their newsletter, sign up for events, or contact AJ and Tom directly at www.campjoyranch.com.

Consciously Participate In Your Own Delicious Expansion!
By Tiffany Dubec

G rowing up in the Bible belt of central Texas, my idea of gratitude was a fleeting theory based mainly on the idea that "things could always be worse, so be happy with what you have." Be humble. Work hard. Be grateful. Grateful you're alive. Grateful you have food, shelter, family, clothing—the basics. Because there are "starving kids in Africa."

It was more of a notion than a feeling—more a concept than a practice.

As I evolved on my spiritual path, I shifted my perception of gratitude to a core feeling of appreciation. A choice. An honoring of my life and the beauty of my experiences. A visceral feeling that taps into the energy, the juice that inspires change, growth, love, and transformation.

I now teach people how to harness the power of appreciation and rewire the brain to seek out things to appreciate. Only then, will you consistently live a life of pure gratitude.

My intention with this article is to give you a glimpse into the influence of appreciation, and how a small shift in mindset and habit can transform your life and allow pleasing manifestations to follow. (Note: For the sake of ease, I will use gratitude and appreciation interchangeably).

In the quantum field of energy, gratitude and appreciation hold one of the highest frequencies measured. This means, when you're under that influence, you are fully tuning in to your natural state of well-being—your true default setting. You are also creating a clear connection to receive guidance from your inner being!

From that place, you're able to move forward and make decisions, have experiences, and feel emotions from a higher vibrational set point. It is a form of pre-paving. Preparing your vibrational atmosphere before the manifestations or conditions arrive.

Your motion forward is inevitable. You can't help it! But you are not here to merely go through the motions. You are here to experience outrageous joy!

You quite literally have the ability to mold and shape the various areas of your life based on how you choose to think, believe, and feel! You are the creator of your reality!

According to the universal laws of quantum physics, the nervous system is basically a transmitter that sends out signals into the environment, and these "waves" of vibration attract similar waves that draw us to certain people and circumstances. Put simply, what you focus on, you feed. And that energy attracts more of the same. So, choosing to feel grateful often, will tune you in to receiving more to feel grateful for.

The field of neuroplasticity tells us that our brains are malleable, continuing to evolve as we respond to new experiences. This gives us the ability to create new patterns of thinking based on the situation. This means we can reshape our neuro-pathways by being intentional with our thoughts and using repetition for new connections of the brain to follow. So, practicing the new habit of gratitude will allow the brain to form new pathways, thus making it easier to feel grateful more often!

Okay, so the science is there, you're on board—now what? How do you leverage this power in your day to day life, and put it into motion?

You do this by meditating, creating a list of appreciation and positive aspects, and looking for things here and now that feel good when you look at them.

The key is to tap into the *feeling* of gratitude.

Find the emotion, and the manifestation is the momentum that will follow every single time!

Close your eyes and think of something you are grateful for. What do you see? Who do you see? Now choose the purest form of the emotion. Who/what evokes that the clearest? Now tune into the feeling—feel the lightness, the swelling of your heart, the openness of your body, the smile it evokes from your lips. Breathe in the energy of appreciation. Let it become a visceral, cellular, systematic experience! Allow it to build, where you feel like you will almost burst from happiness and gratitude. That is the power! Talk about it out loud, put it into words, create a rampage of gratitude, and get as detailed as feels good to you.

Ask yourself, "What is easy for me to appreciate right now in this moment?"

For me, it is sitting outside with my bare feet in the grass, soaking up vitamin D with meditation music playing, my dog lounging beside me, and my cat stretched out on my son's playhouse. The space to create.

Maybe you also appreciate the simple pleasures. Sunrises and sunsets. The taste of clean air and the bliss of deep breaths. The choice to choose freedom!

Maybe it's the gentle sway of your body to music. Cheeks being sore from laughing with a friend. The rush of exhilaration with a new love connection. The purity of petting an animal. The serenity of stillness. Exploring in nature. Sleeping in. Naps without guilt. Knowledge and information at your fingertips. The body's innate ability to heal. Wisdom with age. The freedom to change your mind.

Now take a deep breath and re-evaluate how you feel. You should feel lighter, relaxed, and most definitely happier! However, do not become discouraged if you're not feeling as chipper as you'd like. Like any new practice, it takes, well, practice.

And the brain will initially reject and discredit the new, improved information. Thank you, reticular activating system.

This is why repetition and consistency are crucial in creating a major positive shift in your life!

You have to change your mind before your life is going to change.

Words unlock our potential. And when paired with the pure essence of the emotion, *magic* happens. Appreciation is the avenue through which blessings sync up to you.

A consistent gratitude practice can be a game-changer for most, and one that will positively influence and uplift every aspect and level of your life physically, mentally, emotionally, and spiritually.

Choosing gratitude and living in that feeling is your superpower!

Bio

Tiffany Dubec is a doctor of chiropractic, energy medicine practitioner, and wellness educator. She specializes in Applied Kinesiology, energetic balancing, and emotion calibration technique. Part of her mission is to provide high-quality nutrigenomics that bio-hack the body and positively influence cellular expression! She is a passionate thought leader, providing therapies and tools for vibrational upliftment. Her desire is to influence people to realize and live their greatness! You can contact Dr. Tiffany Dubec, DC at adjust2lifechiropractic@gmail.com.

Planting A Garden Of Hope
Using Seeds Of Gratitude
By Dr. Tonya Featherston

I learned the power of gratitude by experiencing some of the toughest challenges in life. I used to think gratitude was all about family and being with the ones that you love, and then I lost two of the most important people in my life, my grandmother and my father. It was difficult to see my way to gratitude in those moments. I then started to believe that gratitude was all about accomplishing and obtaining things in life, but then I lost many of the things that I cherished the most. I now know the fullness of gratitude and understand that it's truly recognizing the value in all of life's experiences, the good and the bad.

Did you know that gratitude can be the secret to helping you live a happy, healthy life? Gratitude and appreciation are two of the highest emotional states that we can be in. It can be easy to find gratitude when life is good, and when things are going the way we want them to go. We live fast-paced lives and often use a lack of time as an excuse for not pausing and showing gratitude and appreciation for what we have in our lives. At some point, we have all tried to keep a gratitude journal or make weekly lists of the things we are grateful for. We all know how powerful having a personal gratitude practice can be, but sometimes it can be hard to keep it going.

When we face difficult times and tragedy in our lives, it can be even harder to embrace gratitude and be appreciative for all of the wonderful things that are happening. Right now, our world is completely changing as we navigate our way through this coronavirus pandemic. People are experiencing a range of emotions, from doubt to fear to panic. When you look around and see people dying, losing their jobs, children out of school for months, and people fearful that they will run out of personal resources, it can be hard to find gratitude. As we watch the news on television and check our social media news feed, the seeds of fear and doubt get planted in our minds. What if I'm off work for months? What if I run out of savings? What if someone in my family has the virus? What if I get the virus? As we continue to cultivate these seeds of fear and doubt, the quicker they will grow into deeply rooted weeds. When our minds run rampant with fear, the two best things to counter those thoughts are gratitude and appreciation. I encourage you during this season of uncertainty to be intentional about planting seeds of gratitude. There's no better time than ever to develop a daily gratitude practice. Gratitude makes your problems seem less daunting and more manageable.

Developing a daily gratitude practice is like planting a garden of hope. Let's think about what happens when we plant a typical flower garden. We put tiny little seeds in the ground, cover them with dirt, and patiently wait. We know that the flowers won't simply spring up overnight, we have to tend to the garden daily to get those flowers to grow. We tend to the garden by watering it, pulling weeds, and providing it with the sun it needs to grow. As you watch the garden, little by little, you start to see those flowers grow until they reach full bloom.

Planting a garden of hope is a similar process. When we create gratitude journals, boxes, and lists, those items are often tucked away where we can't see them, so we often lose sight of the practice. The key to sustaining a gratitude practice is to make it a living and breathing practice. So, let's bring your gratitude practice to life by planting a garden of hope!

The first thing we need to do is decide what method we will use to create our garden of hope. The method I most often recommend is creating a gratitude wall. Choose an open wall somewhere in your home that you frequently pass by. It could be in your living room, kitchen, bedroom, or anywhere you like. You can cover the wall with a large piece of paper or you can plant your seeds directly on the wall. To create your gratitude seeds, you can use sticky notes or paper shape cut-outs such as hearts, stars, or circles. Now it's time to plant some seeds in your garden. Sit quietly, close your eyes, put one hand on your heart, and ask yourself this question: What am I grateful for in this moment? Whatever comes to mind, write it down on your paper shapes and place it on the wall. Be intentional about doing this at least once a day. You can also add seeds to the garden randomly throughout the day as you pass the wall and are reminded of things that you are grateful for.

As the days pass, you will begin to see your garden of hope grow. Your gratitude wall will become a living garden of gratitude and appreciation. Our soul is nourished by the foods of gratitude, appreciation, love, laughter, and joy, but it all begins with gratitude. The more seeds of gratitude you plant, the more you will grow food for your soul. The more you nourish your soul, the quicker you will release doubt and fear and transform every area of your life. People who continuously plant seeds of gratitude have cultivated better health, better sleep, more happiness, better relationships, increased resilience, and a stronger immune system. Gratitude strengthens your heart, mind, body, and soul. My daily gratitude practice has changed my life tremendously, and it continuously reminds me to appreciate each new day and all the challenges and opportunities it brings. I hope this helps you find your way to making gratitude a daily part of your journey in life.

Bio

Dr. Tonya Featherston is an educational psychologist, wellness coach, and meditation teacher with a passion for sharing information about alternative wellness practices. She is the co-founder/Executive Director of The Center for Social Emotional Wellness, an organization that seeks to promote positive mental health in individuals, organizations, and communities. Dr. Tonya currently offers coaching and support groups for women who are seeking assistance with stress management and improving their overall mental health. She also offers guided imagery and meditations on her website and the Well Space Teacher Wellness App. She can be contacted at www.askdrtonya.com or by email at drtonya@centerforsew.com.

A Toast To Three-Legged Dogs
By Vanessa Plimley

I fumble into my bikini in the dark, feeling for the tags, so I don't wear it inside out again. Quietly, so as not to wake my husband, I fill my shoulder bag with a laptop and a phone, draping a long-sleeved shirt around the strap before adjusting my crutches. I clop out into the twinkling dark.

Hop, clop, hop, clop. I light some candles and cautiously inspect my shirt for scorpions.

I grin at the quickly fading stars, climb into my rocking chair with one foot propped on a stack of pillows and enjoy my tea, as night recedes and the quick tropical change to a new day begins.

Dawn is my favorite hour, especially in our heart-home of northern Nicaragua.

Life can be a bit wild here in the *campo*, and it's certainly not for everyone. We live in a place that is open-air except for the bedrooms. Bats sleep in the palm-frond roof, a resident skunk occasionally cruises through the kitchen, and opossums race each other in the ceiling of our spare room.

As dawn light sweeps across the sky, I see my dog finishing her perimeter check of our property. She stops and spends a moment hanging out with the rooster, Bartolito, and the cat, Mousing. They must have called a truce for the morning.

A swath of ants moves their eggs to a new location. Normally, this would not be weird, but they're coming from under our couch, moving through the kitchen and out beneath a rock by the BBQ. I cheer them on and snort at how stupid I must look, my mouth agape at the wonder of their efficiency. An industrial half-hour of work, and they are gone without a trace.

My attention is drawn outward, and I notice our neighbors' pig as she ambles down to the water's edge and rolls around happily in the tropical sea. A herd of escaped horses cruise the beach.

From the field behind us, grackles and turtledoves stop on the edge of our pool to wash their peanuts or worms. They fluff their feathers and bathe thoroughly before taking off to their secret home.

I notice and cherish all of these things. I've achieved one of my biggest life goals: to live in the tropics for chunks of the year. A simple life of flip flops, few clothes, and time to enjoy the special moments that are sometimes missed when living a busy life elsewhere.

This year, that lifestyle is somewhat different than expected. Three weeks ago, I badly sprained my ankle and have been in a cast ever since. Rehab will take months. My intention this trip was to build a new website, write more, and learn more songs on my ukulele, but the surf has been exceptionally good, and knowing myself, I would have let my goals slide if the Universe didn't have such an ironic sense of humor. Now I turn my focus to non-sport activities and shift my life into a more balanced rhythm.

My husband recently called me "Lucky." I've been plagued by health issues over the years, both illness and injury. I'm partially deaf, I've spent years on the floor with back injuries, I suffer from severe chronic migraines, and now there's a cast up to my knee. He jokingly describes me as his old one-eyed, ripped-ear blue heeler.

If I could describe myself, I'm like that truly stoked three-legged dog. Playing with her toys, hopping around, and still pumped about everything life has to offer: cheese, play, cuddles, repeat.

Our place is on a cliff, overlooking a beach where I can spy on everyone from my chair. A friend asked if I was losing my mind, watching everyone surf below me.

I replied with a contemplative no. Every morning, I list all the things I am thankful for: my supportive husband who's off work, and makes me belly-laugh often, to be in a country where I can get cheap healthcare, to live in a one-level house, and to have friends who stop by to draw on my cast, play music, and drink beer. I focus on only the things I can do and not let anything else in. .

There's a Native American legend of the two wolves within: one light, one dark, good and evil. They fight in every person, every day. The question, "Which one will win?" is answered, "The one you feed."

Like yoga or meditation, running, or playing an instrument, choosing which wolf will win is a great practice. With every choice, you decide which way to turn. Feed the light or feed the dark.

I still have a good cry on occasion as I watch the future I'd planned vaporize in front of me. I feel blessed that my reactions are increasingly rare or short-lived. I quickly reassess and come up with a new plan.

I got into life coaching to help others find perspective while facing deep challenges, to help them create a space where they can take a good look at their current situation, and hopefully clarify the steps that will move them in a direction that excites them and feels attainable.

I encourage my clients to create a practice of joy. Perhaps it's taking an extra five minutes in the morning, sipping coffee as the world wakens around them. Maybe it's a long walk in the fresh air with a dog trotting alongside. Maybe it's listing things to be thankful for, as they embark on their daily commute. It's amazing how one's perspective can shift toward the light with little time or effort.

So, as I rock happily in my chair, I honor this learned philosophy. I wiggle my toes, decorate my cast with paint pens, and with twinkling eyes and a glowing heart, I wonder what other gifts this new day will bring.

Bio

Vanessa Plimley is a surfer, angler, and soul on a holiday. When not playing in the outdoors, she is a life coach, writer, and personal trainer specializing in post-rehab exercise. She splits her time between North America and Nicaragua. www.stokeyourfire.com.

How 9/11 Sparked My Gratitude
By Wendy Yu

Sometimes it takes something of magnitude to shake you up, wake you up, and teach you how to appreciate life and live with gratitude.

In 2001, I decided to move to New York. Things at home weren't working in my favor. Life was boring, work was not rewarding, and things weren't moving along. So, I took a leave from my job, packed up my bags, and moved to New York—a city I always dreamed of living in.

Things in the Big Apple weren't much better. Everything was expensive, the streets were crowded, and people were rude. But I was here to give it a go, so I did—until that fateful day.

September 11, 2001, started like any other day. The sun was shining, and the air was crisp as I set off from my temporary housing on Staten Island to day seven of my new job. I entered my new workplace, an office tower in downtown Manhattan. I was hired to teach high school and had just started my chemistry lesson when we felt the building shake.

"Must be an earthquake," I commented casually, ready to take cover.

"We don't have earthquakes in New York, Miss," replied one of the students.

As we looked out the window, we saw papers floating around like giant snowflakes. Then, the assistant principal came on the PA and announced that a plane had "accidentally" flown into one of the Twin Towers, and as a precaution, we were to stay away from the windows and congregate in the center of our floor. A short time later, we were directed to evacuate the building and made our way down the stairs and through the exit doors.

Everyone scattered in their individual directions once we evacuated. A couple of us walked away from the Twin Towers toward the Staten Island Ferry. As we walked, we saw the first building start to crumble right before our eyes. It felt as if everything was in slow motion, and I was on a set of an adventure movie. When the slow-motion frame stopped, we turned and started running in the opposite direction from the disintegrating building. We could see the street start to be covered in dust as it rolled towards us. Fortunately, we made it on the ferry and over to Staten Island.

The next few days were confusing and uncertain. There was no way out of New York by plane. My only means of escape was by hitching a ride with the safest-looking people I could find (a nice elderly couple who were driving to Canada) and catching a plane near Toronto to fly home to Vancouver.

As uncertainty brewed in the world around me, a transformation was taking place within me that I didn't even realize. I was too busy trying to make it back to safety and get home.

After getting home, the first time I realized that I had "changed" was when a car cut me off in traffic. There's nothing that brings out the worst in people more than rush hour traffic. A car cut me off, and I didn't give him the finger, I didn't shout an obscenity, I didn't even make an off-handed remark. I simply let him in.

Things around me were looking up too. Although in reality, nothing had truly changed. Only my outlook on things. I started to appreciate things around me—nature, possessions, and mostly, people. I stopped judging others and started accepting them for who they were. I think, more importantly, I stopped judging myself and started accepting me.

It turns out that although I always wanted to live in New York, my reasons for moving there were all wrong. Turns out, it wasn't that things weren't working in my favor. I had my focus all wrong. I didn't have a grateful heart.

About a month later, I returned to New York to gather up some forgotten things, and the city had totally changed—well, my view of the city had totally changed. Not everything in New York was expensive; you just had to know where to go. The streets weren't crowded, they were alive with activity and fun. And the people weren't rude, they were direct and to-the-point. New York had some of the kindest, most caring people in the world.

This experience was traumatic and life-changing. And I wouldn't wish it on anyone. But the effects of it I would hope for everyone. It taught me how to appreciate the things I have and to focus on the positive. And it certainly sparked my gratitude.

Be thankful for what you have; you'll end up having more.
If you concentrate on what you don't have, you will never,
ever have enough. ~ Oprah Winfrey

Bio

Wendy Yu is an educator in Coquitlam, British Columbia, Canada, where she enjoys donning brightly colored umbrellas under the gray skies of the West Coast. She lives with her husband, three young children, and Siamese fighting fish that just won't die. She stays fits by running after her children and goes to bed each night grateful that her family keeps her busy and happy.

Final Thoughts From The Publisher

We are extremely grateful for our amazing authors. At As You Wish Publishing we know that every story matters. The heart and soul of our authors pour out on to every page. Thank you dear authors for having the courage, the love and the willingness to speak your truth and bring your stories of gratitude to the world. You are all incredibly special to us.

If you would like some daily gratitude please join our free Facebook group: www.facebook.com/groups/gratefulsouls

Want to learn more about how you can become a published author? Check out www.asyouwishpublishing.com for free webinars and other adventures to choose from for your writing journey.

Find more bestselling books like these visit us at www.asyouwishpublishing.com/our-books

Recent Titles Include:

Inspirations: 101 Uplifting Stories For Daily Happiness

Manifestations: True Stories Of Bringing The Imagined Into Reality